ASIA

IN NEW YORK CITY

a cultural travel guide

ASIA

IN NEW YORK CITY

a cultural travel guide

Asia
Society

FOREWORD BY NICHOLAS PLATT, PRESIDENT
INTRODUCTION BY KAREN KARP,
V.P., MARKETING AND COMMUNICATIONS

with contributions by:

Sandee Brawarsky, Daryl Chin, Alvin Eng, Geoffrey Eu,
Letha Hadady, Bruce Edward Hall, Betty Hallock,
Reena Jana, Theresa Kimm, Alexis Lipsitz,
Arthur J. Pais, and Kenneth Wapner
Photographs by Carrie Boretz

BALLIETT & FITZGERALD INC.
AND
AVALON TRAVEL PUBLISHING

AVALON
TRAVEL
publishing

Asia In New York City: A Cultural Travel Guide

Published by
Balliett & Fitzgerald Inc.
66 West Broadway, Suite 602
New York, NY 10007
and
Avalon Travel Publishing
5855 Beaudry St.
Emeryville, CA 94608, USA

Please send all comments, corrections, additions, amendments, and critiques to:
Asia In New York City
AVALON TRAVEL PUBLISHING
5855 BEAUDRY ST.
EMERYVILLE, CA 94608, USA
email: info@travelmatters.com
www.travelmatters.com

1st edition—October 2000
5 4 3 2 1

Library of Congress Cataloging-in-Publication Data
Asia in New York City : a cultural travel guide / by the Asia Society ; with contribu-
tions by Sandee Brawarsky ... [et al.] ; foreword by Nicholas Platt ; introduction by
Karen Karp.—1st ed.
      p. cm.
    Includes index.
    ISBN 1-56691-217-2 (alk. paper)
    1. Asian Americans—New York (State)—New York—Social life and customs. 2. Asian
American arts—New York (State)—New York. 3. New York (N.Y.)—Guidebooks. I. Asia
Society.

F128.9.O6 A85 2000
917.47'10444'08995073—dc21   00-045440

Front cover photos: © Corky Lee (top, center); all others © Carrie Boretz

Distributed in the United States and Canada by Publishers Group West.

Printed in the United States by Bertlesmann Services.

contents

Film & Performing Arts
Film by Daryl Chin
Performing Arts by Alvin Eng
[213]

[**Asia in Brooklyn** • by Geoffrey Eu]
[248]

Diversions by Day & Night
by Alexis Lipsitz
[258]

[**Little Manila** • by Theresa Kimm]
[283]

Services
by Theresa Kimm
[288]

foreword

for almost half a century, the Asia Society has educated Americans about Asia in a variety of ways. We present major art exhibitions, films and performances; publish scholarly analyses on history and contemporary affairs; sponsor lectures, seminars and international conferences; and create innovative materials for students and teachers.

But what better way is there to learn firsthand about diverse cultures than by trying new foods, wearing contemporary fashions inspired by traditional designs and fabrics, discovering the benefits of health remedies devised thousands of years ago, or meandering through this great city's streets where a tremendous mix of people forms truly global neighborhoods?

That's why we have created Asia in New York City: A Cultural Travel Guide. Through these pages, you will embark on an exciting Asian adventure right in your own backyard. Encouraging you to explore and experience Asian cultures, and to celebrate them, is what it is all about. We think you will enjoy it. And we invite you to come to the Asia Society's many wonderful programs and visit our websites—AsiaSociety.org, AskAsia.org, and AsiaSource.org—to make the rewards of this stimulating and fun journey to Asia last and grow, without ever having to leave New York.

NICHOLAS PLATT
President, Asia Society
Fall 2000

introduction

New York City has always welcomed people from all over the world, from tourists seeking its rich cultural offerings to newcomers starting their lives anew in what has become the capital of opportunity. But what is striking today is the vast diversity of new immigrants—in particular, the extraordinary representation from all parts of Asia. Prompted by movements on both a global and local scale, Chinese, Japanese, Indians, Koreans, Cambodians, Pakistanis, Thais, Malaysians, Tibetans, Filipinos, Burmese, Taiwanese, and many others have come in vast waves to make New York their home.

In 1956 when John D. Rockefeller 3rd established the Asia Society as an educational public institution to help bridge what he perceived to be a gap of understanding about Asia in this country, he probably never imagined that Asian culture would become such a prominent part of his own culture. Yet nearly 50 years later, in response to that prominence, and to the recognition that Asians and Asian Americans are changing the way New Yorkers view the world, the Asia Society has created *Asia in New York City: A Cultural Travel Guide*. A guide to, and celebration of, all things Asian in the metropolitan area, this unique book is not only a savvy travel companion for visitors but an eye-opening entrée into Asian New York for all.

An official 1998 count put the number of Asians in the New York area at more than 1.3 million. And in this country, from 1980 to 1990 the number of Asians and Pacific Islanders grew by 108 percent. This number is estimated at more than 10 million today and is projected to increase another five-fold by the year 2050. Here in the nation's largest city, the result is Asian New York—an eclectic collection of neighborhoods, music, cuisine, art, and ideas that is practically as diverse as Asia itself.

Manhattan's Chinatown—the first in the country and a thriving commercial center with more than 100,000 residents—is now joined by a second Chinatown in Flushing, and yet a third in Sunset Park, Brooklyn, the fastest-growing of the three enclaves. Awash in color and activity, Indian restaurants and boutiques selling jewel-hued saris line bustling 74th Street in the Jackson Heights area of Queens, and Flushing has become the millennial, Asian equivalent of the formerly heavily eastern European Lower East Side. A lively mix of Chinese herbal medicine shops, 24-hour Korean barbecue houses, and Asian American communities have helped create a tremendously dynamic corridor along many of these communities' link to Manhattan, the Number 7 IRT subway line.

But Asia's influence in New York City runs deeper than sheer numbers reflecting increased immigration. Changing neighborhoods are just the tip of the iceberg. People from Karachi to Kyoto from Bangkok to Beijing infuse the city with the heritage of some of the world's oldest cultures while transforming its composition and taste in a way that is 100 percent contemporary. As a result, the boundaries between more defined Asian neighborhoods and the center of New York City are no longer distinct. Things Asian have gone mainstream.

Examples abound. Americans' growing interest in Eastern philosophies and religions has led to a flowering of monasteries, ashrams, and meditation centers along with a new generation of teachers adapting ancient traditions for those in search of new spiritual paths. And East and West meet not just in the burgeoning number of restaurants which fuse Asian and Western methods and ingredients to create revolutionary flavors, but also in the hordes of New Yorkers who have made the simultaneous proliferation of authentic Asian cuisines their own.

But food for the body and spirit is not all that is being consumed by New Yorkers. Voracious readers snap up prize-winning bestsellers by Asian American authors, while fashionistas turn to Asian-flavored designs and the remarkable work of acclaimed Asian designers. Others seek out Asian healing techniques, chanting om shanti on their livingroom floors, while yoga classes are oversubscribed at the city's hottest health clubs and spas. The city's visual and performing artists often draw upon Asian and Western idioms in strikingly original work, while indigenous holiday festivals that punctuate the seasons with colorful celebration liven up the streets in all five boroughs.

Asia in New York City should give you a deeper sense of the history, people, and ideas shaping what's best and most interesting in New York's visual and performing arts, food, fashion, entertainment, health, religion, and much more. It is an engaging and easy-to-access map to the vast and dynamic palate of Asian cultures that fill this city. The book was written with many audiences in mind and covers neighborhoods, trends and activities that can be explored both alone and by the whole family.

As America's foremost public education institution with a focus on the diversity of Asia, in Asia in New York City we have tried to use our experience and networks to identify a great range of the city's best Asia-related resources. Our talented writers have attempted to illuminate within these pages the people, places, ideas, and trends that are changing the face of the city and the style of its residents. We invite you to walk through the streets with us and enter these worlds of delicious tastes, new fragrances, dizzying creativity, and cultural interaction. At the new millennium's dawning, we hope that you will join us in discovering that, in New York especially, Asia is not just a link to a vast and venerable heritage, but a gateway to the future.

KAREN KARP
V.P., Marketing and Communications
Asia Society

editor's note:

Every effort has been made to make *Asia in New York City: A Cultural Travel Guide* as accurate and up-to-date as possible. But, such information can change rapidly—stores close, new restaurants open. Still, we feel the material here has a fresh and timeless quality all its own. The world of Asia in New York is itself ever-changing, and that's part of the fun of exploring the city. We hope that our selections help lead you to new places, as well as inspiring you to make discoveries of your own.

Our writers voices are as unique and diverse as the subjects they cover, providing a real variety of tastes from the banquet that is Asian culture in New York.

You may find authors of different sections talking about the same, or related, topics or events—the richness of the material at hand warrants complementary perspectives. In the same vein, we should note that our chapter listings are clearly selective, but we have taken great pains to supply a rich and representative sampling for each category—amounting to hundreds of listings throughout the book.

We chose not to include prices in these listings—our concern for accuracy precluded providing them, with New York being the ever-changing place that it is. But we did make every effort to indicate a sense of cost level in our descriptions, when appropriate.

We should also note that our index consists of a comprehensive compilation of the venue listings. You can look up the items set in boldface in the text, and readily discover the multiple mentions of the same venue throughout the book.

Finally, you'll find terms throughout that are unique to Asian cultures in New York. Terms like *desi*—a friendly term that Southeast Asians use to refer to each other—or *pinoy*, also a friendly term but referring to Filipinos, are used contextually here and there. We've italicized other terms that may be new to our readers; their meanings have been made clear in the text.

· I ·

art & design

"New York will continue to be one of the most active centers for Asian art in the 21st century. With the vast holdings at the Met and the Brooklyn Museum, and exhibitions at the Asia Society, Japan Society—and even the Guggenheim, Bard Center, and other places—New Yorkers and visitors have constant chances to see Asian art, both traditional and contemporary. And with organizations like the Asian American Arts Center and the Asian American Arts Alliance, there is an increasingly greater attention paid to Asian American artists in the city."

—VISHAKHA N. DESAI, Senior Vice President, Asia Society and Museum

Asian Art in America: The View from New York

Although historians might point to California and the West Coast as centers for Asian culture in America because of their coastal proximity to the East, New York City has long been a major portal for the flow of Asian art into America. More than that, the city has been an important and fertile breeding ground for East-West artistic fusion. American patrons of the arts began a serious pursuit of Asian art during the era of Japonisme, in the 19th century, when Westerners became enamored of Eastern art forms. Collectors at that time were intrigued by the mysterious imagery depicted in the works and grew curious about the unusual techniques of the artists. New York's elite rode the trend, as did the French Impressionists and the graphic artists of the Art Nouveau movement, whose work was greatly influenced by the dramatic, colorful designs of Japanese printmakers. Even Vincent Van Gogh directly copied work by Japanese artists, appropriating the visions of 19th-century printmaker Hiroshige in oil paint. In the 1880s,

Overleaf: Copper 13th-century Bodhisattva from Nepal. (Photo © Lynton Gardiner)

Japanese wood-block print by Toshusai Sharaku, from the Edo period in the late 1700s. (Photo © Lynton Gardiner)

firms dealing in Japanese art did brisk business in New York, as highly regarded interior decorators—such as Louis Comfort Tiffany—incorporated Japanese aesthetics into their designs. Many of Tiffany's lamps and windows borrowed from Japanese styling; symbols found repeatedly in Japanese illustration, such as the peacock, became familiar Tiffany design elements.

The ornate Manhattan homes of America's reigning Gilded Age families, including the Vanderbilts and the Havemeyers, were among the first in the country to incorporate Oriental art into interior design. The Asian references were informed and far-flung: The Havemeyer family library was designed to reflect the bright hues of ancient Noh dance robes, and its walls were painted a shade of green that was inspired by a lacquer panel by Ritsuo, a Japanese printmaker of the 16th century.

New Yorkers were introduced to Japanese wood-block prints by Shugio Hiromichi, the director of the First Japan Manufacturing and Trading Company, a Japanese importer of porcelain and parasols. In 1889, Shugio curated the first significant show of ukiyo-e ("pictures of the floating world")—colorful wood-block prints and posters representing urban and natural pleasures, such as geisha in outdoor revelry or theater actors in costume. These lyrical, contemplative prints inspired a host of turn-of-the-century painters. James Whistler, in particular, borrowed from the ukiyo-e abstract sensibility in his work, saying, "If the man who paints only the tree, or flower, or other surface he sees before him were an artist, the king of artists would be the photographer. It is for the artist to do something beyond this."

Public collections of Asian art also began in the late 19th century, with New York as a hub of sorts for such collecting activity. Howard Mansfield, a trustee of the **Metropolitan Museum of Art,** was the first acting curator of Asian art at the institution (a staff curator was added in 1915). Mansfield's personal collection included Japanese paintings and pottery; Mansfield's fellow trustee, Charles Stewart Smith (also a founder of the Met), bought 1,700 ukiyo-e and 522 Japanese ceramics, which he donated to the museum. Today, visitors to the Met will find the most comprehensive holdings of Asian art in the Western world: a collection of more than 60,000 pieces spanning more than 2,300 years. Completed in 1998, an entire wing of the museum is devoted to Asian art, occupying an astonishing 64,500 square feet. Nineteenth-century Japanese printmaker Hokusai's famous *Great Wave at Kanagawa* (from the series *Thirty-six Views of Mount Fuji*) is part of the collection, as well as the 8th-century Chinese master Han Gan's *Night-Shining White* ink drawing.

The pieces on display are presented chronologically and by region, yet similarities in themes and techniques are conveyed in the placement of the objects. For example, traditional blue-and-white Chinese porcelain is showcased in an installation that explores the influence of Asian ceramics on European ceramic design as well as the similarities between Chinese porcelain and that of Korea, Vietnam, and Japan.

Not to be missed is the Astor Court, which is modeled after a scholar's courtyard in Suzhou, a region in China renowned for its innovative garden architecture. The design of the simulated courtyard, which opened to the public in 1981, dates back to the Ming dynasty (1368–1644 A.D.).

The breadth of the Met's collection can be dizzying. The Charlotte C. Weber Galleries for the Arts of Ancient China feature Neolithic Chinese bronzes and jades, dating from 4500 to 2000 B.C., and rare Buddhist images from the Tang (618–907 A.D.) and Ming dynasties. The Douglas Dillon Galleries, the C. C. Wang Gallery, and the Francis Young Tang Galleries feature scholarly and courtly paintings and calligraphy from the 8th through 18th centuries, as well as works from 19th- and 20th-century China. The Arts of Japan Galleries feature 11 rooms that represent the entire range of Japanese art—from Neolithic ceramics to Edo Period (1615–1868 A.D.) wood-block prints.

The Arts of Korea Gallery, an unusual hybrid of contemporary, sleek interior architecture and traditional Korean details, such as wooden plank floors, highlights Buddhist paintings from the Koryo (918–1292 A.D.) and Choson (1392–1910 A.D.) dynasties. And the Florence and Herbert Irving Galleries for the Arts of South and Southeast Asia show Indian, Pakistani, Afghani, Bangladeshi, Sri Lankan, Burmese, Cambodian, Thai, Indonesian, and Vietnamese art in 15 rooms. Standouts include early Southeast Asian metalwork and Khmer Empire sculptures.

Ganesha—the son of Shiva and considered the God of Good Fortune—from Uttar Pradesh, India. Carved from sandstone in the 8th century. (Photo © Lynton Gardiner)

knockout collections:
public and private

"Before I had my stroke, I would often go to the Asia
Society's galleries. Why? I'd go there to look and get
inspired. I've used Buddha figures a lot in my work, and
the Asia Society has the best collection of Buddhas—
Japanese Buddhas, Indonesian Buddhas. I also go to the
Korean galleries at the Met, which have a very private
feel to them. I get in touch with my Asian background
at both of these wonderful galleries, which are so open
to the public."—Nam June Paik

Beyond the Met's sprawling galleries, New York is home to a
wide array of both public and private collections of astonishing
Asian art. The **Asia Society** is a key destination for the true fan
of Asian art. In 1956, the Asia Society was founded by John D.
Rockefeller 3rd on the belief that art is a key factor in cultivating
better understanding between America and Asia. Art exhibitions
became a lively focus of the overall programming of the institution, with the first show taking place on the opening night of
Asia House, the original name of the gallery spaces. In 1979,
Mr. and Mrs. John D. Rockefeller 3rd granted the Asia Society
nearly 300 works acquired over 25 years of visiting Asia and
collecting Asian art. These masterworks in various media from
South Asia, Southeast Asia, and East Asia, dating from 2000 B.C.
to the 19th century—ranging from paintings to ceramics to
sculpture—reflect the breathtaking diversity of Asian arts and
cultures.

The Rockefellers' collection now constitutes the basis of the
Society's permanent collection. While smaller than the American
collections of other well-known patrons of Asian art (namely
Charles Lang Freer and Avery Brundage), its large number of
acknowledged masterpieces makes it one of the most significant
assemblages of Asian art in the United States. Works include an

11th-century copper statue of a kneeling woman from Cambodia, a many-armed copper sculpture of an Indonesian goddess dating from the 9th century, and a 17th-century watercolor-and-ink courtly painting from the Malwa Region in India.

No question, impressive permanent collections of traditional Asian art abound in Manhattan. A short East Side tour devoted to Asian art spanning centuries and continents could begin with a visit to the Islamic and Indian miniature paintings that are part of the permanent collections at the **J. Pierpont Morgan Library**—the personal library designed for the turn-of-the-century industrialist by the firm of McKim, Mead & White—home to more than a thousand such works, located on East 36th Street. Eleven blocks north, the **Japan Society Gallery,** located at the Japan Society—an institution created to foster enlightened relations between Japan and the West—feature ukiyo-e prints, paintings, ceramics, and folk art, as well as design and architecture. Three-dimensional mandalas, colorful, complex diagrams of the Buddhist spiritual universe (usually paintings), grace the gallery of **Tibet House,** an organization dedicated to increasing understanding of Tibet. The permanent collection of the city's singular design museum, the **Cooper-Hewitt National Design Museum,** located uptown on East 91st Street, includes charming Indonesian shadow puppets and superb examples of Asian textiles.

Outside of Manhattan, the **Brooklyn Museum of Art** boasts one of America's most significant collections of Korean art. That the early 20th century was indeed a golden time for collectors of Asian art is reflected in the museum's holdings. Many of the most important works seen in the Brooklyn Museum of Art—including the stupendous Korean art collection and the works from Iran's Qajar dynasty—were unearthed by the museum's first curator of ethnology, Stewart Culin, during expeditions into East and South Asia in 1903. Around 1911, a medical missionary named Dr. Albert L. Shelton was collecting the rich cache of Tibetan art that is now housed at the **Newark Museum** (including a Buddhist altar that was consecrated by the Dalai Lama)—a museum whose pan-Asian holdings include pieces from Bali, Burma, Sri Lanka, and Mongolia. Housed in charming buildings and terraced stone gardens styled after Himalayan monasteries, the **Jacques Marchais Museum of Tibetan Art** on Staten Island features exhibitions and cultural programs related to Tibet and other Asian civilizations.

On the commercial front, exquisite pieces of antique Asian art, furniture, and porcelain are sold by private dealers on the Upper East Side of Manhattan, mainly from a slew of tony galleries in and around the East '60s and Madison Avenue. **Kaikodo,** housed in an elegant townhouse, is a must-see for its fine works of Chinese art; it also publishes an excellent scholarly journal complete with beautiful color plates. Indeed, if you are inspired by the collections—once private—now on display in New York's institutions, you will find that you can actually acquire almost any sort of Asian art piece in New York: Traditional Indian art is found at **Art of the Past;** Chinese furniture at **Ming Furniture Ltd.;** Japanese and Korean works at **Suzanne Mitchell Asian Fine Arts;** lacquerware at **Naga Antiques;** and rare jades at **Weisbrod Chinese Art Ltd.**

Asia Through Modern Eyes:
Late 20th-century Asian Art

The golden age of Asian art in New York is far from over. New York City is not only a purveyor of Asian arts of the past; it is also becoming an important center for the exhibition and collection of Asian and Asian American art created in the 20th century and beyond. The Asia Society and the Japan Society, for example, have presented thrilling shows of modern and contemporary Asian and Asian American art. The groundbreaking exhibitions "Traditions/Tensions: Contemporary Art in Asia," featuring work by an array of thought-provoking artists from different nations in Asia; "Asia/America: Identities in Contemporary Asian American Art," an exhibition of work created by artists of Asian descent who reside in the United States; and "Inside Out: New Chinese Art,"

Isamu Noguchi installation in the lobby of 666 Fifth Avenue.

an exhibition of contemporary Chinese artists (shown jointly at Asia Society and P.S. 1 Contemporary Art Center in Long Island City, Queens), were all organized by the Asia Society and have traveled across the nation and around the world. All were considered groundbreaking because they were some of the first high-profile exhibitions of contemporary Asian and Asian American art seen in the United States.

Modern Asian works are much in demand by many other museums. Recently, the Japan Society hosted a show of works by contemporary Japanese photographer Daido Moriyama, whose edgy black-and-white documentary photographs were simultaneously featured in an exhibition at the Met.

One of the most popular modern Asian artists, Japanese American sculptor Isamu Noguchi, is a presence all over New York, his graceful sculptures set in tranquil gardens and minimalist galleries. Manhattan alone has a good sampling of Noguchi sculpture, including a brushed aluminum piece at **100 Broadway,** and, indoors at **666 Fifth Avenue,** a remarkable "waterfall" fashioned of steel and corrugated glass. Noguchi's works may have found the ultimate environment for their natural forms, however, at the **Isamu Noguchi Garden Museum** in Long Island City, Queens.

The electronic art of Nam June Paik

One of the most celebrated modern Asian artists in New York, Nam June Paik, may be pushing 70, but he continues to innovate with the best of them. The man who coined the term "electronic superhighway," some 24 years ago, was in early 2000 celebrated with a major retrospective at the Solomon R. Guggenheim Museum, in "The Worlds of Nam June Paik." What's all the fuss? Paik has been a pioneer in the creation of "video art," creating dynamic new artistic expressions through the integration of technology and the media—using film, television, and video, said John G. Hanhart, senior curator of video arts at the Guggenheim, as "flexible and dynamic multitextural art forms."

The Korean-born Paik studied composition in Germany in the '50s and '60s, where he met the avant-garde composer John Cage. He moved to New York City in 1964, and became involved in avant-garde performance art, working with such well-known '60s performance artists as Yoko Ono. At that time he began to embrace video as an instrument of artistic expression. Living downtown in Soho, he collaborated in designing the first video synthesizer, which creates images without using a camera. One reason Paik lived where he did—and continues to live there—was his access to Canal Street's many small electrical-supply shops, which sell case upon case of surplus electrical equipment at bargain rates.

The recent show at the Guggenheim featured pieces from throughout his career, many of them recreated for this show. One installation piece—a video garden—has small TV sets amid living plants. The piece covers an area approximately 10 by 12 feet on the ground, and also runs up the wall. Other pieces include a huge wall collage, about 8 by 20 feet, made up of hundreds of TV monitors, and robots made completely out of different-size televisions. Paik worked with the performance-art cellist Charlotte Moorman to design a "TV bra"—a bra literally made out of two TVs—for her to play in.

Video artist Tom Zafian recalls meeting Paik in 1973 at the Avant-Garde Festival, held on a boat at the South Street Seaport. While they were looking through the show—which featured scores of electric-powered displays—the power supply suddenly went out, and the place went dark. At that moment, says Zafian, Paik looked around with a Buddha-like calm, and said, "without electric, you can have no art."

For the Hip and the New:
An International Epicenter

New York has always been a destination for artists from around the globe. Because of its wealth of world-class galleries and museums, and because of the city's long tradition of cosmopolitan open-mindedness, the city is a welcome home for painters, sculptors, photographers, designers, and other artists seeking to pursue their careers on an international level. Asian artists are no different, finding the fast pace of the thriving Manhattan commercial gallery scene in Chelsea, Soho, and Midtown, or the bohemian communities in Brooklyn, exhilarating environments in which creativity is valued and nurtured. As artist Shahzia Sikander says, "NYC is the place for me as it allows me to be local and global at the same time. . . . I never feel conscious of who I am or where I am from, which is a very common issue anywhere else in the U.S. I can transcend ethnicity here."

A handful of hip commercial galleries have cropped up in downtown Manhattan specializing in modern and contemporary Asian art. Chelsea, the current epicenter of the international art world, is a fine destination for a Saturday gallery stroll—

subway asia   A surprising venue for contemporary Asian and Asian American art in New York is subway stations. Increasingly, the Metropolitan Transit Authority has commissioned public artworks for display at selected stations, many by Asian and Asian Americans. *Eclipsed Time*, a two-part sculpture by Maya Lin, is on view near the 7th Avenue-line token booth in Pennsylvania Station, and *Signal*, a series of stainless steel and glass sculptures by Mel Chin, is at the Broadway-Lafayette station. *Empress Voyage* by Bing Lee, is a colorful ceramic tile mural with mosaic banding at the N, R, 6 Canal Street station. *Happy World* by Ik-Joong Kang, is a giddily joyous ceramic tile mural at the Main Street/Flushing station in Queens. *Q is for Queens*, by Yumi Heo, is an installation of brightly colored murals in glass, located in a number of Queens stations on the 7 line.

One of the striking stained-glass pieces in Yumi Heo's *Q is for Queens* series, in a station on the #7 subway line.

with a focus on Asian art. Two galleries showcasing 20th-century East Indian art have recently opened their doors in this neighborhood: **Admit One Gallery** and **Bose Pacia Modern**. Admit One often displays photography and represents hot young South Asian artists like Rina Banerjee; one of her mixed-media installations—which often employ totemic Indian materials such as sari cloth and incense—was featured in the 2000 Whitney Biennial. Bose Pacia deals in paintings and other works of art by such artists as Manjit Bawa, a prominent Punjab-born modern painter who uses a bright, colorful palette and energetic forms.

Shows of today's Asian artists are organized by independent curator Miyako Yoshinaga at **M. Y. Art Prospects,** also in the Chelsea area. **Sepia International, Inc./ the Alkazi Collection of Photography** is both a commercial gallery and research center focusing on the 19th- and 20th-century photography of India, Burma, and Sri Lanka; it's also in Chelsea.

In the Flatiron district, just across town from Chelsea on the East Side, the recently opened **Paisley,** a store featuring Asian furniture and objects, hosts exhibitions of contemporary Indian art, often in conjunction with Bose Pacia. Farther downtown, in Soho,

Ceiling portion of Maya Lin's floor-and-ceiling installation, *Eclipsed Time,* near the IRT entrance in New York's Penn Station.

the recently opened **Dialectica** presents international art, with an emphasis on Asian (namely South Asian) artists; **Ise Art Foundation,** also in Soho, presents contemporary Japanese (and other Asian) art. In Tribeca, **Ethan Cohen Fine Arts** presents work by internationally recognized contemporary Chinese artists such as Xu Bing and C. C. Wang.

Uptown, on the West Side, **Gallery Dai Ichi Arts, Ltd.,** presents updated versions of Japanese ceramics (often based on or referencing traditional designs); the **Tolman Collection of Tokyo** is a must for those interested in fine contemporary Japanese prints. On the East Side, **Lawrence of Beijing** is an outpost of the China-based dealer, who represents contemporary Chinese artists with a bent for traditional imagery. Also on the Upper East Side is the **Elizabeth Wang Gallery,** which showcases works by artists of Chinese ancestry.

Perhaps the most powerful testimony to the high level of awareness for contemporary Asian art in New York is the fact that many of the world's leading contemporary Asian artists have chosen to live and work in New York: Avant-garde Chinese artists Gu Wenda and Xu Bing (a recent MacArthur Foundation genius grant recipient) live here, as well as the Pakistani painter Shahzia Sikander (a Whitney Biennial star), Japanese photographer Mariko Mori, and Thai conceptual artist Rikrit Tiranvanija.

Another New York–based Asian artist fomenting a lot of buzz is Romon Yang, aka Ro-Starr, who was recently named one of the world's hottest designers under the age of 30 by ID magazine. The Korean-born Ro-Starr has devised an East-meets-West visual style that's recognized internationally; he has art-directed futuristic fashion layouts for Spin magazine and designed graphics for the likes of MTV, Nike, and Swatch. His firm, Starr Foundation, creates cutting-edge logos and album covers.

Dr. Arani Bose, a co-owner of Bose Pacia, captures the spirit of Asia in the New York art world today when he says, "The traditional art of South Asia really meets the contemporary art world in New York. The Brooklyn Museum's collection of classic Indian miniatures is great; you can also go to Paisley for a lively look at what is going on in contemporary Indian art and design. Plus, Asia Week, which occurs every spring, is a focal point of the Asian art community, bringing people together from around the world right here in Manhattan. It's an exciting time to be here for anyone interested in Asian art. We're in the middle of an Asian art world that is currently a work in progress. It's exhilarating."

Asian Visions Everywhere: Architecture and Garden Design

The skyscraper is a uniquely American icon, but a good portion of the city's skyline—and many signature Manhattan buildings— were designed by Asian architects. The muscular twin towers of the **World Trade Center** at the island's base, for example, were designed by Minoru Yamasaki & Associates, with Emery Roth & Sons. In 1929, architect Yasuo Matsui codesigned **32-40 Wall Street,** an example of a classic 1920s Manhattan skyscraper.

I. M. Pei's versatility is evident throughout the city; his oeuvre includes an unusually positioned apartment complex at **100-110 Bleecker Street** and the sprawling, glass-and-steel **Jacob Javits Convention Center.** Pei's refined tower at **88 Pine Street** (Wall Street Plaza) is considered one of the architect's more significant works.

The contemporary architect/sculptor/designer Maya Lin (who may be most famous for her design of the celebrated *Vietnam War Veterans' Memorial* in Washington, D.C., and who operates a design studio in New York) reveals her signature elegance in the streamlined spaces of the Asia/Pacific/American Studies Department of New York University and the Museum for African Art.

A modern update of a traditional Japanese garden can be enjoyed, believe it or not, in midtown Manhattan. Here, at **Greenacre Park,** is a little jewel of a landscape, packing into a small space woodland plantings, a soothing waterfall, and a stream; it was designed in 1971 by Hideo Sasaki, the former chairman of Harvard University's Landscape Architecture Department, and his design firm.

When urban exploration of Asian art and design wears you down, escape Manhattan and discover a multitude of peaceful environments that reflect the serenity of Eastern design sensibilities. America's oldest and most extensive collection of bonsai trees—dedicated to the distinctly Japanese art of growing beautifully formed miniature plants—can be seen at the **Brooklyn Botanic Garden's C. V. Starr Bonsai Museum.** Another revital-

Tiny but tranquil Greenacre Park, tucked between skyscrapers on East 51st Street, in Midtown.

izing place to venture in the Brooklyn Botanic Garden is the **Japanese Hill-and-Pond Garden,** a small-scale landscape featuring cherry trees and other flora set amid classical elements of Japanese environmental design, including traditional Japanese torii gates, lanterns, shrines, and bridges. It was designed by the Japanese landscape architect Takeo Shiota in 1914 as a "mirror of nature" and was recently restored to its original glory. The **Queens Botanical Garden** offers plantings native to various Asian environs as well as the austere tranquility of its Cherry Circle landscape installation.

But it is in Staten Island, approximately a mile from the Staten Island ferry terminal, where one of the most remarkable public gardens in the metropolitan area can be found. Here is the country's only authentic classical Chinese garden. Many of the elements of the **New York Chinese Scholar's Garden** at the Snug Harbor Cultural Center were assembled in Suzhou, China. The tranquil grounds include a Ming dynasty teahouse, a lotus pond, and bridges—all forming the perfect milieu for the latter-day Chinese scholar to meditate and plot the world's future among original Taihu rocks from lakes in China.

Hands-on Asian Art: classes and workshops

If merely looking at Asian art and design isn't enough, and you want to try your hand at some of the techniques seen in galleries and other institutions around New York, finding classes and workshops for learning traditional Asian art forms isn't difficult in this area, where many Asian communities believe that instructing younger generations will help keep traditions alive. Korean calligraphy, for example, is taught at the **Korean Calligraphy Center** as well as at the **Korean Culture Society of Eastern USA**—both located in Flushing, Queens, home to the second-largest Korean community in America (the largest is in Los Angeles). Korean flower arranging is also offered at the Korean Culture Society.

Courses in Chinese painting, ceramics, and calligraphy are taught at the **China Institute** on the Upper East Side as well as at the **New York Chinese Cultural Center** on lower Broadway.

Sumi-e and Japanese calligraphy classes are offered at the **Koho School of Sumi-e**. Both sumi-e and ikebana—Japanese flower arranging—are occasionally taught at the Brooklyn

The nearby Asian community makes its mark at the Queens Botanical Garden, which features plantings native to Asian countries and special events like the traditional Chinese tea ceremony.

Botanic Garden, which, along with the Queens Botanical Garden, offers classes in bonsai pruning. *Ikebana* demonstrations are available seasonally at the **Metropolitan Museum of Art** and through Ikebana International (212 876-2157). Private lessons in the fine art of the classic Japanese tea ceremony can be booked at the **Urasenke Chanoyu Center Tea Ceremony Society.** It is also possible to observe the Chinese tea ceremony at the Queens Botanical Garden at different times throughout the year.

Classes in Tibetan painting and other art forms are occasionally offered at the **Jacques Marchais Museum of Tibetan Art,** where you can participate in centuries-old traditions from this far-flung Himalayan region.

For the tourist and native alike, New York can serve as a fascinating place in which a cross-section of pan-Asian art and design can be experienced and enjoyed on many different levels. Those interested in the astonishingly long history of Asian art, not to mention the wide varieties of traditions from a staggering number of Asian nations, will be more than satisfied by the offerings at the city's major cultural institutions. Anyone with a yen to start a collection of Asian antiques or a desire to snap up works by Asian's hottest contemporary artists can do either—or both—with ease in Manhattan. Or if you're inspired to partake in creating artwork in a traditional Asian style or technique, opportunities abound to learn centuries-old craftmaking skills. Even if one is on a budget and wants only to enter a traditional Asian landscape garden, the experience can be had. In other words, New York City offers the rare chance to experience the glorious, varied, centuries-old and cutting-edge art and design that all of Asia has to offer—from Cambodia to China to India to Japan to the Philippines to Vietnam—in a single, concentrated area of the East Coast of the United States that has made a rich contribution of its own to the history of Asian art.

art & design
THE LISTINGS

Museums

Asia Society. With a mission to help foster American understanding of Asian culture, history, and current affairs, the Asia Society houses some of the most popular and respected venues for viewing not only traditional pan-Asian art but also cutting-edge exhibitions of contemporary Asian and Asian American art (725 Park Ave., NY; 212 517-ASIA [2742]; www.asiasociety.org; 6 train to 68th St. Note: During renovations, the Asia Society is housed [until Fall 2001] at 502 Park Ave.; 4, 5, 6, N, R train to 59th St./Lexington Ave.).

The Bronx Museum of the Arts. Founded in 1971, this institution is recognized as a multicultural contemporary museum, with an active program of acquiring work by artists of Asian descent (1040 Grand Concourse, Bronx; 718 681-6000; 4, B train to 161st St./Yankee Stadium, D train [from Manhattan before 4 p.m. only] to 161st St./Yankee Stadium or 167th St.).

Brooklyn Museum of Art. Featuring one of the most important collections of Korean art in the United States, this museum also boasts some of greater New York's most comprehensive holdings of Asian art, including works from Cambodia, China, India, Iran, Japan, Thailand, Tibet, and Turkey (200 Eastern Parkway, Brooklyn; 718 638-5000; www.brooklynart.org; 2, 3 train to Eastern Parkway/Brooklyn Museum).

China Institute. Dedicated to the appreciation and enjoyment of traditional and contemporary Chinese civilization, culture, and heritage, the China Institute offers a number of different programs to the city of New York. Art exhibitions showcase Chinese paintings, calligraphy, textiles, and architecture; classes are offered in Chinese ceramics, painting, and calligraphy as well; Mandarin language classes are offered for all levels of proficiency; and lectures, book signings, films, and cultural performances of the Institute are open to the public. Programs especially for

[20]

corporations and educators are also available. (125 E. 65th St., NY; 212 744-8181; www. chinainstitute,org; 6 train to 68th St.)

Cooper-Hewitt National Design Museum. This design museum includes in its holdings Asian ceramics, lacquerwork, Japanese prints, Indonesian shadow puppets, and textiles from India, Persia, and China (2 E. 91st St., NY; 212 849-8400; www.si.edu/ndm; 6 train to 96th St.).

Jacques Marchais Museum of Tibetan Art. Museum resembling Tibetan mountain temple contains artifacts from the 17th to 19th centuries; sculpture garden and lily and fish pond on-site. Classes in Tibetan art are offered occasionally (338 Lighthouse Ave., Staten Island; 718 987-3478; www.tibetmuseum.com; Staten Island Ferry to S74 bus to Lighthouse Ave).

Japan Society Gallery. Whether you're a connoisseur or simply a fan of contemporary art, you'll find the best of Japanese painting, prints, ceramics, folk art, architecture and design, and sculpture here (333 E. 47th St., NY; 212 832-1155; www.japansociety.org; 6, E, F train to 51st St./Lexington Ave.).

Korea Gallery, The Consulate General of the Republic of Korea. Regularly features displays of Korean artifacts and traditional arts (460 Park Ave., 6th floor, NY; 212 759-9550; 4, 5, 6, N, R train to 59th St./Lexington Ave.).

The Metropolitan Museum of Art. Largest collection of Asian art in the West, with pieces from the second millennium B.C. to the 20th century (1000 Fifth Ave., NY; 212 879-5500; www.metmuseum.org; 4, 5, 6 train to 86th St.).

The Morgan Library. Designed in the style of a Renaissance palazzo, this elegant building houses over one thousand Indian and Islamic miniature paintings dating from the 13th through the 19th centuries (29 E. 36th St., NY; 212 685-0610; www.morganlibrary.org; 6 train to 33rd St.).

Museum of Chinese in the Americas. Changing exhibits that address the history of Chinatown's residents are featured here, ranging from documentary photography to contemporary art by refugees (70 Mulberry St., NY; 212 619-4785; www.mocanyc.org; A, C, E, N, R, J, M, Z, 6 train to Canal St.).

Newark Museum. Pan-Asian decorative and fine arts are featured here—including a Tibetan Buddhist altar on permanent display. While Tibetan art and Chinese and Japanese decorative arts are this museum's strong suits, Afghanistan, Bali, Bhutan, Burma, Cambodia, India,

Indonesia, Iran, Iraq, Korea, Mongolia, Nepal, the Philippines, Sri Lanka, Syria, Thailand, and Turkey are all represented as well (43 Washington St., Newark, NJ; 201 733-6600; www.newarkmuseum.org; PATH train to Newark's Pennsylvania Station, then Loop shuttle bus to Museum).

The Philippine Center, the Consulate General of the Philippines. Exhibitions curated to promote Filipino culture can be found in the gallery of this seven-story building, the New York home of the branch offices of agencies of the Republic of the Philippines (556 Fifth Ave., NY; 212 764-1330; E, F train to 5th Ave.; by appointment only).

Tibet House Gallery. Three-dimensional mandalas and works from the Tibet House Repatriation Art Collection are included in the permanent collection of this gallery; exhibits of work inspired by Tibet and Buddhism are featured in temporary shows, ranging from traditional to contemporary (22 W. 15th St., NY; 212 807-0563; www.tibethouse.org; F train to 14th St.).

Architecture and Landscape

88 Pine St. (Wall Street Plaza.) Designed by I. M. Pei & Partners, 1973. Cool and refined, this very modern building is notable for its simple, elegant design; nearby, at Pine and William streets, is Isamu Noguchi's Sunken Water Garden at Chase Manhattan Plaza (on Water St. between Pine St. and Maiden La., NY; 2, 3 train to Wall St.).

32-40 Wall Street. Designed by H. Craig Severance and Yasuo Matsui, 1929. This building is a toned-down version of the typically flamboyant skyscraper that has come to symbolize the boom of the 1920s, yet it still "dresses up" the Street (between William and Nassau sts., NY; 2, 3 train to Wall St.).

100-110 Bleecker Street. I. M. Pei & Partners, 1966. These N.Y.U.-owned residential buildings, convey a remarkable sense of refined balance that only Pei could infuse into such a basic design. The complex's three towers are arranged in an unusual, curvelike composition (between Mercer St. and LaGuardia Pl., NY; 6 train to Bleecker St.).

100 Broadway. Bruce Price/Kajima International. This Beaux-Arts building, constructed in 1895, was renovated for the Bank of Tokyo in 1975. Kajima International restored the facade and created a new glass wall on the ground floor. The space is also accented by a brushed-aluminum sculpture by Isamu Noguchi (SE corner of Pine St., NY; A, C, M, 2, 3, 4, 5 train to Fulton St.).

Brooklyn Botanic Garden. At the **C. V. Starr Bonsai Museum,** you'll find the nation's largest and oldest collection of bonsai. The **Japanese Hill-and-Pond Garden** features a miniaturized environment consisting of torii gates, shrines, bridges, stone lanterns, and pruned trees and shrubs. Classes on bonsai, *ikebana*, and *sumi-e* are also sometimes offered (1000 Washington Ave., Brooklyn; 718 623-7200; www.bbg.org; D, Q train to Prospect Park, 2, 3 train to Eastern Parkway/Brooklyn Museum).

Greenacre Park. Sasaki, Dawson, DeMay Associates, 1971. This midtown oasis features a peaceful stream and waterfall, stone walls, and woodland plantings—a design intended to bring a bit of nature into the heart of Manhattan (217–221 E. 51st St., between Second and Third aves., NY; 6 train to 51st St.).

Isamu Noguchi Garden Museum. Need some respite from the harried pace of Manhattan? You won't find a more peaceful setting than this spot in Queens. Elegant stone sculptures populate both the spare galleries and an outdoor setting that emphasizes Noguchi's keen understanding of natural forms, evident in his graceful creations (32-37 Vernon Blvd., Long Island City, Queens; 718 545-8842; www.noguchi.org; N train to Broadway).

Jacob Javits Convention Center. Five blocks long, covering a whopping 1.8 million square feet, this glass-clad behemoth of a building was designed by I. M. Pei. The astonishing, 150-foot-high lobby has been dubbed "the crystal palace" because of its modern grandeur (11th Ave. between 34th and 35th sts., NY; 212 216-2000; A, C, E train to 34th St.).

Kips Bay Plaza. I. M. Pei and Partners, S. J. Kessler, 1960, 1965. These concrete rectangles signify early 1960s architectural aesthetics, and while they may seem "outdated," they predict the design of Pei's highly respected complex of apartment buildings at 100-110 Bleecker St., and can thus help us understand how his design vision evolved (E. 30th–E. 33rd sts., First to Second aves., NY; 6 train to 33rd St.).

New York Chinese Scholar's Garden at the Staten Island Botanical Garden/Snug Harbor Cultural Center. This site is the home of the only authentic classical Chinese garden to be built in the United States, created by a team of Chinese artists and artisans. A triumph of garden design (1000 Richmond Terrace, Staten Island; 718 273-8200; www.sibg.org; Staten Island Ferry from Battery Park, then S40 Bus to Snug Harbor).

Queens Botanical Garden. Features plantings native to Asian environs as well as classes—including Tai Chi, bonsai pruning and Ikebana—and activities that respond to the nearby Asian communities. Seasonal displays of flowers and a variety of plants and trees in 39 verdant acres of beauty and tranquility in the heart of Queens (43-50 Main St., Flushing, Queens; 718 886-3800; www.geocities.com/qbgarden; 7 train to Flushing/Main St.)

World Trade Center. Minoru Yamasaki & Sons, with Emery Roth & Sons, 1970–77. The tallest points on the Manhattan skyline, these iconic twin towers have come to define New York City. Some might call them simple in design, but the towers have the sleek presence of minimalist sculpture (bordered by Church, Vesey, West, and Liberty sts., NY; E train to World Trade Center, 1, 9 train to Cortlandt St.).

Public Artworks

10 Degrees North. Maya Lin, Rockefeller Foundation (420 Fifth Ave., NY; 212 869-8500; B, D, F, Q, N, R train to 34th St./Herald Sq.).

666 Fifth Avenue, sculpture by Isamu Noguchi. The lobby of this edifice boasts a 40-foot-wide "waterfall" fountain by Noguchi, created out of curvy constructions of stainless steel, corrugated glass, and, of course, trickling water (NY; E, F train to Fifth Ave.).

Associated Press Building at Rockefeller Center, sculpture by Isamu Noguchi. For a Noguchi fix while shopping in midtown, visit this rhythmic, dynamic work of art, incorporated seamlessly into its surrounding architecture (50 Rockefeller Plaza, NY; B, D, F train to 47–50th sts./Rockefeller Ctr.).

Eclipsed Time. Long Island Rail Road, Pennsylvania Station, Maya Lin. Look up at the ceiling and see what appears to be a giant scientific apparatus, look down at the ground and see a magnificent sun dial. Both ominous and elegant, it's actually a frosted glass, aluminum, stainless steel, and fiber-optic sculpture by the celebrated architect (NY; 1, 2, 3, 9, A, C, E train to 34th St./Penn. Sta.).

Empress Voyage, 2.22.1784. Canal Street MTA station, Bing Lee. Platform walls and the connecting passageway are decorated with this artist's colorful ceramic tile mural and mosaic banding (NY; A, C, E, J, M, Z, N, R, 6 train to Canal St.).

Happy World. Ik-Joong Kang. Colorful and playful cartoonlike imagery makes up the ceramic tile mural in this subway station's mezzanine wall (Main St. station, Flushing, Queens; 7 train to Main St./Flushing).

Q is for Queens. The mezzanine and platform of the 33rd, 40th, and 46th street Queens MTA stations are spruced up with an installation of faceted glass murals from A to Z, by children's book illustrator Yumi Heo (Queens, 7 train to 33rd, 40th, 46th sts.).

Signal. Stainless steel and glass sculptures by Mel Chin, at the Broadway-Lafayette Street MTA station are installed on this station's mezzanine columns; they're accompanied by ceramic tiles on the station's walls (B, D, F, Q, train to Broadway-Lafayette).

Sounding Stones. Maya Lin fountain installation involves water bubbling around and through four black blocks—often more heard than seen (500 Pearl St., NY; 4, 5, 6, N, R train to City Hall).

Antiques

Art of the Past. An excellent source for traditional Indian art (1242 Madison Ave., NY; 212 860-7070; 4, 5, 6 train to 86th St.).

Carole Davenport. The place to buy—or at least view—a 17th-century Edo Period Noh mask (131 E. 83rd St., NY; 212 734-4859; 4, 5, 6 train to 86th St.).

Chinese Porcelain Company. Of course you'll find lovely porcelain from China here, but other fine Asian antiques are available as well (475 Park Ave., NY; 212 838-7744; 4, 5, 6, N, R train to 59th St./Lexington Ave.).

Dimson Homma. Extremely tasteful midtown Manhattan gallery displaying some of the finer things in life. There's an interesting mix of antique and contemporary items, including Tibetan tiger rugs, rare Japanese dinnerware, Burmese buddhas, and Chinese scholar rocks (20 E. 67th St.; 212 439-7950; 6 train to 68th St.)

E. & J. Frankel Ltd. When making the Madison Avenue rounds for Asian art, stop by this outpost of beautiful treasures. Recent offerings included a Tang dynasty horse sculpture (1040 Madison Ave., NY; 212 879-5733; 6 train to 77th St.).

Far Eastern Antiques and Arts. A mouthwatering range of antique and contemporary pieces from China, Japan, India, and Southeast Asia. Owner Stephen Gano has been in the business for over 25 years and will be able to help you decide on how best to decorate your home or office (799 Broadway, NY; 212 460-5030; N, R, L, 4, 5, 6 train to 14th St./Union Sq.).

Flying Cranes Antiques Ltd. Lovers and collectors of Japanese antiques will have a field day here, where offerings have included works by Meiji Period masters (1050 Second Ave., NY; 212 223-4600; 4, 5, 6, N, R train to 59th St./Lexington Ave.).

Imperial Oriental Art, Inc. Fine Chinese porcelain and other antiques can be purchased here (790 Madison Ave., NY; 212 717-5383; 6 train to 68th St.).

J. J. Lally & Co. One of the leading dealers in early Chinese bronzes, ceramics, jades, and other works of art. Special exhibitions at this gallery during Asia Week in March are stunning. (41 E. 57th St., NY; 212 371-3380; N,R train to Fifth Ave.).

Liza Hyde. Ah, there's nothing so lovely as an antique Japanese screen. Hooked? This dealer specializes in them (565 Park Ave., NY; 212 752-3851; 4, 5, 6, N, R train to 59th St./Lexington Ave.).

M. D. Flacks Ltd. Beautiful, intriguing Asian antiques and sculptures can be found here (38 E. 57th St., NY; 212 838-4575; N, R train to Fifth Ave.).

Ming Furniture Ltd. Witness the timelessness of antique Chinese furniture, like the 18th-century Qing dynasty spindleback designs at this gallery (31 E. 64th St., NY; 212 734-9524; 6 train to 68th St.).

Naga Antiques. Exquisite Japanese screens from the 16th century onwards, plus a variety of antique baskets and ceramics, lacquerware, and other treasures can be purchased here (145 E. 61st St., NY; 212 593-2788; 4, 5, 6, N, R train to 59th St./Lexington Ave.).

Orientations Gallery. This gallery specializes in antique Japanese masterpieces. Wood and ivory carvings, netsuke, and bronzes are some of the fine offerings (P.O. Box 1018, Lenox Hill Station, NY, NY 10021; 212 772-7705; www.orientationsgallery.com; by appointment only).

R. H. Ellsworth Ltd. If you've got the budget to collect Asian antiquities, such as sculptures from, for example, 8th- or 7th-century Siberia, you can find these and other examples of fine art here (960 Fifth Ave., NY; 212 535-9249; 6 train to 77th St.).

Robert Haber and Associates, Inc. If you're in the market for exquisite, rare antiquities, such as Sino-Siberian harness ornaments dating back to the 4th or 3rd century B.C., this is a good place to look (16 W. 23rd St., NY; 212 243-3656; F train to 23rd St.).

Sepia International, Inc./The Alkazi Collection of Photography. Part commercial gallery, part research center, part privately owned archive, this gallery showcases 19th- and early-20th-century photographs of South Asia, namely India, Burma, and Sri Lanka (148 W. 24th St., 11th floor, NY; 212 645-9444; www.sepia.org; 1, 9 train to 23rd St.).

Suzanne Mitchell Asian Fine Arts. Hanging scrolls from the 18th century are among the Japanese and Korean works of art for sale (17 E. 71st St., NY; 212 535-1700; 6 train to 68th St.).

Weisbrod Chinese Art Ltd. Gorgeous traditional Chinese treasures. For example, a recent show included very rare jades from the 2nd to 3rd centuries A.D. (36 E. 57th St., 3rd floor, NY; 212 319-1335; N, R train to Fifth Ave.).

William Lipton Ltd. Excellent gallery of Asian art, with a pleasant outdoor courtyard. This well-established dealer carries a full range of antique Chinese furniture, with a special emphasis on desk objects. A recent exhibition focused on the "wondrous and amenable Chinese stool" (27 E. 61st St., NY; 212 751-8131; 4, 5, 6, N, R train to 59th St./Lexington Ave.).

Contemporary Art Galleries

Admit One Gallery. Located in the Chelsea arts district, this newly opened gallery is devoted to East Indian contemporary art, with an emphasis on photography (529 W. 20th St., 4th floor, NY; 212 463-0164; www.artnet.com/admitone.html; C, E train to 23rd St.).

Bose Pacia Modern. Modern and contemporary artists, such as the painter Manjit Bawa, are shown at this sleek gallery located in the heart of the ultra-hip Chelsea art world (508 W. 26th St., 11th floor, NY,; 212 989-7074; www.bosepaciamodern.com; C, E train to 23rd St.).

China 2000 Fine Art. At this gallery, you can discover modern and contemporary Chinese art that bridges both past and present, created by artists from mainland China (5 E. 57th St., NY; 212 588-1198; N, R train to Fifth Ave.).

Dialectica. Although not necessarily "Indocentric," this new, exclusive international art gallery in Soho often features art by the all-stars of modern Indian art; its inaugural exhibition, for example, included works by Rabindranath Tagore (415 West Broadway, NY; 212 226-8921; C, E, train to Spring St., N, R train to Prince St.).

Elizabeth Wang Gallery. Modern works by artists of Chinese ancestry—not necessarily concentrating on Chinese subject matter—are offered by this dealer (20 E. 63rd St., NY; 4, 5, 6, N, R train to 59th St./Lexington Ave.; by appointment only).

Ethan Cohen Fine Arts. Street-level Tribeca gallery shows contemporary work, like the updated versions of calligraphy by C. C. Wang, plus exhibitions featuring current art-world darlings like Xu Bing and Gu Wenda (37 Walker St., NY; 212 625-1250; 1, 9 train to Franklin St.).

Gallery Dai Ichi Arts, Ltd. Curious as to how traditional Japanese ceramics have evolved? This gallery specializes in contemporary

Japanese vessels and ceramic sculptures (24 W. 57th St., 6th floor, NY;
212 262-0239; www. daiichiarts.com; N, R train to 57th St.).
Ise Art Foundation. View contemporary Asian art here during a Soho
jaunt (555 Broadway, NY; 212 925-1649; N, R train to Prince St., B, D,
F, Q train to Broadway-Lafayette).
Kaikodo. Superb shows of both traditional and newer East Asian art,
supplemented with a gorgeous, scholarly journal, can be found at this
gallery (164 E. 64th St., NY; 212 223-0121; 6 train to 68th St.).
Lawrence of Beijing. The New York arm of this China-based dealer
represents contemporary Chinese artists whose works bridge past and
present (63 E. 79th St., 5-A, NY; 212 866-0525; 6 train to 77th St.).
M. Y. Art Prospects. A Chelsea outpost for contemporary Asian (and
other international) art run by independent curator Miyako Yoshinaga
(135 W. 29th St., Ste. 1002, NY; 212 268-7132; 1, 9 train to 23rd St.).
Paisley. This hip Flatiron district store/gallery/cafe/lounge not only
features Asian furniture and objects, but it also showcases modern and
contemporary Indian art (49 E. 21st St., NY; 212 353-8833; N, R, 6
train to 23rd St.).
Tolman Collection of Tokyo. If contemporary Japanese prints are your
cup of tea, this is a source for limited-edition lithographs (350 W. 50th
St., NY; 212 489-7696; C, E train to 50th St.; by appointment only).

Arts Organizations and Community Groups

Akira Ikeda Gallery. Although this New York branch of a long-open
Japanese gallery is no longer an exhibition space, it serves as a bridge
between U.S. artists and galleries and arts institutions in Japan (17 Cornelia St., 1-C, NY; 212 266-5449; A, C, E, B, D, F, Q train to W. 4th St.).
Asian American Arts Alliance. Founded in 1983, this nonprofit arts
service organization exists to raise awareness of Asian American arts.
Publications, roundtables, and a resource library are available to artists
and the public (74 Varick St., Ste. 302, NY; 212 941-9208;
www.aaarsalliance.org; 1, 9 train to Canal St.).
Asian American Arts Center. This Chinatown space offers a range of
community programs (26 Bowery, NY; 212 233-2154; A, C, E, N, R, J,
M, Z, 6 train to Canal St.).
Indus Arts & Community Service. Both contemporary and traditional
Indian American art is supported by this organization (P.O. Box 1249,
Wall Street Station, NY, NY 10268-1459; 212 840-2300).
Japanese Artists Association. This nonprofit membership organization

exists to help Japanese artists organize exhibitions in the New York area (14 Harrison St., NY; 212 966-9850; 1, 9 train to Franklin St.).

Asian Arts Classes
(*see also* **Museums listings**)

Koho School of Sumi-e. Offers small classes on the art of *sumi-e* and calligraphy—complete with instruction on proper breathing and posture, as well as ink preparation and brush positioning, of course (64 MacDougal St., NY; 212 673-5190; 1, 9 train to Houston St.).

Korean Calligraphy Center. This Koreatown establishment offers $50 lessons in the painting of Korean letters on long strips of pale-hued cloth (35-14 Farrington St., 2nd floor, Flushing, Queens; 718 461-3190, 718 279-4577; 7 train to Main St./Flushing; call for appointment).

Korean Culture Society of Eastern USA. Exhibitions and classes on calligraphy and flower arranging are offered at this nonprofit multicultural center (42-40 Bowne St., Flushing, Queens; 718 358-5010; 7 train to Main St./Flushing).

New York Chinese Cultural Center. Among the offerings at this community-based arts organization are classes in traditional Chinese visual arts such as Chinese landscape painting and Chinese calligraphy (390 Broadway, NY; 212 334-3764; A, C, E, N, R, J, M, Z, 6 train to Canal St.).

Riverside Church. Calligraphy and batik are some of the Asian crafts courses offered to the public both in the day and in the evening (490 Riverside Dr., NY; 212 749-8140; 1, 9 train to 116th St.).

Urasenke Tea Ceremony Society/Urasenke Chanoyu Center. Private lessons in the classic ritual are given by the tea teachers (153 E. 69th St., NY; 212 988-6161; 6 train to 68th St.; by appointment only).

little tokyo

J apan is alive and well in several distinct communities throughout New York City. Here are a few of the city's outposts of Japanese life and culture.

east village: sushi in *bohemu*

New York and Japan converge in Manhattan's Little Tokyo, on land that was once Dutch governor Peter Stuyvesant's country estate. For the last 15 years, the East Village around 9th and Stuyvesant streets has been the convergence point for a flood of Japanese students and expatriates. It's not quite as big and brassy as Tokyo's trendy Shibuya district—but the block between Second and Third avenues has its own lively, distinctive character, serving Japanese expats with a variety of Japanese restaurants, along with a hair salon, video store, sake bar, and grocery.

Drawn by the colorful unconventionality that is the East Village, hundreds of Japanese students, artists, and musicians migrated here in the mid-1980s as Japan's bubble economy ballooned and the yen pummeled the dollar. The neighborhood, traditionally an area with a high tolerance for individual expression and a low tolerance for rules and strong-arm authority tactics, has for decades been a mecca for like-minded artists, political anarchists, and students. Even when those same qualities attracted junkies, prostitutes, and drug dealers in the '60s,

Japanese hip-hop dancers perform at a fundraising event in the East Village. (Photo © Corky Lee)

'70s, and early '80s, the community had a certain seedy charm and cranky survivalist spirit—as well as a deep commitment to the pleasure principle.

Gradual gentrification over the last ten years has muscled out the area's more unsavory elements. Still, with its multitude of bars, shops, restaurants, clubs, and cafes, the neighborhood has retained a festive atmosphere of multiethnic *bohemu*, or bohemia (not to mention more liquor licenses per square block than almost any other neighborhood in the city). Energized by the youthful spirit of the Village streets, the young Japanese expats established their own community—a community that has since swelled into the thousands. The New York City Department of Planning estimates that some 3,200 Japanese moved to the Big Apple between 1990 and 1994, with the highest concentration of those immigrants settling on the Lower East Side. That trend has continued since then, according to the latest available figures.

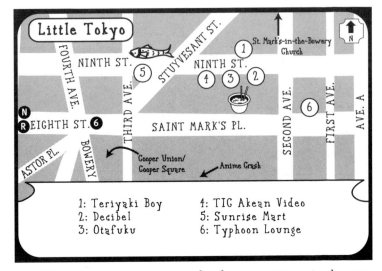

Little Tokyo

NINTH ST.
FOURTH AVE.
STUYVESANT ST.
NINTH ST.
St. Mark's-in-the-Bowery Church
N
EIGHTH ST.
THIRD AVE.
SAINT MARK'S PL.
SECOND AVE.
FIRST AVE.
AVE. A
ASTOR PL.
BOWERY
Cooper Union/
Cooper Square
Anime Crash

1: Teriyaki Boy
2: Decibel
3: Otafuku
4: TIC Akean Video
5: Sunrise Mart
6: Typhoon Lounge

While the Japanese presence has been a constant in the area around 9th Street since the '80s, Little Tokyo in the Village has gone through a series of incarnations. Fifteen years ago, Japanese expatriates made the scene at Counterpoint—a bar that has since become a takeout shop called **Teriyaki Boy**—and at one of the city's first karaoke bars, Candy B1, which is now the **Decibel** sake bar. Much like Little Tokyo itself, Decibel has a funky Gotham vibe and a decidedly Japanese spirit. Descend a flight of stairs, ring the buzzer, and enter the dark, friendly space, where the list of sakes is long and the martinis are mixed with litchi juice. The bar is owned by entrepreneur Bon Yagi, who in 1984 opened the first Japanese restaurant on the street—the sushi bar **Hasaki,** named after his hometown. The sushi bar faces a quaint Old New York tableau of Federal-style rowhouses, and skyward, toward 10th Street and Second Avenue, is the steeple of Saint Mark's-in-the-Bowery Church, one of New York's oldest churches, built in 1799. But step into **Yajirobei,** a second-floor restaurant a block away on Stuyvesant Street, and you'll think you're in a bustling *izakaya* sake house in Japan.

Sunrise Mart, the Japanese market next door, opened in 1995. The bulletin board at the entrance advertises moving sales, rooms for rent, clubs, art shows, and Japanese and English lan-

public transportation

EAST VILLAGE (9th St. between 2nd Ave. and Bowery)
SUBWAY: 6 to Astor Pl. BUS: M101, M102, M103 on 3rd Ave. and
Lexington Ave. to Astor Pl.; M15 on 2nd Ave. to 9th St.
MIDTOWN (5th and 6th Ave. between 40th and 60th sts.)
SUBWAY: B, D, F, Q to 42nd St., 7 to 5th Ave. BUS: M6 on 6th Ave.
and Broadway to 42nd St.; M2, M3, M5 on 5th Ave.

guage lessons. The **TIC Akean** video store on 9th Street toward
Second Avenue rents Japanese videos (not subtitled) and sells
Japanese books and magazines. Mr. Yagi most recently opened
Otafuku across the street, a tiny stand for *takoyaki* (octopus cro-
quettes) and *okonomiyaki* pancakes—*yatai* snacks, the foods found
at Japanese fairs and festivals. "I wanted a place that fit with the
nature of the East Village and its atmosphere of festivities," Mr.
Yagi says.

midtown: not all business

When Tokyo's Mitsubishi Estate Company in 1989 bought a 51
percent stake in the Rockefeller Group, owners of Rockefeller
Center, the headline on the front page of the *New York Times* read:
"Japanese Buy New York Cachet With Deal for Rockefeller
Center." The deal was only the most high-profile of many
Japanese investments in New York real estate. Japanese companies
have since divested themselves of some of their Manhattan holdings, but certainly not all, and a Japanese-interpreted New York
hipness continues to vibrate through midtown.

Executives on corporate assignment, for example, still favor
making business agreements over sake and sushi. Midtown
Japanese restaurants are well established—some have been there
since the '70s—and their sleek, inconspicuous facades are seamlessly incorporated into midtown's towering skyscape. **Sushisay,
Sushi Zen, Kuruma Zushi, Sushiden,** and **Hatsuhana** are known

for the quality of their sushi. **Chikubu, Naniwa,** and **Yodo** offer dinners of *fugu*, or blowfish, the Japanese delicacy infamous for the neurotoxin that, if not carefully removed, can be deadly (though deaths are very rare). **Inagiku,** set in the Waldorf-Astoria Hotel, offers expensive, elegant meals—seasonal offerings of minikin proportions.

Exclusive, discreet clubs, or *kurabu*, such as **Usagi** and **Stella** on 49th Street, cater to Japanese businessmen whose expense accounts cover such incidentals as $150 bottles of Cognac. But the shuttered door at one club seems an unfortunate sign of the Japanese economy's prolonged slump. Since the early '90s, Japanese companies have reduced their staffing in the United States, and the number of Japanese executives based in New York has fallen.

Yet, if the crowds of patrons are any evidence, Japanese midtown establishments that reach a much broader market have fared well. Fifth Avenue shoppers file into the Japanese department store **Takashimaya** for beautifully arranged flowers, Shu Uemura cosmetics, unusual gifts, and teas and confections in the basement Tea Box. Bookstores **Kinokuniya** on 49th Street off Fifth Avenue and **Asahiya** on Vanderbilt Street near Grand Central carry Japanese books, magazines, and stationery. They're the best places to look for hard-to-find English editions of Haruki Murakami novels, for example. Next to Kinokuniya is **Minamoto Kitchoan,** where the glass counters encase precious *wagashi* confections like bean jelly in dried persimmons, chestnuts and sweet red beans in green tea pancakes, and plum wine jelly sprinkled with gold powder.

Opened in 1973, the **Kitano Hotel,** at 38th Street and Park Avenue, was the first Japanese-owned hotel in New York. The brick and brownstone building was built in 1926 by the Rockefellers. The hotel closed from 1991 to 1995 to undergo a $50 million reconstruction. Rates start at $275, but a night in a tatami suite and a formal *kaiseki* meal at the hotel restaurant **Nadaman Hakubai** can cost as much as $2,000 for two.

seasonal festivals

In 1936, the Reverend Hozen Seki, who had moved to Los Angeles from Japan in 1930, flew to New York from the West Coast in a single-engine airplane piloted by two of his church members. The following year, Reverend Seki established the first Buddhist institution chartered in New York State—the **New York Buddhist Church**. For more than 50 years this church on New York's Upper West Side has held an annual *Obon* festival. According to a Buddhist sutra, a disciple of the Buddha liberated his mother from the tortures of the land of death with his selfless prayers. *Obon odori*, a celebratory occasion, commemorates the deceased with traditional music and dance. The festival is held the second Sunday in July across the street from the church in Riverside Park.

Every October for the past few years, the **Japan Society** has sponsored a street festival on 47th Street, featuring a *mikoshi* shrine procession. As is tradition, the shrine is carried along the street to pay respects to local gods and give thanks for good fortune. The block becomes a stage for *taiko* drumming performances, traditional music played on the *koto* and *shakuhachi* instruments, and martial arts demonstrations, while food stands offer such festival fare as *yakisoba* noodles and *mochi* rice cakes.

When the coming of spring brings cherry blossoms to Tokyo, millions of visitors descend upon Ueno Park to view the pink-petaled splendor. In New York, the **Brooklyn Botanic Garden** holds an annual *Sakura Matsuri*, or cherry-blossom festival, in late April to celebrate the flowering of the Kwanzan cherry trees that line the garden's cherry esplanade. The blossoming begins in March and culminates in a festival that might include an exhibit of bonsai trees, a kimono show, displays of traditional arts, and performances of traditional dance, all amid a sea of pink and white petals.

shopping, fashion & beauty

The happy collision of Eastern and Western fashion cultures can be traced back to the Middle Ages, when mariners sailing the Spice Route stowed traditional Asian garments amid tins of fragrant cinnamon, ginger, and cumin. Western artists over the centuries have been equally enthralled with the cuts and colors of Asian clothing; most memorably, in the 19th century, Monet painted a portrait of his wife in a kimono. In the 1960s, the Beatles triggered a brief flirtation with the Nehru jacket. More recently, fashionistas of the Western world—notably, that trend-monger Madonna—have taken a fancy to colorful East Indian saris and the art of mehndi, or painting henna designs on hands and feet, a practice that evolved out of ancient Egypt.

Still, there is a palpable sense of excitement and discovery whenever another successful stylistic merger of East and West is announced each spring or fall season. This fusion of East-West style isn't limited to the runways of New York fashion shows; it's out on the streets as well, in glorious Indian-inspired prints, in handcrafted Tibetan earrings, and in jeweled slippers from a Chinatown street vendor. Throughout New York, the Asian-inspired look is a firm fixture in the fashion encyclopedia.

An array of Tibetan-style hats, as seen through the window of Dö Kham, in Soho.

The aesthetic and commercial success of this once-unlikely marriage of East and West is indisputable, albeit a little surprising, given the different philosophical standpoints from which Eastern and Western cultures derive their inspiration. The Chinese, for instance, are deeply influenced by the teachings of Confucious, who preached a lifestyle devoted to the "golden mean"—a strict adherence to following the "middle way." This balanced approach is also intrinsic to the Eastern religions of Buddhism and Taoism. Around 320 A.D., the Taoist scholar Ko Hung published *Nei Pien*, a book of teachings that emphasized the relationship between health and moderation. To maintain harmony in life, he wrote, "one must not look, listen, sit, drink, eat, work, rest, sleep, walk, exercise, talk, or dress too much."

Ko Hung would not have been too popular in modern-day New York, where his admonitions represent the polar opposite of a "successful" New York lifestyle. Andy Warhol, the notorious Manhattan style-setter and inveterate party-goer, was one of the city's most active advocates of excess and extravagance. "Fantasy and clothes go together a lot," he once declared. And in the hotbed New York context of recent decades past, who could argue?

The Warholian vision prevailed through the '70s and '80s, until it hit a roadblock of New-Age sensibility—a shift toward the less-is-more dynamic of the new millennium, an Eastern ethos of inner harmony and outer serenity. That, along with the increasingly diverse ethnicity of New York itself, provided an ideal platform for the fusion of cultures. The Asian aesthetic in the Big Apple now encompasses everything from sashimi and sitar music to Ming meditation chairs for the living room and Ayurvedic beauty treatments for the living body. These days, *wabi*, the centuries-old Japanese concept of unostentatious refinement, can just as easily be applied to the philosophy of contemporary designers like Giorgio Armani, whose design creed eliminates the superfluous and emphasizes the comfortable, adhering to a time-tested dictum of simplicity and elegance.

shopping for asia in nyc

Faster than you can say "(Vera) Wang! (Shanghai) Tang! Thank you ma'am!" the ascendancy of Asian designers and Asian-accented design in New York has cemented its reputation as the shopping capital of the world. The city's cosmopolitan and uniquely multicultural makeup ensures that shopping here provides the quintessential East-West experience, with enough mind-numbing variety to satisfy cross-cultural neophytes and discerning fashionistas alike.

Armed with a precise plan of attack on several shopping fronts, shoppers with substantial war chests will head directly for posh Madison Avenue on the Upper East Side, where expensive designer brands are more prevalent than pollen on a spring morning. Department store devotees might prefer the quietly classy confines of Japanese retail giant **Takashimaya** for unusual gifts, fine furnishings, and accessories (as well as a pot of tea), while no-nonsense traditionalists can hop on the subway to Canal Street and pay homage to **Pearl River Mart,** the legendary China-

Ting's Gift Shop, in an historic building in Chinatown, with its intriguing display of toys and other wares.

toys, toy, toys

Chinatown is full of toy and novelty stores, but an increasing homogeneity has crept in at these enterprises, bringing with it the kinds of New York–centric souvenir tchotchkes you could find anywhere in the metropolitan area. At the top of curling Doyers Street, at the corner of Pell, one of the oldest businesses in Chinatown is a wonderful exception. **Ting's Gift Shop,** with its high tin ceiling overlooking old wooden shelves, is crammed with quality Chinese toys, kites, cheongsam (the distinctive long Chinese sheath dress), lanterns—you name it. The shop has been in business for 45 years, dating back to when the neighborhood population was largely Cantonese, and has been run by the same family all those years. According to Tammy Ting—who, with her husband, Y. H. Ting, has been the store's proprietor since her 94-year-old uncle died—the building is also one of the neighborhood's oldest, originally housing a Chinese herb shop.

town emporium that inspires designers each fashion season; or stop at the seemingly-unaffected-by-time 100-years-old **Mott Street General Store** to peruse the pottery and other household goods; toys and other fun stuff at the equally historic **Ting's Gift Shop;** or **Sinotique** for an eclectic selection of Chinese artifacts, from ancient to pop history. At other points along the way, Indian jewelry, Indonesian textiles, Korean cabinets, and Vietnamese lacquerware can be found in myriad stores throughout Manhattan. On the east side you'll find Japanese kitchenware at **Katagiri** and 18th- and 19th-century wood-block prints at **Things Japanese.** For books, cards, and a well-selected range of Asian ephemera, you'll want to visit the **Asia Society Store** as well as **Kinokuniya** and **Asahiya.** Midtown, especially in the thirties, is also where you'll find the heaviest concentration of stores selling rugs of all Asian origins. You might want to stop at the **Tibet Carpet Center,** or **Bolour** if you're further uptown, for fabulous antique carpets. Also home to a number of stores with Asia-related offerings is the Flatiron area, including the incredible one-of-a-kind home furnishings store **ABC Carpet and Home** and **Far Eastern Antiques and Arts.** Chinatown, Soho, Nolita, Greenwich Village, and the Lower East Side remain the primary neighborhoods in which to discover Asia in New York. Textiles and home accessories with a cutting edge blend of traditional with contemporary can be found at spots like **Paisley, Shï,** and **Leekan Designs.** But you'll want to go to **Zakka** for a true taste of an ultra-modern Asian environment.

No one likes to pay full price, and as any New Yorker will tell you, the key word in the shopping lexicon is "sale," defined as the sacrifice of personal dignity in the pursuit of the greater goods. Unless you schedule a trip to coincide with a sale period or tax-free shopping week, negotiating the retail jungle in New York can be painfully expensive. That's why you shouldn't worry about getting down and dirty with the hordes at sale time, because the payoff—stretching those shopping greenbacks a little further—is no small matter, especially if it means converting the savings to an extra embroidered shawl or two. Sale time or not, there's no doubt that Asia has made its presence felt in New York. East meets West indeed.

Mott Street General Store dates back to the late 19th century; while the household goods sold there do not, you will still get a taste of the early days of New York's Chinatown.

Asian Fashion Traditions:
A Bit of Background

It is not difficult to understand why designers from the West look east for inspiration. Eastern garments are the ultimate realization of the design tenet "Form Follows Function"—but, what form! Asian-influenced fashions will always be prevalent because they have "an uncomplicated ease to them, and they're so attractive to the eye," says Jane Agnew Schelling, senior fashion editor at *Town and Country* magazine.

The sari—a necessary yet perfect response to India's oppressive heat—has been called the most feminine costume in the world, magically concealing as much as it reveals. With apologies to proponents of the Roman toga, there is no more graceful way to drape six yards of colorful silk or cotton around the female form. Although wearing a sari in New York poses its own special problems, it has certain unique advantages as well. Shoba Narayan wrote in *Newsweek* that squeezing into a crowded subway car was risky for fear of inadvertent entanglement, but when she tried to hail a taxi, "Indian cab drivers raced across lanes and screeched to a halt in front of me." In New York's Little India you can readily indulge your curiosity and consider the beautiful fabrics at the **Om Saree Palace** and the **Little India Emporium.**

Japan's kimono, a flowing full-length robe graced with long, wide sleeves, is worn by both men and women and is versatile enough to accommodate both courtly geishas and portly sumo wrestlers. Anyone who has ever tried to kneel or sit cross-legged on a tatami mat can readily appreciate the ease and comfort afforded by a kimono, as opposed to the discomfort caused by a tight cocktail dress or fitted pants. The kimono is by no means an informal costume, however. In centuries past, there were times when the occasion demanded that ladies of the Japanese court wear up to 12 layers of kimono. For her traditional wedding to Japan's Crown Prince Naruhito in 1993, Masako Owada's elaborate 12-layer costume weighed a hefty 30 pounds. You will find an intriguing range of vintage and modern—and

Dressed in traditional Korean *hanbok*, two Korean women go for a walk in Flushing, Queens. (Photo © Gorky Lee)

far less hefty—kimonos at the **Kimono House** in the East Village. **Nakazawa** in Soho will custom make a kimono for you.

While the color and design of Western dress are very much personal statements—made to reflect an individual's personality or to enhance a person's skin tone—garment colors, motifs, and fabric type all serve a clearly defined social, religious, or cere-monial purpose in Asian culture. In Chinese society, red denotes happy occasions such as weddings, while white is worn for funerals. Red is also a color of strength: The golfer Tiger Woods, whose mother is Thai, always wears power red on tournament Sundays. In Imperial China, bright yellow was reserved for roy-alty. The dazzling "dragon robes" worn by Chinese nobility had a strict hierarchical system dictated by color and style, incorpo-rating elaborately embroidered dragons (representing the emperor), clouds (heaven), mountains (earth), and other auspi-cious symbols such as waves, cranes, and flowers. Costume

Sari fabrics, in a kaleidoscope of colors and patterns, are sold in Little India.

colors were also based on the "five-elements theory" (yin-yang wu-hsing) of Chinese cosmology: blue equals east, white is west, black is north, red is south, and yellow is the center.

Similarly, Japanese floral patterns featuring cherry or plum blossoms and designs based on the four seasons represent the innate characteristics of the country. And in Korea, the beauty of the hanbok lies in its deceptively simple form, carefully chosen color juxtapositions, and elegant, flowing lines. In Asia, harmony in life is assured by the proper combination of clothing and colors.

cross-cultural fashion

Even as Asia's customs and cultural heritage are being seriously eroded by the steady influx of Western ideas and influences, Western designers are helping to preserve these traditions by applying Asian design principles to the concept of haute couture. So, while fashion-conscious teens in Bombay, Bangkok, and Beijing rush to identify with MTV icons by hip-hopping around town in Levi's and Polos, sarong-clad supermodels in braided Balinese hairdos and Japanese whiteface traipse the runways of Paris and New York. It's a cross-cultural stew of multiple influences: Men and women of every Asian persuasion populate top design houses, bringing global culture to the rarefied stratosphere of high fashion.

Jane Agnew Schelling cites a who's-who of name-brand designers who have, in their own way, tapped into the Asian theme: "John, Giorgio, Ralph, Donna—designers are inspired by traveling to different cultures and driven by the need to do something different." Still, when it comes to defining a fashion ideal, successful designers are not identified by their ethnic backgrounds. Says Calvin Tsao, a New York architect and arbiter of good taste, "Asian-influenced design is not based on racial lines but on cultural affinity—having an Asian sensibility is the important thing."

The happy result of all this cross-cultural fashion fertilization can be seen on a stroll through New York's shopping streets, from the upper reaches of exclusive Madison Avenue

Paisley, in the Flatiron district, is known for its contemporary Indian and other Asian-influenced furnishings, textiles, and art.

and midtown Manhattan to gentrified Soho, trendy Nolita, and the cutting-edge creations of Tribeca and the Lower East Side. Label-conscious types can sweep up a funky top from **Anna Sui,** an exquisitely crafted **Vera Wang** gown, an ethnic knit from **Yohji Yamamoto,** or a **Comme des Garçons** original, while intrepid shoppers are likely to find such prizes as an exotic Tibetan fur hat, a stunning Indian silk jacket, or an intricate beaded blouse with dragon-and-ox motif. The "Asianization" of the New York fashion world is irrefutable and irreversible.

Asian Designers in New York

Thanks to its seductive blend of money, power, and glamour, New York is the stage on which the stars of the fashion firmament shine brightest. Fashion legend **Issey Miyake** was certainly among the first to fuse an Eastern aesthetic with the world of high fashion. In 1978 he published a summary of his work, East Meets West. His unique exploration of form, function, and beauty brought him enduring global recognition. "Curiosity and pleasure are at the heart of my work," says Miyake. At a New York retrospective in 2000, he defined design as "not a static process; it is the constant exchange of ideas, aesthetics, and emotions."

While the high-wattage Asian designers have a significant presence in New York, the Big Apple is also home to many up-and-coming designers. To commemorate the Year of the Dragon in 2000, handbag designer **Amy Chan** commissioned an impressive paper-and-wire sculpture of the mythical beast to decorate the window front of her fashionable Nolita store. In the Chinese horoscope, dragons are propitious creatures, associated with the twin virtues of wisdom and generosity. In a clever and not-so-subtle nod to the industry, each of Chan's carefully constructed paper "scales" covering the sculpture was cut from the page of a fashion magazine. Inside her store, the numeral 8—an auspicious number in Chinese thinking—features prominently, from the large figure on one of the walls to the tiny eights hanging from the light fixtures. Her store tags feature this pithy

Amy Chan brings Chinese tradition into the concepts and presentation of her modern handbag designs.

nugget, translated from the Chinese pronunciation of eight: $(\text{Harmony}+\text{Progress}+\text{Happiness})^2 = 8$. "Eight is a harmonious number, so we also decided to make it our logo," says Chan, who grew up steeped in Chinese folklore. "It's the idea of passing good energy around through my designs. It's fabulous to be able to maintain tradition in some shape or form while being futuristic at the same time." While the designer in her acknowledges the need to create beautiful bags that are highly functional, Chan will continue to draw inspiration from the East, because "so much in our culture has yet to be fully explored."

Chan is a relative newcomer to the New York fashion scene, while Josie Natori is a Philippines-born designer who "made it" here over two decades ago. Her signature line of lingerie, sleepwear, and accessories is sold in department stores nationwide. Natori, a pioneer of the Asian aesthetic, attributes the popularity of her line to "the East-West sensibility, the fluidity of fabrics and shapes. When

Vivienne Tam outside her clothing store in Soho.

I do classic, there's more of a twist to it. Exoticness is our trademark." With ideas from the East now easily accessible, Natori is optimistic that the influx of talented young Asian-influenced designers will cement the Asian cultural aesthetic in the fashion mainstream. "We bring something to the table that's different," she says.

Respected Malaysia-born designer Yeohlee Teng is often described by industry watchers as an "intellectual maker" of clothing. Her functional, design-driven style, combined with her effective and innovative use of fabrics, has earned her accolades from around the world. While there is nothing overtly "Asian" about her clothes, she says "there are certain values you grow up with. I believe in things that are very simple and natural. I'm interested in how space is defined around the body. There must be balance, proportion, simplicity. It's debatable whether you can attribute that to personal style or my Asian heritage." What's important, she says, is that "my clothes empower the wearer— not in ways that are very obvious, but a more subtle fusion." Teng traces the current fascination with Asian-influenced fashion back to the 1970s, when designers like Yamamoto, Kawakubo, Miyake, and Kenzo took Paris by storm. "That was the definitive moment in time—we can still see its influence today."

the tao of vivienne tam

Decorative Chinese elements—a dragon wall carving, antique screen doors, hanging lanterns, and a pair of mythic fu dogs standing sentinel-like at the entrance—lend an Eastern charm to **Vivienne Tam**'s unique Soho store. Tam's popular, distinctive designs blend a dose of playfulness with traditional Chinese motifs and a functional modernity, reflecting her Hong Kong roots. "It's a combination of what I experienced when I was growing up in Hong Kong, and where I am now in New York," she says. She is intent on producing what she calls "harmonious and beautiful clothing that enhances one's personality."

What Vivienne Tam never intended was for her clothes to become museum pieces. But that's exactly what happened. Her design sensibility was further sparked by a visit to China in 1979. She was mesmerized by "shocking-pink peonies, playful pandas, and the bright red Chinese double-happiness symbol," all of which deeply influenced her subsequent collections. Her signature style—exemplified by her "Mao Print" dress that created a sensation in the mid-1990s—put Tam on the fashion map and into the permanent collections of art-world institutions like the Metropolitan Museum of Art in New York and the Victoria & Albert Museum in London.

At **Kinnu,** a refreshingly unusual Nolita gallery housed in a former noodle factory, beautiful clothes decorate the walls like so much wearable art. Owner John Panikar is quick to distinguish his delectable designs from the run-of-the-mill stuff. "We use Indian textiles in a different way, beyond the crafts and ethnic process," he says. Working with skilled artisans from villages in Gujarat in western India, Panikar and wife Kinnari design their own hand-sewn fabrics in resplendent cottons and silks. Panikar calls the iridescent look of the fabrics, achieved by blending Eastern tradition with Western technology, a "light and shadow" design. The Panikars are adamant about preserving Indian culture and protecting the artisans they work with. "Good design means not only being a good designer, but understanding the culture of a place and respecting it," he says. "Knowing the social pattern of a place and how to work in tandem with the locals is an integral part of the process." Kinnu's

one-of-a-kind fashions, from the gold-embossed tie-dye bedspreads to the embroidered jackets and appliqué sarongs, are evidence of that commitment.

Shaw Behzad also bridges the gap between East and West—
almost literally. The Iranian-born designer is based in New
York's Fashion District, while his 12-year-old Rimini By Shaw
line of women's clothing is manufactured for U.S. department
stores exclusively in Asia. "All the dresses I design have some
kind of embellishment, be it handwork or embroidery," he says.
Shaw, who visits the Far East frequently, explains that he has
"always been inspired by the handwork, by the colors—the
whole Asian spirit." He believes that Eastern concepts are more
understood now. "Asians come from a rich cultural background, and now that their cultures are much more known to
the world, designers are inspired to reinterpret them aesthetically." He adds that Asian designers working in New York "do
not necessarily do anything Asian-inspired, but they just have
that inbred sensitivity to pay attention to aesthetics—they have
a very good 'hand.'"

Xuan, a young Saigon-born designer of "high-end sports-
wear" in the city's Garment District, reaffirms Shaw's assessment.
While he says his design style "definitely has a cosmopolitan
sensibility," he tries to include at least one detail that is somehow
Asian, perhaps in the stitching, the color, the neckline, or the
length of skirt. "It's not a self-conscious thing," Xuan says. "It
just comes." Working in multicultural New York provides inspiration and accessibility not available in other cities, he says. Ideas
speak to him at any moment: "Dining in a pan-Asian restaurant,
walking down the street," he says. "On my way here, I saw an
African American woman on the train. She had on a lambskin
coat, copper-colored—let's call them Chinese gold—low-heeled
leather shoes, and pink floral socks. It's impossible not to feed off
the energy."

In the dynamic, disorderly, and gloriously creative cauldron
that is the fashion world, inspiration is only a pair of pink socks
away. Meanwhile, Asian fashion is here in New York to stay.

Beauty in NYC: The Eastern Approach

An anthem of sorts is being played out daily in softly lit, sweet-scented, and hushed spaces around the city. The song of beauty is big business, and stressed-out New Yorkers are shelling out millions of dollars annually to lie in Zen-like oases and enjoy pampering body treatments and services. Urbanites are finding particular comfort in Asian-style treatments, which emphasize spiritual well-being as much as physical and psychological health. The result is a mini-boom of Eastern-style salons and spas throughout the city.

The Asian approach to personal beautification and health has its roots in centuries-old traditions, such as Ayurveda, a 5,000-year-old practice that uses herbal treatments for everything from stretch marks to dark circles under the eyes. If the prospect of warm herbs and essential oils being slowly dripped onto your forehead holds a certain karmic appeal, then Shirodhara, a classic Indian Ayurvedic treatment, is the ideal way to relax those hard-to-reach places. When your head feels as if it is in a vise and your back and shoulder muscles are painfully knotted from hours at the computer, then the Javanese Lulur—two hours of pampered bliss, including a full-body massage, an exfoliating rice scrub, a soothing yogurt slather, and a flower-filled loofah bath—is a miracle cure. If you want your skin to have that soft and healthy glow, try a Korean-style sauna and exfoliation. Of course, miracle workers don't come cheap—especially in New York. Expect to pay, on average, about $80 an hour for a no-frills massage and $100 an hour for something more elaborate or luxurious. Intrepid types in search of some local flavor and lower prices should head to Manhattan's Chinatown for traditional treatments at less than princely sums. Just don't expect the royal treatment.

[shopping, fashion & beauty]

THE LISTINGS

Bookstores

Asahiya. Japanese expatriates and students frequent this store, located across the street from Grand Central Station, for a taste of home. Apart from the usual books and magazines, there's a small CD section and some English-language books as well (52 Vanderbilt Ave., NY; 212 883-0011; 4, 5, 6, 7 train to Grand Central/42nd St.).

Asia Society Store. Who says you can't toot your own horn? Probably the most comprehensive collection of Asian-subject books in town. Topics range from history and culture to art and religion. There are also gift items featuring arts and crafts from all over Asia (725 Park Ave., NY; 212 517-ASIA [2742]; www.asiasociety.org; 6 train to 68th St. Note: During renovations, the Asia Society is housed [until Fall 2001] at 502 Park Ave.; 4, 5, 6, N, R train to 59th St./Lexington Ave.).

Asian American Writers' Workshop Bookstore. Interested in learning more about the Asian diaspora? This niche bookstore, located below a Gap clothing store, features fiction, poetry, and anthologies by Asians in America (27 St. Marks Pl., NY; 212 494-0061; 6 train to Astor Pl.).

East West Books. Specialty bookstore for enlightened readers. Self-help yourself to titles on meditation, Eastern religions, alternative medicine, and astrology. Sample titles include *The Tao of Contemplation, Optimal Wellness,* and *Autobiography of a Yogi.* You get the picture (78 Fifth Ave., NY; 212 243-5994; N, R, L, 4, 5, 6 train to 14th St./Union Sq.).

Kinokuniya. The most comprehensive store in Manhattan for books from and about Japan (10 W. 49th St., NY; 212 765-7766; www. kinokuniya.com; B, D, F, Q to 47–50th Sts./Rockefeller Ctr.).

K-Mei Inc. Neighborhood joint with Chinese-language books and magazines, dictionaries, and stationery (81-B Bayard St., NY; 212 693-1989; A, C, E, N, R, J, M, Z, 6 train to Canal St.).

Koryo Books. Korean translations of English-language bestsellers, Korean paperbacks, videos, CDs, toys, and gift items in the heart of Manhattan's Koreatown. There are also some English-language books on Korea (35 W. 32nd St., NY; 212 564-1844; B, D, F, Q, N, R train to Herald Sq.).

Ming Fay Book Store. Chinese equivalent of the local newsstand, stocked with books, videos, and entertainment magazines, together with dozens of English titles on such esoteric topics as feng shui, tai chi, and traditional Chinese medicine (42 Mott St., NY; 212 406-1957; A, C, E, N, R, J, M, Z, 6 train to Canal St.).

Oriental Book and Stationery Co. Two Chinatown locations carry a comprehensive assortment of Chinese-language books and magazines, plus English-language children's books, toys, and stationery (29 East Broadway, NY; 212 962-3634; F train to East Broadway; 131 Bowery, NY; 212 343-0780; B, D, Q train to Grand St.).

Oriental Culture Enterprise. This second-floor space has a large selection of popular Chinese paperbacks. There's also a section on CDs and cassettes, Chinese musical instruments, and supplies for calligraphy (13 Elizabeth St., NY; 212 226-8461; A, C, E, N, R, J, M, Z, 6 train to Canal St.).

Zakka. Looking like a transplant from Tokyo's Shinjuku district, this Japanese bookstore with an industrial-chic interior carries English-language titles on graphic design, architecture, and illustration. Two glass-enclosed shelves showcase a collection of toy characters from Japanese comic books and anime films (147 Grand St., NY; 212 431-3961; A, C, E, N, R, J, M, Z, 6 train to Canal St.).

Kitchen, Sundries, and Kids

Chinese American Trading Company. A traditional Chinese provision shop that's worth a look to get an idea of what's available in the dry goods and dinnerware department. There's a section on Chinese herbal medicine as well (91 Mulberry St., NY; 212 267-5223; A, C, E, N, R, J, M, Z, 6 train to Canal St.).

Katagiri. Neighborhood place for Japanese dinnerware, kitchenware, and simple gift items. Two doors away is a supermarket of the same name, where you can pick up Japanese groceries, or have them delivered to your home (226 E. 59th St., NY; 212 838-5453; www.katagiri.com; 4, 5, 6, N, R train to 59th St./Lexington Ave.).

Mott Street General Store. An old-fashioned taste of Chinatown. This great space is the oldest store in Manhattan's Chinatown—and it reeks of history. Owner Paul Lee's grandfather started the business in 1891 and the store still retains its original 19th-century facade. Inside, the wooden floors and high tin ceiling evoke an earlier age. The shelves are cluttered with household goods, dinnerware, and assorted knick-knacks (32 Mott St., NY; 212 962-6280; A, C, E, N, R, J, M, Z, 6 train to Canal St.).

Things Japanese. This cozy second-floor space is cluttered with sec-ondhand art books, trays and baskets, porcelain, and dolls. But if you're looking for fine 18th- to 20th-century woodblock prints, you'll be even more pleased. There is a good selection available (127 E. 60th St., NY; 212 371-4661; www.thingsjapanese.com; 4, 5, 6, N, R train to 59th St./Lexington Ave.).

Ting's Gift Shop (Ting Yu Hong Co.) Find gifts for every occasion at one of Chinatown's oldest toy stores (18 Doyers St., NY; 212 962-1081; A, C, E, N, R, J, M, Z, 6 train to Canal St.).

Wing On Wo and Co. How much is that porcelain piggy in the window? Chinese tea sets, decorative porcelain plates, plus dinnerware and home accessories. Nothing fancy, but good if you're looking for Asian essentials for your home (26 Mott St., NY; 212 962-3577; A, C, E, N, R, J, M, Z, 6 train to Canal St.).

Furniture, Rugs, and Other Home Accessories

ABC Carpet and Home. A Manhattan "must-see" destination. Go crazy over the incredible selection of household goods (not to mention the uptown prices) at this downtown favorite. You won't find any depart-ment store like this in your hometown. Eclectic and innovative mer-chandising blends food, furniture, and home accessories, in a magical space (888 Broadway, NY; 212 473-3000; www.abchome.com; N, R, 4, 5, 6 train to 14th St./Union Sq.).

Alpine Design. "Museum quality," says owner John Kang succinctly when asked to describe the beautiful pieces in his antiques-filled store. Appreciative visitors will encounter Japanese cabinets, Korean book chests, Chinese altar tables, and many other decorative items that more than fit the bill (230 Fifth Ave., NY, 212 532-5067; N, R train to 28th St.).

Beyül. Owner Matthew Carrigan makes regular trips to China, Tibet, Nepal, and Southeast Asia; his dedication shows. Beyül—"hidden

Rug traditions from the Near and Far East are represented in the vast selection of rugs at ABC Carpet, and elsewhere in the city.

realm" in Tibetan—is a welcome anomaly on a quiet street in Manhattan's meatpacking district. It is a treasure trove of high quality, functional antique furniture, great for adorning the home. There is an especially impressive collection of restored Chinese window lattices and painted Tibetan chests (353 W. 12th St., NY; 212 989-2533; A, C, E train to 14th St.).

Bolour, Inc. Wonderful antique carpets can be purchased here (595 Madison Ave., NY; 212 752-0222; 4, 5, 6, N, R train to 59th St./Lexington Ave.).

Dynasty Arts/Qian Long Palace. This furniture store is on a little side street, just down from the corner of Chinatown's famous "Egg Cake Lady." Lacquer and pine cabinets, tables, drawers, and other decorative pieces for the home (103 Mosco St., NY; 212 566-6882; A, C, E, N, R, J, M, Z, 6 train to Canal St.).

Eleanor Abraham Asian Art. Having been a collector since the 1960s and a dealer for over 20 years, Eleanor Abraham has a varied selection of Asian art and antiques to choose from. There's stone and bronze sculpture from India, Tibet, Pakistan, and Southeast Asia, tribal jewelry from Central Asia, Indian village jewelry, and intricately embroidered wedding shawls (345 E. 52nd St., NY; 212 688-1667; E, F, 6 train to Lexington Ave./51st St.; by appointment only).

Equator. Tropical wooden furniture, decorative arts, and accessories

to be or knot to be: some basic rug facts for first-time buyers

The origins of Oriental carpets can be traced back thousands of years. In 1949, the remains of a carpet discovered in a cave in Outer Mongolia were found to date back to the 5th century B.C.

Each of the following places in Asia has a distinct carpet-making tradition: Afghanistan, China, India, Kashmir, Pakistan, Iran (Persia), the Russian republics (the Caucasus), and Turkey. Persian carpets are made using a double-knotted technique; all the other countries make rugs that feature both single and double knotting.

The golden age of Chinese carpets took place during the Tang dynasty (618–907), when arts and crafts were at their most refined. The equivalent period for India was during the reign of the mighty Moghuls (1526–1857).

Tribal rugs, which were used primarily for the home, always feature symbols that have a positive connotation or are meant to dispel evil spirits. Many rugs have poetic-sounding symbols, such as a "window to prosperity."

Each color in a Chinese carpet has specific meaning. For example, blue—the color of the sky—signifies purity, while yellow—the color of the earth—is reserved strictly for the emperor. There is a similar code for animals, birds, and mythical creatures—tigers, cranes, dragons, unicorns, and the like.

A good quality 5- × 8-foot silk carpet with 500 to 600 knots per square inch will take one to two years to make. Carpets with 900 knots per square inch and above will require three to four years to finish. Top-notch master weavers skilled enough to scale the Everest of fine rugs—about 1,100 knots per square inch—can only stay in front of the loom for one or two hours at a time.

from Indonesia and other parts of Southeast Asia (98 Greene St., NY; 212 219-3708; 6 train to Spring St.).

Felissimo. Upscale multicultural, multilevel specialty and lifestyle store. Tons of tabletop merchandise. An exercise in quiet restraint, this is a great place to browse for unusual and well-packaged gifts, even though the prices are likely to raise your blood pressure (10 W. 56th St., NY; 212 247-5656; E, F train to Fifth Ave.).

Global Table. As its name suggests, this Asian-accented Soho store has an interesting selection of tastefully refined decorative items (107 Sullivan St., NY; 212 431-5839; C, E train to Spring St.).

Jacques Carcanagues Inc. Large, elegant, and well-decorated furniture and antiques store, featuring a first-rate range of items from China, Japan, Korea, and parts of Southeast Asia (106 Spring St., NY; 212 925-8110; www.artseensoho.com; 6 train to Spring St.).

Jamson Whyte. Wood, wood, everywhere! A large selection of well-made Indonesian furniture and household items. Owners Byron Jeong and John Erdos will help acquaint you with the rustic charm of tropical furniture (47 Wooster St., NY; 212 965-9405; 6 train to Spring St.).

Kashmir. This swanky midtown establishment offers a typical range of decorative items from North India, including marble tabletops with colorful inlays, handsome carpets, papier-mâché trays, and embroidered cushion covers (157 E. 64th St., NY; 212 861-6464; 6 train to 68th St.).

Leekan Designs. Tastefully quirky items from all around Asia, including delicate Chinese lanterns and birdcages, Indonesian shadow puppets, wooden tribal sculptures, and yes, the ubiquitous mah jongg sets. A bead bar—the choice is huge—dominates the middle of the store (93 Mercer St., NY; 212 226-7226; 6 train to Spring St.).

Paisley. This hip Flatiron district store/gallery/cafe/lounge not only features Asian furniture and objects, but it also showcases modern and contemporary Indian art (49 E. 21st St., NY; 212 353-8833; N, R, 6 train to 23rd St.).

Pondicherri. Indian and Tibetan textile and handicrafts, Indonesian furniture, and a variety of Asian knickknacks (454 Columbus Ave, NY; 212 875-1609; B, C train to 81st St.).

Robb Steck. This store has an impeccable Zenlike sensibility. Wander in to admire the Asian-influenced tableware and other accessories, including vases and candles (131 Thompson St., NY; 212 388-0828; C, E train to Spring St.).

Rustika. If weekend furniture browsing is a favored pastime, this Southeast Asian (mainly Indonesian) home furnishings store should be on the agenda (63 Crosby St., NY; 212 965-0004; 6 train to Spring St.).

Sara. Japanese ceramics and delicate glassware on Manhattan's Upper East Side. There is also a selection of pretty gift items (952 Lexington Ave., NY; 212 772-3243; 6 train to 68th St.).

Sarajo. An ocean of exotic Indian imports, including ethnic-design textiles, carved tribal art, and furniture from the Indian subcontinent (130 Greene St., NY; 212 966-6156; B, D, F, Q train to Broadway-Lafayette).

Shï. This interesting home and gift spot has a particular emphasis on design. European, Japanese, and American houseware items are the order of the day. The store is tucked away on a favorite Nolita street along with several chic stores and restaurants (233 Elizabeth St., NY; 212 334-4330; F train to Second Ave.).

Sinotique. Standing out from the plethora of restaurants and souvenir stores in Manhattan's Chinatown, this long and narrow oasis of calm attracts collectors of Chinese artifacts, accessories, and antique furniture. Interesting and unusual items abound, such as 19th-century Chinese shop signs and apothecary jars (19A Mott St., NY; 212 587-2393; A, C, E, N, R, J, M, Z, 6 train to Canal St.).

Spirit World. A modest storefront in the West Village, Spirit World specializes in the crafts, cultures, and religions of Thailand, Laos, and Burma. Featured items include Buddhist statuary, Burmese lacquerware, hand-woven textiles, and silver. Most items have been directly commissioned from artists and cooperatives (541 Hudson St., NY; 212 352-0326; seasiancrafts.com; 1, 9 train to Christopher St.).

Takashimaya. Opulent, understated store that exudes good taste—or, in the store's own words, it's "a cross-cultural forum" that reflects "a singular commingling of Eastern and Western aesthetics." Feel free to commingle with the fancy gifts and accessories, well-crafted clothing, and fine furnishings, then head for the Christian Tortu flower shop and basement tea room (693 Fifth Ave., NY; 212 350-0100; E, F train to Fifth Ave.).

Tibet Carpet Center. Manufacturer and wholesaler of Ralo Tibetan carpets, which are spun-knotted and dyed by hand, using fine Tibetan wool (127 Madison Ave., NY; 212 686-7811; www.tibetcarpet.com; 6 train to 33rd St.).

WaterMoon. Nancy Murphy developed a taste for Asian art while she was a lawyer in China, becoming an authority on fine Chinese furniture in the process. Her well-appointed store is a cultured showcase for top-drawer collector's pieces and decorative items, tribal textiles, and Chinese and Tibetan furniture (211 West Broadway, NY; 212 925-5556; A, C, E, N, R, J, M, Z, 6 train to Canal St.).

Traditional Clothing and Accessories

China Silk and Handicrafts Corp. There are dozens of gift and souvenir stores in the heart of Manhattan's Chinatown, and you'd be well advised to give many of them a wide berth. This is one of the more interesting ones, especially for anyone in search of traditional silk costumes, porcelain vases and figurines, embroidered purses, and other household paraphernalia (18 Mott St., NY; 212 385-9856; A, C, E, N, R, J, M, Z, 6 train to Canal St.).

Himalayan Vision II. The proliferation of Tibetan shops in NY means the availability of a wide range of *Chuba* (Tibetan dress), *kap che* (tops), and religious artifacts (127 Second Ave., NY; 212 254-1952; 6 train to Astor Pl.; 1584 First Ave., NY; 212 988-6573; 4, 5, 6 train to 86th St.).

Kimono House. Vintage and modern kimonos, slippers, antique dolls, pottery, and prints in a cramped but charming East Village space (93 E. 7th St., NY; 212 505-0232; 6 train to Astor Pl.).

Little India Emporium. If you must have that gold lamé jacket or a sari to sashay in, this is the place. Custom-made outfits, hand-embroidered cushion covers, and even natural henna tattoos are also available, as are men's Punjabi suits and costume jewelry. Bangles, bangles, everywhere. The Emporium is on the second floor. Downstairs is the Little India Store, which stocks Indian groceries, magazines, and videos (128 East 28th St., NY; 212 481-032; 6 train to 28th St.).

LNK Custom Tailoring. Don't be put off by the graffiti-covered wall and that clipping in the window from a men's magazine, circa 1980. If the disco outfit depicted there doesn't suit your needs, this Hong Kong–style tailor can produce a more contemporary cut. Two weeks or less, at prices between $650 and $1,100, including material (178 Mulberry St., NY; 212 226-7755; B, D, Q train to Grand St.).

Nakazawa. Custom-made kimonos from this husband-and-wife team, plus Japanese gift items (137 Thompson St., NY; 212 505-7768; B, D, F, Q train to Broadway-Lafayette).

New Age Designer Inc. Tailor-made *cheongsams* and traditional jackets, catering mainly to Chinatown regulars. There is a good selection of Chinese silks and satins (38 Mott St., NY; 212 349-0818; A, C, E, N, R, J, M, Z, 6 train to Canal St.).

Om Saree Palace. In a neighborhood flush with South Asian restaurants, this pocket-size showroom specializing in custom-made saris has a dazzling array of materials to choose from (134 E. 27th St., NY; 212 532-5620; 6 train to 28th St.).

Oriental Gifts and Products, Inc. For those inclined to slip into something a little more comfortable, this basic Chinatown store has a good range of Chinese slippers and sandals spilling out onto the sidewalk. Size it up, slip something on, then take a stroll in Columbus Park, just across the street (96 Bayard St., NY; 212 608-6670; A, C, E, N, R, J, M, Z, 6 train to Canal St.).

Pearl River Mart. Ground zero for all things Chinese. This Manhattan Chinatown emporium's influence on inspiration-seeking designers cannot be overstated. The two-level store could do with a touch-up, but it houses an impressive selection of *cheongsams*, silk jackets, kung fu pants, and other clothes, as well as many household products and traditional gift items. The Grand Street location is much smaller, though well displayed and no less fascinating (277 Canal St., NY; 212 431-4770; A, C, E, N, R, J, M, Z, 6 train to Canal St.; 200 Grand St., NY; 212 966-1010; B, D, Q to Grand St.).

Royal Sari House. Custom-made traditional Indian saris. The shelves in this conveniently located corner store are lined with colorful Indian fabrics, scarves, and jewelry. Step inside and be transported to another world (264 Fifth Ave., NY; 212 679-0732; N, R train to 28th St.).

Shanghai Mei Li Fashions. Chinatown-style custom tailoring for traditional and contemporary outfits. Bring your own material or choose from a selection of brightly colored silk (7 Elizabeth St., NY; 212 431-3855; A, C, E, N, R, J, M, Z, 6 train to Canal St.).

Tibet Arts and Crafts. This Village favorite has ritual objects, pashmina shawls, jewelry, and the usual assortment of handicrafts from Tibet and Nepal (144 Sullivan St., NY; 212 529-4344; 197 Bleecker St., NY; 212 260-5880; A, C, E, B, D, F, Q train to W. 4th St.).

Vision of Tibet. Himalayan arts and crafts, shawls, scarves, and jewelry, plus a sampling of books and stationery (167 Thompson St., NY; 212 995-9276; B, D, Q, F train to Broadway-Lafayette).

Contemporary Clothing and Accessories

Alpana Bawa. Colorful beaded and embroidered clothing from this Indian-inspired designer, who has an obvious love of art and nature. Innovative, imaginative use of traditional fabrics and techniques with contemporary styles. Popular items include a backless embroidered wrap skirt and Chinese silk brocade dresses. Printed shirts for men are also available (41 Grand St., NY; 212 965-0559; A, C, E, N, R, J, M, Z, 6 train to Canal St.).

Amy Chan. This Hong Kong–born, U.S.-raised designer is known for her groovy must-have handbags in a variety of attractive, whimsical designs and innovative materials—note her signature "mosaic tile" look. Asian touches abound in this uniquely New York store (247 Mulberry St., NY; 212 966-3417; 6 train to Spring St.).

Anna Sui. Leader of the hip parade. Visitors to Sui's Soho boutique, decorated in Wild West, early-bordello style, will not immediately notice an Asian connection, although the embroidered tops and beaded bags may give a hint. Fun, frilly, and funkadelic clothing and accessories from this in-demand designer of cutting-edge downtown chic. "Live your dream," says Anna Sui. And she does—in spades (113 Greene St., NY; 212 941-8406; N, R train to Prince St.).

Atsuro Tayama. This Yohji disciple's clothes are well made and exceedingly wearable and come in a range of styles, from avant-garde to contemporary. The sweaters and tops are exceedingly popular (120 Wooster St., NY; 212 334-6002; N, R train to Prince St.).

Comme des Garçons. Designer Rei Kawakubo is to fashion as rock 'n' roll is to music. Stunning, visually stimulating clothes that are artistic, edgy, and unpredictable. Appropriately located in Chelsea's gallery district (520 W. 22nd St., NY; 212 604-9200; C, E train to 23rd St.)

Dö Kham. Himalayan hip. Known for its colorfully exotic fur hats, this top-end store also has a variety of authentic and well-made Tibetan-style clothing—loose cotton tops, trendy monk's satchels, pashmina shawls and scarves, and religious art (51 Prince St., NY; 212 966-2404; N, R train to Prince St.; 304 East 5th St.; 212 358-1010; F train to 2nd Ave.).

DOSA. Delicate dresses in lightweight Asian fabrics and pastel shades with an ethereal quality and a subtle Eastern influence. The simple styles have attracted a loyal following, and there's a strong dose of DOSA in many a New York wardrobe (107 Thompson St., NY; 212 431-1733; N, R train to Prince St.).

Duh. Former film student Etsuko Kizawa has found her true calling with these simple, one-of-a-kind fabric bags, made from a variety of Asian-inspired furniture fabrics. Her Lower East Side work space is worth seeking out (102 Suffolk St., NY.; 212 253-1158; F train to Delancey/Essex).

Handloom Batik. Despite its dingy exterior and kitschy Balinese souvenirs in the window, this store offers handmade fabrics from India and Indonesia that will appeal to the sarong-savvy crowd (214 Mulberry St., NY; 212 925-9542; 6 train to Spring St.).

Issey Miyake. Stylish, pioneering exponent of the East-West aesthetic, this artist-as-designer is still very much at the top of his game (992 Madison Ave., NY; 212 439-7822; 6 train to 77th St.).

Jade. This Nolita standout offers a smart and sexy range of exotic Indian- and Asian-inspired clothing and accessories (280 Mulberry St., NY; 212 925-6544; N, R train to Prince St.).

JIMINLEE translatio. This well-traveled designer effortlessly transcends the East-West culture gap. "Translatio" refers to the morphing of various basic principles from both sides of the fashion divide into one distinct identity. The beautifully unique clothes are a seamless juxtaposition of the designer's Korean roots and her global perspective (13 White St., NY; 212 219-9146; 1, 9 to Franklin St.).

Jimmy Choo. Malaysian-born, London-based Choo was put on the map by celebrities like Princess Diana. Now, royalty, showbiz types, and native New Yorkers alike have been brought to heel by his stylish and extremely well-crafted shoes (645 Fifth Ave., NY; 212 593-0800; E, F train to Fifth Ave.).

Jussara. Samba style with a Korean twist. Elegant, well-made clothes and must-have matching accessories from designer Jussara Lee, who grew up in Brazil (125 Greene St., NY; 212 353-5050; N, R to Prince St.).

Kazuyo Nakano. Working with bold colors and unique materials like snakeskin and antique kimono prints, this Nolita-based designer gives handbags a modern-day spin (223 Mott St., NY; 212 941-7093; 6 train to Spring St.).

Kinnu. Designer couple John and Kinnari Panikar's gallery-like space features clothing-as-art: one-of-a-kind handwoven designs in airy, ethereal silks and cottons and iridescent colors. Gold-embossed bedspreads and fine, tie-dyed linens complement the collection, produced by skilled Indian craftsmen in Ahmedabad (43 Spring St., NY; 212 334-4775; 6 train to Spring St.).

Language. Sleek, chic European-style boutique, infused with an Asian sensibility. Art and fashion is creatively combined. This is a showcase for hip women's fashions—beaded shawls and bags, cutting-edge jewelry—and there is a funky art space in the rear to boot (238 Mulberry St., NY; 212 431-5566 6 train to Spring St.).

Margie Tsai. Fashion insiders are justifiably upbeat about this designer with a world view on wearable contemporary clothing and accessories. Fun and functional clothes for the young, and the young at heart (4B Prince St., NY; 212 334-2540; B, D, Q train to Grand St.).

Min Lee 105. This store in the interesting "bargain district" on Manhattan's Lower East Side is fashionably hip and carries an eclectic mix of contemporary men's and women's clothes, including European imports and lines from young designers like Min Lee and Anni Kuan (105 Stanton St., NY; 212 375-0304; F train to Delancey/Essex.).

Pleats Please. Miyake's signature pleated clothing is also priced to please at this venue. As the name suggests, lightweight pleated clothing is the order of the day (128 Wooster St., NY; 212 226-3600; www.pleatsplease.com; N, R train to Prince St.)

Purdy Girl. Located on a downtown street littered with shopping discoveries, this innocuous-looking store features contemporary clothing and accessories. The embroidered fabrics and Asian themes will appeal to the younger crowd (220 Thompson St., NY; 212 529-8385; A, C, E, B, D, F, Q train to W. 4th St.).

Selia Yang. This Korean designer caters to confident career types who "aren't afraid to look like a woman," according to sister Jenny Yang. Simple silk dresses and elegant wedding gowns form the core of the collection (328 E. 9th St., NY; 212 254-9073; 6 train to Astor Pl.).

Shamballa. Fine ethnic jewelry from around the globe in a variety of traditional and contemporary designs, including a selection of exquisite 22-carat handcrafted items from India. The wedding bands based on traditional Indian and Byzantine designs are especially popular (92 Thompson St., NY; 212 941-6505; www.shamballajewelry.com; C, E to Spring St.).

Shanghai Tang. This reincarnation of an earlier attempt to tap into the Manhattan market focuses on what made the Hong Kong original such a hit: an unlikely yet chic combo of Mao and Mickey—silk and satin Mandarin jackets and the like in a riot of cartoon colors. While prices are still hard to swallow, the five-story townhouse is a beaut (714 Madison Ave., NY; 212 888-0111; B, Q train to Lexington Ave.).

Shin Choi. Korean designer of classic contemporary clothing, catering to a youngish, fashion-conscious clientele (119 Mercer St., NY; 212 625-9202; N, R train to Prince St.).

Vera Wang. The epitome of wedding gown chic. This much-sought-after designer is defined by stylish, sophisticated, and beautifully made dresses that would make any woman rush to the altar (991 Madison Ave., NY; 212 628-3400; www.verawang.com; 6 train to 77th St.).

Vivienne Tam. Prominent proponent of "China Chic"—a tastefully elegant, delicately feminine, and innovative blend of wearable contemporary clothing, reflecting her Eastern roots and a large dose of Western style. Savvy shoppers will find "double happiness" at this designer's fashionably exotic downtown Manhattan boutique. Tam's spacious, eye-catching flagship store is a radiant example of "Asia in New York" (99 Greene St., NY; 212 966-2398; N, R train to Prince St.).

Yohji Yamamoto. You know it's exclusive when you have to be buzzed in. One of Japan's original Big Three, Yohji is never out of fashion. This inventive designer does amazing things with the color black; his white shirts aren't too shabby, either. It's high-fashion engineering at its best (103 Grand St., NY; 212 966-9066; www.yohjiyamamoto.co.jp; A, C, E, N, R, J, M, Z, 6 train to Canal St.).

Yolanda Kwan. From her workshop in the back of the store, Hong Kong–born, Tokyo-trained Kwan uses rich, textured fabrics like Chinese brocade, Thai silk, and Indian cotton to attain her signature look in a selection of handmade clothes, scarves, and home accessories (6 Prince St., NY; 212 625-3348; 6 train to Spring St.).

Yu. If avant-garde designers are your thing, put this consignment "resale" store in the once-bohemian, now horribly hip Lower East Side at the top of your list. Eiko Berkowitz started off with her own Japanese collectibles, but now carries clothing from assorted Chinese, Thai, and Filipino designers—all of which are in pristine condition (151 Ludlow St., NY; 212 979-9370; F train to Delancey/Essex).

Zao. Groovy, baby! Looking like a set from an Austin Powers movie, this sleek, slick, ultra-trendy "lifestyle" store has been labeled a "pop-culture supermarket." It carries clothing by Asian designers and showcases an unusual selection of design-driven accessories. There is also a gallery space in the rear, with new exhibitions every six weeks (175 Orchard St., NY; 212 505-0500; F train to Second Ave.).

Spas and Other Beauty Treatments
(see also Bodywork listings in **Health and Fitness***)*

Ajune. Try the "Eastern Influence," an acupuncture-based treatment. The spa offers reflexology, body wraps, ginger massages, and on-site specialists to give you a rundown on your personal well-being, followed by a relaxing rubdown (1294 Third Ave., NY; 212 628-0044; 6 train to 77th St.).

Away Spa. Many are lured here by the Lulur—a blissful two-hour treatment of massage, scrubs, and slathering—that was once only reserved for the Indonesian royal family (New York Hotel; 541 Lexington Ave., NY; 212 407-2970; E, F, 6 train to 51st St./Lexington Ave.).

Bliss 57. Uptown branch of Bliss Spa (19 E. 57th St., NY; 212 219-8970; N, R to Fifth Ave.).

Bliss Spa. This downtown star also has a newer uptown branch. Featuring a full slate of luxury treatments, it makes for a heavyweight tandem on the city's spa circuit (568 Broadway, NY; 212 219-8970; www.blissworld.com; N, R train to Prince St.)

Bon-Sofi Ladies Spa. Although most of the better-known establishments for Korean-style sauna and exfoliation are farther afield in Flushing and Fort Lee, this ladies-only Koreatown favorite provides a quick fixer-upper (2 W. 33rd St., NY; 212 244-5949; B, D, F, Q, N, R train to Herald Sq.).

Jin Soon Natural Hand and Foot Spa. Entrust your hands and feet to Jin Soon, who works wonders with essential-oil infusions and natural scrubs. It's an indulgence you won't soon forget (56 E 4th St., NY; 212 473-2047; 6 train to Astor Pl.).

Joean Skin Care. Face-off (otherwise known as exfoliation) at this no-frills Chinatown salon. A full facial will leave you feeling relaxed and your wallet feeling none the worse for wear. (163 Hester St., NY; 212 966-3668; A, C, E, N, R, J, M, Z, 6 train to Canal St.).

Karen Wu Beauty & Wellness Spa. An East-meets-West combination of traditional Chinese therapy and European skin care in Manhattan. Trained Chinese doctors are on the spot to assess your body and ensure harmony of mind and spirit (1044 Madison Ave.; 212 737-3545/1377 Third Ave., NY ; 212 585-2044; 6 train to 77th St.).

Kozue Aesthetic Spa. Exclusively Japanese-based spa techniques are used at this salon, which bases its treatments on the ancient healing art of ki to attain both inner peace and outer beauty (795 Madison Ave., NY; 212 734-8600; 6 train to 68th St.).

Ling Skin Care. Asian-influenced facial treatments and curative methods for all skin types. Wrinkle-reducing herbal masks that use ginseng and seaweed and pearl powder are especially popular. Ling skincare products are also for sale (128 Thompson St., NY; 212 982-8833; www.ling-skincare.com; C, E train to Spring St.; 12 E. 16th St., NY; 212 989-8833; N, R, L, 4, 5, 6 train to Union Sq.; 105 W. 77th St., NY; 212 877-2883; 1, 9 train to 79th St.).

Prema Nolita. "We're about beauty and wellness," says part-owner Celeste Induddi of her tiny bamboo-floored spa and store in trendy Nolita. There is a single treatment room, and after a restorative Thai massage, you'll probably wish you'd booked it for the whole day (252 Elizabeth St., NY; 212 226-3972; F train to Second Ave.).

Shangri-La Day Spa. Heavenly rewards await those who come to Shangri-La, a tranquil Tibetan-owned operation that focuses on Himalayan-style treatments (247 W. 72nd St., NY; 212 579-0615; 1, 2, 3, 9 train to 72nd St.).

Shiseido Studio. This innovative, high-tech "interactive beauty station" invites you to enjoy facials and massages or attend skincare class—and it's all for free. Try the makeup navigator, a sophisticated screen that can "visualize" you in various types of makeup, without putting anything on your own face (155 Spring St., NY; 212 625-8820; www.shiseido.com; C, E to Spring St.).

Soho Integrative Health Center (Mezzanine Spa). Treat your body to a well-deserved makeover at this medically supervised super-spa. There is a comprehensive medical center downstairs, while on the upper levels, Ayurveda and acupuncture are the treatments of choice (62 Crosby St., NY; 212 431-1600; 6 train to Spring St.).

Soho Sanctuary. Yin, yang, and yoga are the draws at this women-only spa. After you've balanced your body with a shiatsu massage, go one-on-one with a yoga instructor (119 Mercer St., NY; 212 334-5550; 6 train to Spring St.).

Wu Lim. After going grocery shopping or antique hunting, this Chinatown (bargain) basement space is the place to go for a quickie back rub or foot massage. If you're pressed for time, no problem—get a 10-minute rub for something like seven bucks. Prices and times go up proportionately, if rather oddly—a 31-minute stay on the massage table will cost you $21; 46 minutes, $32; and so on (145 Grand St., NY; 212 925-1276; 6 train to Spring St.).

asia in queens

Out on the streets of Jackson Heights, food carts beckon with a South Asian treat: betel leafs layered with lime paste, rose petals, betel nuts, anise, cloves, cardamom seeds, and other spices, then folded over into a bite-size packet. *Paan*, as this snack is known, is considered a breath freshener and an aid to digestion, to be chewed slowly either after a meal or as a midday treat. Abdul Momin Hamid, who runs Shaheen's Palace on 37th Avenue and other locations, describes the sensation of eating the filled betel leaf as an "encounter with 35 distinctive flavors."

The act of chewing *paan* is no modern street fad—in fact, this Ayurvedic tradition, reportedly dating back some 8,000 years, is far older than the city into which it has migrated. Still, you would be hard-pressed to find *paan* on the streets of any other neighborhood—aside from along Lexington Avenue in the twenties—in New York City. The constant intertwining of old and new cultures is typical of Queens, the most ethnically diverse borough in New York City, and perhaps in the United States: 167 nations are represented by its residents. Many Queens neighborhoods are populated by a mix of old and new immigrants, and you can see this rich diversity reflected in the sidewalk storefronts—where Colombian bakeries sell their wares next door to Indian grocers and Korean herbal medicine shops.

Of all the ethnic groups that have made the borough their home, however, it is the Asian communities in Queens that are

The #7 train—recently granted landmark status in recognition of its rich heritage of conveying new populations between home and work—runs from Manhattan, making local stops throughout Queens.

growing at the fastest pace. According to a New York University study, the largest groups include immigrants from China, Korea, Taiwan, and South Asia (India, Pakistan, Sri Lanka, and Bangladesh); there are also growing numbers of Asian emigres from the Philippines, Cambodia, Vietnam, Japan, Afghanistan, Laos, and Thailand. The languages, cultures, foods, folkways, and dreams they have all brought to the streets of Queens are visibly present and thriving in the borough's vibrant daily life.

"we're all immigrants"

Historically, the borough has been attracting new immigrants since the 1840s. At the beginning of the 20th century, the building of bridges, railroads, and the subway system helped to transform the borough from a series of farms and small villages into an urban outpost, easily accessible from Manhattan. The greatest growth in immigrant populations occurred after 1965, when amended immigration laws shifted from a quota system to a policy based on family reunification and labor skills. Among the reasons frequently given as to why Queens became such a magnet for immigrant groups are the availability of affordable housing, its proximity to New York's airports, and its highly developed hospital system, which has provided jobs for many immigrants in medical-related fields. Some experts cite the 1964–65 World's Fair, held in Flushing Meadows Park, as the catalyst that brought many people from all over the world to Queens for the first time. Finally, there is no doubt that immigrants attract other immigrants: Most newcomers prefer to settle where they have relatives or friends—or at least some countrymen—as they begin to build a new home in a new place. That's why you'll often hear Queens residents of all backgrounds say, "We're all immigrants."

Exploring the Jigsaw puzzle

A map of Queens reveals a jigsaw puzzle of neighborhoods. The majority of the Asian population lives in northern Queens. The neighborhoods containing the largest Asian communities—Flushing, Elmhurst, Jackson Heights, and Woodside—boast a great diversity among those populations. Although certain streets are ethnic enclaves for shopping, residential neighborhoods are often home to many different peoples. One block, for example, might house families from Korea, Pakistan, Hong Kong, and Vietnam, as well as many non-Asians.

People who wish to explore the Asian neighborhoods of Queens need only hop on the 7 train (with a few detours to places along other subway lines). Recently designated a National Millennium Trail by the White House, the train—sometimes called "the International Express"—follows a seven-mile route from Times Square in Manhattan to Main Street, Flushing. Inside the train is a montage of newspapers in many languages, faces that spell diversity, and lively non-English conversation. Outside the train windows are advertisements and signs in multilingual typography, while beneath the elevated train, many colorful, vital ethnic worlds—straddling the old country and the new—commune.

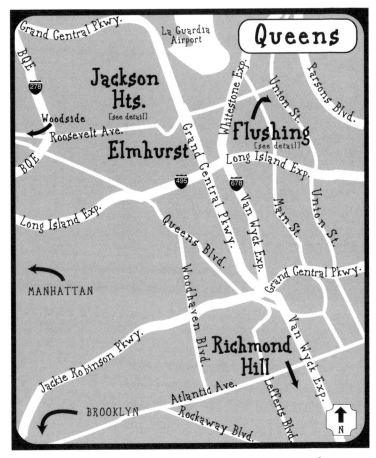

For many New Yorkers, a trip to Queens is a chance to sample the rich array of delicacies found in the borough's Asian restaurants and food shops. "Food isn't just food," explains Dr. Ilana Harlow, folk arts program director at the Queens Council on the Arts. "It's nostalgia, evoking memories of the homeland." For visitors who don't share communal memories, food can be a welcome introduction to a culture. Collecting takeout menus on a single block holds the potential for an international feast, full of flavors both subtle and complex, from dried fish imported from the Philippines to fragrant Indian curries.

Asian communities are not limited to the neighborhoods mentioned above. They are also found in increasing numbers in

Long Island City, Astoria, Forest Hills, and Rego Park. New immigrants arrive daily in these areas, bringing fresh energy and a stream of new businesses with them. Meanwhile, neighborhood artists continue to interpret the Asian American experience as it is evolving. Still, too few books have been written about Queens and the extraordinary multicultural forces at work shaping its neighborhoods. One fine exception is Roger Sanjek's 1998 book, *The Future of Us All: Race and Neighborhood Politics in New York City,* a compelling portrait of civic life in Elmhurst and Corona from 1983 to the present. The title is prescient indeed: Queens, in all its rich diversity and sunny penchant for tolerance, offers a promising glimpse of America's future.

Come along on a neighborhood tour of Asia in Queens.

flushing

The first stop in Flushing—where half the residents are of Asian backgrounds—isn't Asian in origin, but it sets the mood for the neighborhood's long tradition of tolerance. The **Bowne House** (37-01 Bowne Street), built in 1661 and the oldest house in Queens, is the site of John Bowne's defense of the Quakers' freedom of religion in defiance of Governor Peter Stuyvesant's ban; the house was also a haven for outcast worshipers. Bowne's precedent-setting act helped to make religious freedom a birthright in the Dutch colony. Today, local officials like to describe Flushing as the birthplace of religious freedom in America. Indeed, Korean churches, Hindu temples, Buddhist temples, Chinese churches, and many other houses of worship coexist on commercial as well as residential streets.

Several blocks south on Bowne Street, the Hindu Temple Society of North America, **Sri Maha Vallabha Ganapati Devasthanam** (45-57 Bowne St.), dedicated to the popular elephant-headed diety, Ganesh, is a stunning sight. Adorned with beautiful ornamental carvings, the gray stone building, much of which was created in India and reassembled here in the 1970s, was dedicated on July 4, 1977. Carved elephants stand

$$\boxed{\text{public transportation}}$$

FLUSHING SUBWAY: 7 to Flushing/Main St.; BUS: Q66 to Main St.

at either side of the staircase leading to the main entrance. The society's logo, in gold on the building's facade, is a light surrounded by the insignia of other religions, signifying the Hindu spirit of tolerance. A brass flag post outside, known as the *dhwajasthambha*, features a deity figure at the top, reflecting the sun; bells chime in the breeze. Visitors are welcome and must leave their shoes outside to enter. A canteen prepares snacks, and also sells deity pictures, prayer books, and videotapes. An adjacent community center, frequently the site of traditional wedding ceremonies, offers cultural programs, youth activities, and classes. Next door is an Indian restaurant, a shop selling coral and jade, and a grocer offering Indian hair dyes, aromatic spices, and fruits and vegetables that would seem exotic in other parts of New York City.

Flushing has the largest Korean community in New York City, as well as a large Chinese population, the majority of which is from Taiwan; the numbers of Indian and Pakistani residents are also growing. Serving the entire Flushing community, the Flushing branch of the **Queens Public Library** at the intersection of Main Street and Kissena Boulevard (41-17 Main St.) is a modern building with a rounded facade, dedicated in June 1998. This sparkling, 76,000-square-foot library is at the heart of Flushing's commercial and transportation center. It has the big, bustling air of a multicultural university; learning is evident everywhere. On a Sunday afternoon (the library is open seven days a week), it's buzzing with activity, with a long, snaking line of young people waiting to check out books. The stacks are lined with newspapers in non-English languages and both Asian and American bestsellers, and the children's sections offer computers.

Nearby, the 7 train and the Long Island Rail Road discharge

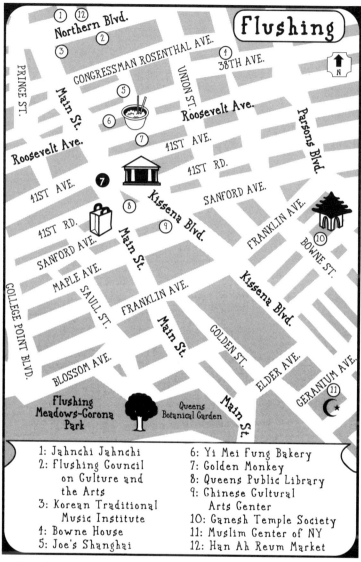

PRINCE ST.

Northern Blvd.

CONGRESSMAN ROSENTHAL AVE.

UNION ST.

38TH AVE.

Flushing

N

Main St.

Roosevelt Ave.

Roosevelt Ave.

41ST AVE.

41ST AVE.

41ST RD.

41ST AVE.

41ST RD.

SANFORD AVE.

Kissena Blvd.

SANFORD AVE.

MAPLE AVE.

SAULL ST.

Main St.

FRANKLIN AVE.

Main St.

GOLDEN ST.

FRANKLIN AVE.

Kissena Blvd.

Parsons Blvd.

BOWNE ST.

ELDER AVE.

GERANIUM AVE.

COLLEGE POINT BLVD.

BLOSSOM AVE.

Main St.

Flushing
Meadows-Corona
Park

Queens
Botanical Garden

1: Jahnchi Jahnchi
2: Flushing Council
   on Culture and
   the Arts
3: Korean Traditional
   Music Institute
4: Bowne House
5: Joe's Shanghai

6: Yi Mei Fung Bakery
7: Golden Monkey
8: Queens Public Library
9: Chinese Cultural
   Arts Center
10: Ganesh Temple Society
11: Muslim Center of NY
12: Han Ah Reum Market

and pick up passengers, and buses disperse to the surrounding areas. The streets are bustling, particularly on weekends, the time everyone seems to do their shopping in the fish stores, green-grocers, and bakeries. Many people enjoy their sweet cakes and buns while walking. Most but not all of the shop clerks speak English. Stationery stores sell calligraphy brushes, drawing paper, learn-to-read books, Chinese greeting cards, and imported toys. Shoppers will find myriad varieties of loose and packaged teas, ginseng, ginger in many forms—raw, sugar-coated, honey-coated, hot and spicy—and traditional medicines, as well as Asian video games, movies, and cosmetics. Several Asian banks serve the area, along with a decidedly non-Asian Starbucks. Many of the Korean businesses, including shops selling wedding dresses and handicrafts, hair salons, and food markets, are along 39th Avenue and Union Street. A few blocks south on Main Street, several South Asian grocers sell Indian and Pakistani products along with halal meat. Although the streets are dense with shops, most buildings aren't more than a few stories tall, so that the sun shines into the streets, filling the area with sparkling light.

Restaurants reflect the area's diversity; here diners can choose from Chinese, Korean, Malaysian, and Indian cuisines. Some of these spots were converted from traditional American diners enjoyed by an earlier generation of Flushing residents. Several of the Korean restaurants feature do-it-yourself barbecue, and others have sushi bars; some establishments stay open all night and feature karaoke singing. A Chinese vegetarian restaurant has kosher certification, attracting Jewish diners.

At the **Chinese Cultural Arts Center** (41-61 Kissena Blvd.), sponsored by the government of Taiwan, traditional Chinese musical instruments and colorful masks are on display. A reading room features Chinese newspapers and books, and the auditorium and classrooms are used by local cultural groups. The Hai-tien Hsiang-Yin Chorus, a 20-year-old group, rehearses here every Sunday afternoon. Their repertoire includes Taiwanese folk songs; Chinese art songs, religious songs, and cantata; and American folk and religious songs sung in English. The choir, led by a noted conductor from Taiwan, Pi-Chu Hsiao, performs in the community at festivals, hospitals, street fairs, and schools, as well as in concerts in Lincoln Center and beyond.

Multi-lingual signage adds flavor to this street scene in Flushing, Queens.

A Crossroads of Culture

Passing cultural traditions on to the generation growing up in New York is of vital importance to many immigrant groups. At the New York Institute of Culture and the Arts (41-75 Bowne St., 718 961-3100), young people from the ages of 3 to 16 study Chinese folk dance, Chinese language, and Chinese music, both in groups and in private lessons. The institute also teaches ballet, piano, and other musical instruments with "cross-cultural combinations of Eastern and Western cultures," as the director, Dr. Hsing-Lih Chou, explains. On weekend afternoons, the school is as crowded as a busy marketplace, not only with Chinese students but with young people from a range of backgrounds, including Korean, Russian, and Latin American. Annual recitals are held for parents and the community.

At the **Korean Traditional Music Institute of New York** (137-45 Northern Blvd.) and other art and music schools, a range of lessons and classes are offered, including instruction in playing the *kayaguem*, a traditional string instrument, and traditional dances like *hwa kwan moo* and *boo chae chom*. The **Korean**

YWCA (42-07 Parsons Blvd.) also offers English classes, as well as many cultural, educational, health, and leadership programs geared to all ages, from young children to senior citizens, including fan dancing and the Evergreen Choir for seniors. The many Korean churches also offer a wide ranges of language and cultural classes and programs.

Early mornings at the **Queens Botanical Garden** (43-50 Main St.), a group of Chinese senior citizens and others get together for an outdoor tai chi class led by a tai chi master, in an open area bordered by two rows of oak trees. The group, which meets every morning at 7:30—except in severely inclement weather—has been exercising here for 15 years. The very fit participants first do a silent warm-up and then, with recorded Chinese instrumental music playing hypnotically in the background, stretch and move in dancelike poses, sometimes using swords and fans.

In recent years, the 39-acre Garden has instituted lectures and programs highlighting the connections between botany and cultural traditions, and has added plants important to the local immigrant communities, such as peonies for the Chinese and Rose of Sharon for the Koreans. It has held Chinese tea ceremonies in the Garden's Cherry Circle, and sometimes the tai chi group does public performances. A winter visitor to the Garden recalls the delight of a group of Malaysian women seeing snow for the first time.

The Botanical Garden is joined via a pedestrian bridge to **Flushing Meadows-Corona Park,** on the site of the 1939 and 1964 World's Fairs. The 1964 Unisphere, a New York City landmark, still stands as a symbol of international unity and peace. The Park houses the Queens Museum of Art, Queens Theater in the Park, New York Hall of Science, Shea Stadium, and the U.S. Tennis Association headquarters, along with public tennis courts, an ice skating rink, and fields where Asian youngsters join in soccer, cricket, and other games. It is also the site of annual festivals celebrating Asian culture.

Flushing Festivals

Every August, the two-day **Hong Kong Dragon Boat Festival** on Meadow Lake features boat racing not unlike canoe racing, with more than 70 teams; paddlers range from teenagers to senior citizens. On land, extensive programs offering a mix of East and West include musical entertainment; lion dances, dragon dances, and contemporary dancing; and arts and crafts demonstrations like paper cutting and calligraphy. And in Flushing Meadows in September, the **Korean Harvest and Folklore Festival** (also known as the Harvest Moon Festival by local Koreans), sponsored by the Korean Produce Retailers Association, features two days of traditional cultural programming, including ceremonies to honor ancestors, folk dancing, kite flying, folk games, music, and Korean food.

Jackson Heights

Here in Jackson Heights, people from South Asia are all "desis," ("countrymen") whether they emigrated from India, Pakistan, or Bangladesh, whether they are Hindu, Muslim, or Sikh, or whether they speak Hindi, Urdu, Punjabi, or any other regional language from the subcontinent. In their home countries, they'd be seen as separate groups and are often in conflict, but in America, the distinctions matter less. In Jackson Heights' "Little India," South Asian cultures commingle peaceably.

Seventy-fourth Street between Roosevelt and 37th avenues is the community's main shopping street, "a mall without walls," as City Council member John Sabini, who represents the area, describes it. Crowded with shoppers from the neighborhood and points beyond, the street is lined with sari shops selling ready-made or custom-made traditional outfits; stores that sell books, videos, and gifts; jewelry stores with bright gold items shimmering in the windows, some inset with stones or etched with fine filigree work; beauty salons that decorate hands and feet with henna designs (mehndi) and apply bindi spots to women's foreheads.

public transportation

JACKSON HEIGHTS SUBWAY: E, F, G, R to Roosevelt Ave./Jackson Hts., 7 to 74th St.-Broadway; BUS: Q32 to 74th St.

Food stores are fragrant with *garam masala*, cumin, pomegranate powder, and a host of other ingredients for South Asian cooking. Many shoppers leave loaded down with 20-pound bags of rice, cartons of mangoes, and whole coconuts. They discover *karela*, or bitter gourd, a vegetable that looks like a cucumber with a spiky outside; and banana flowers, used in cooking certain fish dishes. The many restaurants on the street represent several regions and styles of cooking, with sweets shops, vegetarian cafes, and all-you-can-eat buffets, all serving flavorful meals that are relatively informal and inexpensive.

Spring, summer, and early fall are particularly interesting times to stroll around the neighborhood; it's warm enough for people to go coatless, so colorful saris and other traditional outfits are visible in full splendor. Careful observers will notice the

A child checks out the wares in Butala Emporium, a general store and book shop, in Jackson Heights, Queens.

bright street murals of artist Mrinal Hague, who came to the United States from Bangladesh in 1995. The 41-year-old artist has created a series of mosaic paintings using ceramic tiles in natural colors, depicting the Bangladeshi liberation war, on the side of the **Subzi Mandi Market** (72-30 37th Ave.), and religious and mythological subjects, on the outside of **Patel Brothers Market** (37-27 74th St.) and elsewhere along 74th Street. Just a few doors down is **Butala Emporium** (37-46 74th St.), a good place to browse for all manner of Indian goods.

Adjacent to the 74th Street subway station (the Roosevelt Avenue stop on the E, F, G, and R trains) is a sign advertising an astrologer, palmist, and matrimonial service offering predictions—in English, Tamil, Hindi, Kannada, Punjabi, and Urdu—regarding the future, love, divorce, green card possibilities, wealth, and more.

Back on Roosevelt Avenue is an unusual but extraordinary multicultural venue: **Championship Ping Pong** (78-14 Roosevelt Ave., 2nd floor), where serious players from Chinese, Korean, and many other backgrounds compete.

Elmhurst/woodside

Within multicultural Queens, the most diverse neighborhood is Elmhurst. Newtown High School (48-01 90th St.) has more ethnic groups represented in its population than any other school in New York City. The stretch of Broadway south of Roosevelt Avenue offers a dazzling lineup of shops and restaurants on a wide, busy boulevard. The breadth and depth of offerings at **Top Line Supermarket,** the large Asian grocery in Elmhurst, would rival that of Zabar's on Manhattan's Upper West Side. Here, among hundreds of other foods, are fresh fish, noodle crackers from Indonesia, and fruit dressing from Malaysia. Down one long aisle are woks, soup bowls and spoons, and plastic dishes with Asian designs. Also on Broadway, several Thai grocers sell Thai specialties, and Thai beauty salons and restaurants join the international assortment of restaurants, herbal centers, and bakeries.

$$\text{public transportation}$$

> **ELMHURST** SUBWAY: 7 to 90th St.-Elmhurst Ave., G, R to Elmhurst Ave. BUS: Q32 to 82nd St. and Roosevelt Ave.
> **WOODSIDE** SUBWAY: 7 to 61st St.-Woodside or 69th St. BUS: Q32 to 61st St. and Roosevelt Ave.

Surrounding the parking lot they share on Broadway near Whitney Avenue are four restaurants specializing, respectively, in Vietnamese seafood, Thai cooking, Chinese Shanghai-style dishes, and Malaysian cuisine (plus a sushi bar). All post newspaper reviews in their windows. In the parking lot, the din of clanking dishes is loud; unlike their spices, the various kitchen noises are indistinguishable.

Get off the 7 train at 69th Street in Woodside and discover a Filipino culinary enclave along Roosevelt Avenue and its side streets. A stretch of restaurants, cafes, and pastry shops, and a grocery filled with an extensive array of imports and prepared takeout Filipino foods, lies literally under the subway tracks. But that hardly takes away from the cozy atmosphere of home cooking in family-run places, redolent of regional Filipino cooking. Places are open all day, from breakfast, featuring *tapsilog* (fried marinated sliced beef) and *longsilog* (homemade sausages), to dinner, with specialties like barbecued meats and seafood, oxtail *kare-kare* (oxtail and tropical vegetables in peanut sauce), and traditional desserts with fruit and crushed ice.

Multiethnic Touchstones

Around the corner on Whitney Avenue is a cluster of churches. The flower sellers outside shift positions as different services let out on Sunday afternoon. The **Elmhurst Baptist Church** (87-37 Whitney Ave.), founded in 1900 and housed in a beautiful old stone building, describes itself as a "caring progressive multiethnic congregation." In addition to its regular worship services, it offers Korean Baptist and Indonesian services. Across the street at **Saint Bartholomew's Roman Catholic Church,** many Fil-

Jackson Heights/Elmhurst

72nd ST.
73rd ST.
74th ST.
75th ST.
37TH AVE.
78th ST.
80th ST.
82nd ST.
ROOSEVELT AVE.
Woodside
BROADWAY
41st AVE.
(69th St. Station)
41st AVE.
BAXTER AVE.
ELMHURST AVE.
WOODSIDE AVE.
N

1: Eagle Theater
2: Subzi Mandi Market
3: Jackson Diner
4: Butala Emporium
5: Delhi Palace
6: Patel Brothers Market
7: Championship Ping Pong
8: Satya Narayan Mandir (Sindhi Temple)
9: New York Chodae Church (Korean Church)

ipinos join in the worship services. The **Christian Testimony Church** (87-11 Whitney Ave.) has services in Mandarin Chinese for adults in the community and in English for young people who are born here.

City Councilman John Sabini says that neighborhood churches, temples, and mosques are "touchstones, where people go back to associate with people from their homeland." Immigrants have reinvigorated old religious institutions and built new ones. As is the case throughout Queens, spiritual spaces are shared. In Woodside, a Korean mission and Spanish *iglesia* share space with the First Bengali Christian Church (76-11 Woodside Ave.).

Down the street is **Satya Narayan Mandir,** a Sindhi temple (75-15 Woodside Ave.). The Sindhis are a community originally from Pakistan who migrated to India in 1947; they speak the Sindhi language, and the majority are Hindus. Gope Chander, a

poet, composer, and singer who is president of the Sindhi Association of New York, explains that Sindhis live in the
Elmhurst/Woodside area as well as in Rego Park and other
Queens neighborhoods, and many live in the suburbs too. Their
services, in the colorfully appointed main room of the temple,
are filled with devotional chanting accompanied by music,
sometimes led by Mr. Chander. Even without knowing the language, it is clear that this is spiritual music, deeply felt. After
Sunday services, congregants join together for a meal in the
temple's basement.

The **New York Cho Dae Church** (71-17 Roosevelt Ave.), a
large Korean church, shares its modern building with the **Thai
Alliance Church**. Sunday morning services are filled with music,
as a choir of young people—including several students from the
Juilliard School in Manhattan—lead the congregation in song.
The calligraphic sign above the doorway leading into the social
hall reads EVERYTHING WILL PROSPER. A fellowship lunch of seaweed
soup with rice, meat, and spicy kimchi follows the services.

Richmond Hill

On an early evening in Richmond Hill, the streets are alive with
men in turbans, walking purposefully. Most likely, they're heading
toward the **Sikh Cultural Society of New York, Gurdwara Sahib**
(95-30 118th St.), a cluster of attached buildings that used to
house a church. Evening services include chanting and reading
from the holy book *Granth Sahib*. In the lower-level *langar*, or
24-hour kitchen, participants dine on a meal of traditional Indian
foods prepared and served by community members, who number
3,000. At the same time, young people in traditional dress—the
boys in a turban variation for youth—study the Punjabi language
and sing religious songs as they learn to play musical instruments
like the harmonium, a kind of boxed piano, and the tabla. Visitors, who must leave shoes outside and cover their heads, are
made to feel welcome. For the Sikhs, the turban is a crown; it signifies that the wearer rules his destiny.

public transportation

RICHMOND HILL SUBWAY: J, Z to 104th St., or E, F to Kew Gardens-Union Tpke.

Richmond Hill is also a magnet for the Indo-Caribbean community, comprised of many residents of Indian descent who have emigrated from Surinam, Guyana, and Trinidad. The **Rajkumari Cultural Center** (no permanent location, for information, call 718 805-8068) works to preserve and present cultural traditions and contemporary creative works, ranging from photography exhibitions to music and dance recitals to spoken word performances. They offer workshops in various locations and an annual Kitchrie festival, featuring music and dance in performance.

Richmond Hill is not on the 7 train line; it's reachable by the Long Island Rail Road or the J or Z subway trains to 121st Street. The main shopping streets, which feature South Asian food stores and restaurants, along with shops that combine South Asian and West Indian products, are Lefferts Boulevard, Liberty Avenue, Atlantic Avenue, Myrtle Avenue, and Jamaica Avenue.

Through its New Americans program, the **Queens Public Library** features cultural programs throughout the 62 branches and the Central Library in Jamaica, reaching out to residents whose first language is not English. Its Lefferts branch (103-34 Lefferts Blvd.) occasionally features Indian storytelling and dance; it is also one of the branches to house the Namaste-Adaab collection, with books and other materials in six South Asian languages.

The neighborhoods of Queens are as diverse and distinctive as the people who live there. Maintaining a slew of ethnic backgrounds and cultural traditions, Queens truly embodies the concentration of a great land area into a tight community that is symbolized in the phrase "Asia in New York City."

health & fitness

"Sick people are sad. I smile and laugh to lift their spirit."
—DR. AI JA LEE, practitioner, traditional Chinese medicine

"We must use our lifestyle to prevent illness."
—DR. NAN LU, founder of the American Taoist Healing Center

From the day's dawning to deep into the night, Eastern healing arts of all kinds are woven into the fabric of New York City life. In Manhattan, Flushing, and Brooklyn—home, collectively, to the largest population of Chinese-speaking people outside of China—thousands of residents start off their day with a half-hour of tai chi movements and a warming cup of green tea. At the same time, members of one of America's largest East Indian communities are saluting the sun with yoga poses and a mug of chai. In each of the city's five boroughs, dozens of massage and acupuncture centers—all specializing in various techniques for guiding healing energy through the body—are stirring, as spiritual sanctuaries scattered throughout the city open their doors for morning rituals of movement/meditation classes.

At **Peridance** on Fourth Avenue in Manhattan, hundreds are signing up for tae kwon do, Thai kick boxing, hatha yoga, or dance classes. Consumers are reaching for herbal medicines, once found exclusively in Asian shops, on chain-store shelves. Acupuncture—formerly the province of traditional Chinese healers—is being offered by everyone from physical therapists

Overleaf: Tae kwon do demonstration at the Festival of Korea, a special event held in conjunction with the Asia Society. (Photo © Hyun Kwan-Uk)

Chinese apothecary on Mott Street in Chinatown.

to Park Avenue MDs as a way to cure aches, stop addictions, enhance sexuality, and improve appearance.

In fact, many of the city's doctors, chiropractors, nurses, midwives, and veterinarians now use some form of Asian medicine in their daily practices, from acupuncture to herbal formulas. For example, New York State employs acupuncturists to correct substance addictions in public clinics such as the Stuyvesant Polyclinic in Manhattan and the clinic at Lincoln Hospital in the Bronx. While certain legal restrictions limit Western medical doctors from practicing some traditional Asian healing arts, more and more Eastern and Western health professionals are working together, melding disciplines and philosophies. The city's bastions of traditional medicine have also turned their eyes to the East: Columbia Presbyterian Hospital in uptown Manhattan and the City University of New York (CUNY) in Queens both host annual alternative medicine conferences that share recent research on Asian health modalities, while the Rosenthal

Center for Complementary and Alternative Medicine is currently researching several Chinese herbs for women's health issues.

The full potential of traditional Asian techniques within the world of Western medicine is still being explored. So far, scientific studies hold much promise. Evidence is conclusive that meditation reduces high blood pressure and is effective in reducing the body's stress response—and practitioners are using it successfully in pain management. Acupuncture, which has been used at the Mayo Pain Clinic since 1974, has been shown to provide relief from chronic localized pain and may even help control menstrual cramp discomfort, lower back pain, and tennis elbow pain. Evidence is mounting that green tea—the favored tea in Asian countries—actually reduces the risk of cancer and heart disease. Researchers have speculated that Japan's low rate of lung cancer may be, at least partially, a result of green tea consumption. Chinese herbs are thought to lessen the side effects of some chemotherapies; ginkgo, used in China since 2800 B.C., may actually improve mental function. (Keep in mind, however, that some herbs may become toxic in certain dosages or in combination with other substances, so it is always best to talk to your doctor or other health care practitioner before taking on an herbal regimen.)

While researchers continue to sift through the evidence, however, growing numbers of New Yorkers are embracing Asian massage, meditation, movement, and other traditional healing practices in their daily lives for a much more subjective reason: For their own part, at least, they've found these millennium-old techniques offer an effective, revitalizing, and relatively inexpensive antidote to the stresses of urban life.

Eastern Medicine: The Three Great Traditions

Regardless of their origin, traditional Asian health and fitness methods focus on influencing vitality, circulation, digestion, breathing, sexuality, and mood. The goal is always to facilitate balance and harmony within oneself and with nature. The mind/body connection—now considered to be one of the frontiers of Western medical research—has been taken for granted in the East for centuries: Foods, herbs, bodywork, exercise, and mental-concentration techniques are applied with the aim of simultaneously healing the patient both physically and psychologically. Sound habits that emphasize strength, agility, and peace of mind are considered to be the path to success and a long, healthy life.

The three major Asian health traditions have all been greatly influenced by the philosophies from which they arose. In general, however, every Eastern healing technique is designed to balance "humors," believed to affect both the body and the mind. The names of these humors are suggestive of their different qualities—such as wind, bile, phlegm, dampness, and stagnation—and the means used to balance a given humor will vary accordingly. Asian health experts tend to rely on direct diagnostic methods as well, including asking extensive questions about symptoms and the taking of a medical history. A careful examination of the patient's tongue, pulse, physical appearance, movements, sensations of pain, and other complaints is also standard.

Traditional Chinese Medicine

Traditional Chinese medicine (often referred to as TCM) takes a holistic perspective based on Taoist philosophy. In this system, the individual is constantly moving either toward health or illness, and the practitioner treats the changing symptoms in relationship to a particular person as a whole. The earliest medical texts, including the Nei Jing, written around 3000 B.C., describe the use of herbs and acupuncture to treat epidemic fever disease, chronic illness, and aging. Anatomy is described through maps of meridians (invisible energy pathways) that link the body's surface to internal processes. The concepts of yin, yang, and chi (sometimes spelled "qi") are used to describe the body's functioning. Yin (body fluids) and yang (functions such as metabolism) support and balance each other, while chi (vital energy) flows through the meridians and enlivens physical and mental activity. Emotions come into play as well, since they are thought to influence yin, yang, and chi. In traditional Chinese medicine, foods, herbs, and acupuncture (the technique of inserting thin, disposable needles into specific points on the body's meridian network) are all employed to regulate the flow of chi and to restore balance between yin and yang.

Ayurvedic Medicine

Ayurvedic medicine (*ayur* means "life" and *ved* means "knowledge") began in India over 5,000 years ago. Dr. Vasant Lad has written that this science is based on the eternal wisdom of the rishi ("seers of truth") who received it through religious introspection and meditation. The oldest Sanskrit texts, called the Vedas, describe many daily health and rejuvenation practices, including the use of seasonal foods, herbs, yoga techniques, powerful cleansing activities, massage, therapeutic aromas, baths and enemas, exposure to beneficial gems and colors, and meditation using repeated prayers called mantras. Three basic body types are believed to correspond to the three predominant humors: *vata* is wind; *pitta* is bile, and *kapha* is phlegm. It is said that the goal of Ayurvedic medicine is not only to prevent and heal illness by balancing humors, but also to create a positive spiritual relationship with the cosmos. Using wellness practices such as yoga and herbs, Ayurveda teaches the practitioner to take responsibility for personal health and spiritual growth.

Tibetan Medicine

Tibetan medicine comes out of the Buddhist tradition, which originated in India. Tibetan doctors—who are often Buddhist monks—believe that illness is caused by 440 possible imbalances of the body and mind, as well as by karmic (cause and effect) problems carried over from previous lifetimes. Much like other Asian doctors, Tibetans use foods, herbs, incense, and a form of acupuncture to balance the three humors corresponding to wind, bile, and phlegm. However, since Tibetan medicine holds that a major component of health is mental clarity (defined as freedom from ignorance, hatred, and greed), the doctor/monk may also suggest prayers, meditations, or other spiritual practices to help the patient transform negative karma (harmful or unkind actions) into positive karma, or to bring emotions into balance. According to Tibetan medicine, kindness, spirituality, and good karma are the keys to health and happiness.

Heαlin♀ Heɾbs & Heαlth ꜰoods

Asian markets and health professionals do not always make a clear distinction between foods and medicines. Ask a traditional Asian doctor to give you a prescription for a particular herbal medicine, and you may well get a recipe. Everyday Asian foods and herbs are traditionally used to address a variety of lifestyle issues, including weight loss; improving energy, endurance, and digestion; sleep problems; beauty; and sexuality.

Susan Lin precisely weighs out herbs to fill a prescription brought to her at the Lin Sisters Herb Shop on the Bowery.

scents for healing

Tibetan doctors make herbal incense, which is used in Tibetan medicine to ground an overactive wind energy. More than 20 pungent ingredients such as evergreens, sandalwood, and tree barks are combined to produce scents designed to soothe the nerves, reduce tension headaches, and improve sleep. Incense herbs blessed by Tibetan monks can also be used to inspire meditation or to offer protection from evil influences.

In Asian medicine, preventing the weakening effects of stress, fatigue, allergies, and emotional upset is key to avoiding illness. When illness does strike, specially chosen foods are taken to enhance any therapy. Asian herbal medicines, now being recognized by Western doctors for their properties as natural antibiotics or anti-inflammatory remedies, have been confidently used for centuries to reduce high blood pressure, fever, or pain in specific areas of the body. Herbal remedies, long recognized by Asian martial artists and currently used by China's vast professional army, have been shown to be effective at speeding the healing of injuries and surgical wounds. Herbs are also recommended to ease arthritis pain, and are used to prevent or treat depression, infertility, heart disease, stroke, diabetes, and various cancers. Traditional Chinese herbs are the most prevalent type of herb sold in New York City. A wide variety of herbal remedies can be purchased in bulk packages in most Chinatown grocery stores, as well as in specialty shops. Many Chinatown herb shops also have a resident herbal doctor who can answer casual questions or give a formal diagnosis for a fee, which can range from $10 to $30 or more. A formal diagnosis involves taking your pulse at various points and looking at your tongue to determine if your chi is strong and flowing smoothly. The doctor will usually ask a few questions to confirm the diagnosis.

Herbal medicines are traditionally administered as teas, soups, bottled extracts, pills, or capsules filled with herbal powders. Bottled herbal mixtures (known as "Chinese patent remedies") contain traditional pill formulas that have changed very little over the last few thousand years. They are often even sold at grocery check-out counters. The herbs are traditionally cooked for up to an hour in a brew, but many Western people complain about the bitter taste, particularly that of cleansing herbs. To remedy this, most stores offer the option of grinding herbs into a powder in order to fill capsules for you. Also, Chinese herbal pills or soup formulas sometimes contain animal products such as insects, dried gecko lizard, bones or tendons, sea shells, cow gallstones, or even processed human placenta. If you wish, you can request vegetarian formulas.

Whether you're searching for a Chinese herb shop or the Ayurvedic or Tibetan equivalent, look for a large herbal selection, a clean setting, and a friendly staff. The best shops have a welcoming atmosphere. Another key sign: The best herbalists— no matter how tiny their shops—always make up their own herbal formulas and use medicinal herbs themselves. These practitioners are more than herb sellers: They are sages, continuing a proud and ancient tradition. Herb shops typically open at 10 a.m. and close at 7 p.m.

Asian food markets

With few exceptions, Asian food markets throughout the city open between 8 and 9 a.m., and close at around 8 in the evening. You may find the same foods called by different names in different locations, and the prices can vary widely as well. In general, the higher uptown you go, the higher the price you'll pay. At deluxe shops in the east fifties, you'll find lotus root selling for $6 a pound and daikon radish at $1.65 a pound—compared against prices of $1.20 per pound and 50 cents per pound, respectively, in Chinatown.

A quick look at three of the biggest Asian-food supermarkets—Kam Man in Manhattan's Chinatown, Patel Brothers in Jackson Heights, Queens, and Katagiri in midtown Manhattan— and one specialty store, will help familiarize you with the most common Asian health foods and herbs. Once you learn to recognize the appearance of these unique natural medicines, you'll be able to find them in stores throughout the world.

Kam Man: A Chinatown Favorite

Kam Man, a Chinese supermarket and cookware store located on Canal Street between Mott and Mulberry, is a favorite of Chinatown residents. In the center of the main floor, dried shiitake mushrooms hang from the ceiling. These mushrooms provide useful nutrients and are also used for their healing powers.

Below those hanging mushrooms is an island display of foods and herbs recommended to cure cough and shortness of breath: A fluffy white fungus, tremella, is featured, along with gingko nuts, fox nuts, lotus nuts, Chinese pearl barley, white chinese yam (*dioscurea*), red jujube dates, and lily bulbs. These ingredients can be blended into a tasty and nutritious soup stock.

The store's herb shop is to the right. Along the wall, you'll see large glass jars containing fat light-colored American ginseng (*quinquefolium*), which is recommended to combat thirst, dry skin, chronic fever, or hot flashes. On the counter is dark brown Chinese ginseng (*panax*), prescribed for weakness and chronic aches. (Experts advise avoiding all ginsengs if you have a cold or flu.) On the counter are containers of small red berries that go by the Latin name of *lycium* but in Mandarin are called *goo gee tse*. These berries are traditionally added to teas or eaten daily to reduce dry eyes, dizziness, and ringing in the ears.

On the counter, not far from the wavy yellow shark's fin (used to flavor soup), are packaged soup stocks made from energizing and "blood-building" Chinese herbs. These ingredients are used by Chinese mothers to prevent fatigue, colds, and allergies. You'll also find the famous blood-building herb *tang kuei* (a dried white root the size of your thumb), which is purported to ease circulation. "Slimming" teas—teas believed to be diet aids—such as Bojenmi are sold in this section of the store, as well.

For more tea choices, wade through the dried fish displays and head downstairs, where you'll find a large variety of tea leaves located in the back of the shop—including tea from China (*camellia senensis*) and India (*camellia asamica*). The taste of these green, black, red, white, and oolong teas will vary depending on how long they've been roasted or fermented. All such teas have been found to contain rejuvenating antioxidants and heart-protecting flavonoids. Harvard Medical School's heart specialist, Dr. Michael Gaziano, recommends drinking at least six cups of freshly brewed tea a day for maximum health and beauty benefits. Green tea is especially recommended for cancer prevention and healthy weight loss.

Patel Brothers: A Bounty in Queens

In Jackson Heights, about half an hour from midtown Manhattan via the E train (at the Roosevelt stop), is **Patel Brothers,** a huge East Indian supermarket. If you have a dime left after passing the fabulous sari and gold jewelry shops that line 74th Street, you'll be knocked out by the tremendous selection of sumptuous fruits and vegetables. Here you'll find Chinese okra (*toori*), bitter melon (*karela chines*), various flat peas (*valor or suri papdi*), and a variety of squash (*golka*).

All the way to the right in the store are Ayurvedic medicines made by Dabur, Zandu, and others. The ingredients are often listed in Sanskrit, although many bottles have directions in English as well. Ashwagandha, a popular vitality tonic, is recommended to "warm up" weak, overworked people and to strengthen the muscles and nerves. The *shilajet* capsules sold here are recommended for rejuvenating internal organs and replenishing sexual fluids—just be sure to avoid this herb and all other moistening herbs when you have a cold or flu, since they are thought to increase mucus.

Katagiri: Japanese Health Foods

A half-block away from Bloomingdale's on 59th Street, you can find one of New York's best selections of Japanese health foods. **Katagiri** sells everything from broiled eel (one of nature's best sources of vitamin D) to green teas, countless varieties of noodles, all sorts of soy products, seaweeds, and mouthwatering

the japanese diet for a long life

Statistically speaking, the Japanese people have the longest life expectancy of any nation on earth. It's normal for Japanese women to live into their nineties. This longevity is often credited to the fact that Japanese people eat mostly grains and soy products such as tofu, raw soy beans, and natto (a longevity food sold at Katagiri, which has been described as "sticky, smelly, fermented soy beans"). Fermented or cultured soy products—such as miso and natto—provide isoflavones, which act as natural estrogen balancers in the body. Fresh fruits and vegetables, fish, seaweeds, and green tea make up the rest of the healthy traditional Japanese diet.

sweet rice and bean confections. Careful, though—you may become addicted to shiritaki noodles, a slimming and wonderfully satisfying diet food. These noodles, made from Japanese white yam, contain no calories.

Foods for the Adventurous

Instead of running to the drugstore for flu remedies like oscillococcinum—which is actually homeopathic duck's liver—Chinese people eat strengthening foods year-round. Chinese butchers such as **Siu Cheong,** at 89 Mulberry Street, have all kinds of unusual items like congealed duck's blood (which looks like calves' liver), sliced eels, quail eggs, frozen pigs' ears, frozen snakes, refrigerated black chickens, bird's nests, and shark fins for soup. Fish markets along Canal, Mulberry, and Elizabeth streets will have squirming live eels, frogs, and fishes.

Acupuncture: painkilling needles

Acupuncture is a healing art based on the traditional Chinese concept of meridians. By freeing the body's natural flow of energy (chi) through careful placement of needles on key meridian points, the acupuncturist invites the body to heal itself. While the theory behind acupuncture has not been accepted by

Western medicine, the treatment itself has been proven to work in controlled studies; the National Institute of Health has recognized acupuncture as an effective treatment for pain and chronic illnesses, and many HMOs now cover treatments. New York State employs acupuncturists to correct substance addictions in public clinics such as Stuyvesant Polyclinic on Second Avenue and Lincoln Hospital in the Bronx.

Finding an Acupuncturist

When searching for an acupuncturist, look for someone you feel comfortable with. Credentials vary: For the most part, Asian- and European-trained acupuncturists are also MDs. Asian American acupuncturists, on the other hand, rarely have medical school training. That's not necessarily a bad thing, however: In New York, non-MD acupuncturists have years' more formal training in traditional Chinese medicine than the required short course in acupuncture given to Western medical doctors.

Asian-trained acupuncturists are used to seeing as many as 50 to 100 patients daily in Asian clinics: As a result, they are not given to lengthy explanations. In general, acupuncturists would rather ease your suffering than explain what they are doing. They may shrug off a question by merely stating that they are bal-

o-frills tcm The city has quite a number of highly qualified Asian-born acupuncture/herbal doctors who do not speak English, relying instead on translators. Their inexpensive treatments and sparse settings sometimes resemble what you might encounter in a Chinese hospital. This is the real thing—TCM without any cosmetic frills. Their private offices are sometimes listed in the Yellow Pages, but practitioners are also frequently associated with Chinese herb shops, and can be contacted through the store's staff. Two notable acupuncturists who fall into this category are **Dr. Lucy Liu,** who does acupuncture at Columbia Hospital uptown but also has a downtown Manhattan office attached; and **Huynh Van O,** a Vietnamese doctor with over 40 years' experience in acupuncture, herbs, and osteopathy, whose office is located downtown.

acupuncture for animals

Attention, animal lovers: Veterinary acupuncture is also becoming increasingly common, as the National Veterinary Acupuncture Association spreads the word about its effectiveness. As with people, acupuncture can be used to ease an animal's arthritis pain, speed healing of injuries or paralysis, regulate digestion or energy problems, or treat depression. The Heart of Chelsea Animal Hospital offers acupuncture, as does the Animal Natural Healing Center, which also uses homeopathy, vitamins, herbs, and Bach Flower remedies to treat pet cancers, arthritis, and allergies.

ancing yin and yang. That is a deceptively simple description of a complex process that involves regulating energy, freeing circulation, and enhancing metabolic function. Meanwhile, Western scientists continue to probe for an explanation as to what makes acupuncture so effective in blocking pain (in China, it's often the only form of anesthesia used in surgery). Some speculate it involves alterations in the body's electromagnetic fields, while others point to the workings of endorphins or hormones, the lymph system, or a change in temperature or circulation. Thus far, no one has been able to figure out definitively why acupuncture works—we just know that it does.

Although the insertion of the needles is usually quite painless, you may experience temporary discomfort for a day or so after first getting treated, as your body readjusts; stay in touch with your acupuncturist or herbal doctor, and report any reactions. It's also a good idea to check back with your healer/doctor at each change of season, in order to harmonize your energy with your new environment.

Below are thumbnail profiles of three different acupuncturists, all leading members of New York's highly respected acupuncture community.

Dr. Lili Wu:
Getting Tough With Illness in Chelsea

A photo of Jeanne Moreau, the French actress, hangs on the wall of the Chelsea office of **Dr. Lili Wu** as a testament to the broad reach of her practice. But Dr. Wu—Lili—remains unaffected by fame, warmly greeting every visitor with dignity and respect. Her office is immaculate, quiet, and professional.

What is striking about Lili is her gentle and hardworking approach. She is the picture of tireless dedication—typical of acupuncturists who have worked in Chinese hospitals—and she goes for a strong, fast cure in her treatments. As one of her patients says, "She gets tough with your illness." Lili graduated at the top of her class in a famous Shanghai school for traditional medicine. Since moving to New York 15 years ago, she has specialized in treating stress-related complaints, as well as arthritis, headaches, back or shoulder pain, sports injuries, menstrual problems, and addictions. Treatments for smoking cessation normally take up to three—and never more than seven—visits.

After Lili finishes doing the Chinese pulse reading at your wrist, she may surprise you by whispering something like, "I'm sorry, but I think you are very angry." By listening to the quality of your pulse, TCM doctors can determine whether you are tense, nervous, hyperactive, depressed, or afraid. Lili's frequent advice to tired New Yorkers: "Sit down and rest sometimes," or, "You work too hard."

After reaching her diagnosis, Lili quickly inserts a number of slender disposable needles into the patient's skin, sometimes all the way from head to foot, and then tiptoes out of the room. You'll find you can actually feel your circulation shift as a treated area becomes free of discomfort; you may also discover yourself letting go of anxiety or even falling asleep as pain recedes. After the acupuncture treatment, Lili may follow up with a short massage on your back. The session typically lasts 45 minutes to an hour.

Dr. Nan Lu performing acupuncture at his American Taoist Healing Center in downtown Manhattan.

Dr. Ai Ja Lee:
Healing Laughter in the Heart of Koreatown

Dr. Ai Ja Lee greets you with a grin, a hug, and her healing laugh. Her approach aims to heal emotional pain with joy. Her office, located just off Fifth Avenue on West 32nd Street, is on restaurant row in the heart of New York's bustling Koreatown. Dr. Lee is a skilled practicioner of TCM and is also a Western-trained pharmacist. She specializes in womens' issues and stress reduction, but her favorite gift is love. "Sick people are sad. I smile and laugh to lift their spirit," she says. Some of her patients tape-record her laugh to play at home. A favorite of models and movie stars, her sliding-scale fees have included bartering for cars, paintings, and even watermelons from poor farmers.

Dr. Nan Lu:
The Tao of Wellness, Downtown Style

"We must use our lifestyle to prevent illness." **Dr. Nan Lu** speaks clearly and looks you straight in the eye, yet there is something distinctly otherworldly about him. He is the founder of the **American Taoist Healing Center,** located on Broadway in downtown Manhattan—and like any dedicated Taoist, his life and healing philosophy are all about balance.

Dr. Lu is an acupuncture doctor who first started out as a martial arts competitor. He now teaches an integrated program for the prevention and treatment of breast cancer that involves a combination of foods, herbs, and wu ming qi gong exercise (see below). The center also features scheduled workshops for bringing your energy into balance according to the season.

Bodywork

If you love being touched, you can choose from a wide variety of Asian-influenced bodywork therapies in New York—from holistic chiropractors and experts in meridian massage to simple massages for healthy pleasure.

Therapeutic Massage

Asian therapeutic massage differs from Western methods such as Swedish massage, which focuses on lightly stroking the body. Instead, Asian massage works more deeply, as the therapist concentrates on lines of energy circulation (meridians) or deep tissue connections. The massage session can also involve stretching or adjustments. The goal of Asian massage and energy work is to balance the body's energy, and bring about a profound healing change in physical and emotional well-being.

chiropractic with an asian spin **Dr. Vittoria Repetto** has used her unique blend of chiropractic technique and traditional Asian healing arts to treat everything from injuries to PMS and chronic fatigue syndrome. In a session at her West Broadway office in downtown Manhattan, she'll spend up to an hour with you using kinesiology, muscle balancing, cranial work, acupressure, Chinese herbs, and homeopathics, along with traditional chiropractic manipulation. Dr. Repetto has also studied Asian martial arts—including karate, jowgar kung fu, and hsing i—and will often prescribe stretches or alignment exercises based on these art forms.

To attain physical well-being, in most Eastern cultures body, mind, and spirit are treated at the same time.

Shiatsu Massage

Shiatsu (literally, "finger pressure") massage has been used in Japan for more than 1,000 years. A shiatsu practitioner uses palm and finger pressure, rotation, and stretching techniques to free up the flow of vital energy through the body. One of the city's best shiatsu massages is offered by **Osaka,** which offers sports and medical massage, as well as herbal steam baths, body wraps and facials, Japanese hot baths, and an Akasuri scrub (using salt and essential oils).

For a less expensive session at the hands of a student—or if you'd like to learn how to do shiatsu yourself—check out the **Do-In Shiatsu Center.** This massage school, founded by Do-In Shiatsu master Dr. Nori Suzuki, offers evening and weekend courses in shiatsu technique.

And on 25th Street in Manhattan, between Sixth and Seventh avenues, you'll find **The Ohashi Institute,** a small corner of serenity overseen by Wataru Ohashi—a Japanese healer who, along with his trained instructors in 50 schools scattered throughout the world, teaches a unique form of bodywork called Ohashiatsu, a technique invented to strengthen the treatment-giver. "My work is my exercise," says Mr. Ohashi. "I have worked for over 30 years and have never been tired or sick. I teach people how to heal themselves while they work on others."

Chinese Massage

Chinese massage focuses on encouraging energy flow through the meridian channels, much as acupuncture does. Tui na, a particularly deep and often painful type of massage, is used to reduce spasms and poor circulation along meridians.

In addition to physical touch, a massage may also include moxibustion—which involves holding a smoking herbal stick a few inches above the skin surface in order to activate circulation or warm an area. Cupping, another method used to free up the circulation of energy, uses small glass jars to form a vacuum over the skin, and may leave temporary bruises.

The range of available treatments will vary depending on the practitioner. **Dr. Qin,** who maintains an office in the Grand Meridian shop on Grand Street in Manhattan, combines internal qi gong (which uses the practitioner's cultivated healing energy to promote chi flow to the internal organs) along with massage to build vitality and reduce pain. In Flushing, Queens, the **Chinese Holistic Center** features acupressure, tui na massage, and acupuncture sessions. The clinic is brisk, with a no-time-for-nonsense attitude and limited English.

movement and meditation

The **International Chun Do Sun Bup Institute,** in Manhattan's Koreatown, is a Korean healing center that offers a 100-day therapeutic program, including movement, sounds, and meditation, aimed at ridding the body, mind, and spirit of toxins. Students, who can choose their learning schedule, are taught ways to free circulation and reverse aging. Individual massage treatments are also available.

Qi Gong Meditation

Besides internal qi gong massage, qi gong also refers to a traditional Chinese form of moving meditation that involves either gentle, slow movements or simply sitting still. The aim of qi gong meditation is to build the practitioner's store of vital energy. Sometimes, after years of dedicated practice, qi gong can then be used to heal others. In China, qi gong is practiced in the early morning in order to awaken the practitoner's chi energy. The movements may look simple, but in fact they are precisely choreographed to promote deep circulation of energy in the meridians and internal organs.

In Chinese hospitals, qi gong is an essential part of treatment: It's taught to patients in order to reverse symptoms of paralysis and weakness, and is even used to engage the body's defenses against cancer. Masahiro Ouchi, the director of the Healing Tao Center of New York, who teaches Kuan Yin qi gong—a version named for the Chinese goddess of compassion—explains that qi gong can be used to "open the heart to the deep expression of unconditional love."

Two other good places to practice these subtle and energizing movements: the **Qi Gong Center**—where Masters Shen Rong-Er and Wu Yi teach several styles, including the Soaring Crane, all intended to improve health, mental clarity, and total well-being—and the **American Taoist Healing Center,** which features wu ming qi gong, designed to promote relaxation, inner focus, and emptiness. The wu ming style uses just a few simple movements, which are done for about ten minutes several times a day. According to the center's Taoist founder, Dr. Nan Lu, "Too often people want to learn elaborate forms, lots of movements, and fancy styles. It's a mistake. The important thing is how you use the form to empty yourself of thought, to forget who you are."

Yoga

For New Yorkers, yoga's subtle stretches, breathing techniques, and chanted prayers can represent either an attempt at a union with universal bliss, or a cushion offering protection against the

A class at The Ohashi Institute in Chelsea focuses on maintaining and improving posture, movement, and well-being.

urban landscape's periodic assaults on their consciousness. A number of different types of yoga are taught in ashrams, gyms, health clubs, and Y's across the city—each type stressing its own traditional approach to physical and mental development. Hatha yoga aims to tone the body and free the mind, while chakra yoga focuses on purifying each of the seven chakras (literally, "wheels of consciousness"), which correspond to various regions of the body. Specific postures may be coupled with sounds, colors, and visualization exercises. Kundalini yoga, a highly transformative style, often combines postures intended to build up a powerful charge of energy with mantras (chanting) and meditations aimed at healing the nerves and glands and opening the flow of energy through organs and meridians. With this particular form, guidance is recommended.

The **Integral Yoga Institute** in Manhattan offers hatha and specialized instruction for menopausal women, prenatal/postpartum yoga, and breathing and meditation classes, as well as teacher training and classes for HIV care and vegetarian cooking. The **Sivananda Yoga Vedanta Center,** founded by Swami Vishu-devananda, teaches asanas (yoga postures), meditation, pranayama (breathing practices), philosophy, vegetarian diet, and chanting.

The center also has retreats in upstate New York, India, the Bahamas, and Grass Valley, California.

The folks at the **Jivamukti Yoga Center,** down in the Village, are proponents of power—highly athletic—yoga. The **Atmananda Yoga Center,** in Soho, is a friendly place that offers 35 weekly classes in yoga and qi gong. They also do Ayurvedic herbal and wax beauty wraps. Uptown, on the West Side, the **Sat Nam Yoga Garden,** features "withdrawal technique, radiant health, Sehaj Bliss, and hatha and japa yoga." Finally, **Yoga Zone** has two Manhattan locations, both specializing in hatha yoga classes (they also sell yoga clothes and health items).

Martial Arts

Martial arts run the gamut from highly combative forms, like karate and kung fu, to activities as benign as tai chi, which is essentially a gentle system of calisthenics. Your own yearnings will have to guide your choice—but you can be assured that any style of martial art will provide you with an unsurpassed physical and mental workout.

The form of martial art you settle on will also determine how you select a teacher. Marita Ramirez, an award-winning Filipina tae kwon do champion turned flamenco dancer, describes how she chooses her martial arts instructors: "First I find out if the instructor has won titles. Then I find out from his students if he really kicks ass." On the other end of the spiritual spectrum, Dr. Nan Lu advocates the gentle martial art of tai chi. In tai chi, he explains, "Everything is a circle. With a circle there is no beginning and no end. It is the tao." Choose a martial arts instructor who best develops your natural style—be it ass-kicking or blissful. You can tell which approach is emphasized right away, by looking around at the school. Are there trophies and swords on the walls, or pictures of clouds?

The **Bond Street Dojo for Aikido** in Manhattan features the subtle art form of aikido, once described as "the best way to let the other guy hit the pavement as he misses you." The kung fu style taught at **Chau's Wu Mei Kung Fu** can be used either for fitness or for mortal combat. Wu Mei kung fu was first developed by Chinese nuns, and later developed into the spinning, high-kicking movements familiar to Bruce Lee fans.

The **NY Martial Arts and Health Center** offers classes in Thai kick boxing, tae kwon do, and hapkido. All these styles rely on kicking movements that are guaranteed to tighten your buns, abs, and thighs—making them a favorite of dancers looking to build strength and balance.

To learn jujitsu—a style first used by the samurai in Japan that involves punching, kicking, and throwing, as well as inward focus and meditation—visit Dino Blanche's studio, **Laughing River Jujitsu,** in Brooklyn. "In jujitsu we do not oppose force against force, but re-channel aggression," says Blanche. "Jujitsu aims to bring the individual into harmonious balance in the midst of conflict."

Kaicho Tadashi Nakamura founded **Seido Karate** over 20 years ago in order to reintegrate Zen meditation into a strict, traditional Japanese style of karate, resulting in a school that is known today not only for producing fierce competitive fighters, but also for its gentle, community-oriented spirit. At Seido's World Headquarters (Honbu) in Manhattan, Kaicho Nakamura's philosophy of "karate for everyone" has resulted in a gamut of classes that invite men and women of all ages and abilities to train hard; in addition, special classes are offered for the blind, the deaf, and homeless children, among others.

Tai Chi

Tai chi, a system of slow, graceful movements, is one of the most popular exercise forms in the world. In China, millions practice it upon waking each morning to prevent illness and ward off the effects of aging.

There are a number of schools of tai chi, based on various teaching traditions. The graceful energy of **William C. C. Chen,** who runs an instructional studio on West 23rd Street in Manhattan, manifests an undisturbed line of tai chi expertise inherited from his late Grand Master, Cheng Man-Ching. Since 1952,

Chen has taught "the body mechanics of tai chi chuan," an approach comprised of 70 gentle movements. As proof of the endurance of his teachings, some of Chen's students (who range in age from 30 to 65 and older) have been with him for some 35 years.

Chen's scientific approach to relaxation emphasizes improvement of balance and centering. "When you do tai chi," he notes, "the important thing is to let energy come up from your feet, and move through your body all the way to the tips of your fingers with no break." At his regular practice sessions, held four times weekly, you can observe Chen's science of relaxation at work: One man will hit a punching bag without tensing a muscle, for example.

Practiced regularly, tai chi is one of the best techniques on earth for improving health and mobility, no matter what your age. In his mid-sixties, Chen is charming, enthusiastic, and constantly on the move. Even his wife is now a believer: "After 19 years of raising kids and doing absolutely nothing physical," she says, "tai chi helped me to lose 50 pounds and move like a teen."

health & fitness

THE LISTINGS

Herbs and Other Foods for Health

Chinese/Vietnamese

Golden Harvest Trading, Inc. In Brooklyn's Chinatown. Chinese herbs and patent medicines for sale and mail-order. Consult with Dr. Sze, a Chinese herbalist who has over 30 years' experience. Her son Nick speaks fluent English (5315 Eighth Ave., Brooklyn; 718 633-0985; N train to Eighth Ave.).

Kam Man. Foods, herbs, teas, herbal soap and shampoo, cookware, dishes. There is no herbal doctor for consultations (200 Canal St., NY; 212 571-0330; A, C, E, N, R, J, M, Z, 6 train to Canal St.).

Kam Tat Herb Shop. Proprietor Grace Ho, one of the first herbalists in Chinatown, offers herbal advice for a wide variety of health problems, including children's issues (54 Mott St., NY; 212 925-8868; B, D, Q train to Grand St.).

Kamwo Herb & Tea Co., Inc. Retail and wholesale, the "largest Chinese herbal pharmacy on the East Coast." Features an attractive tea shop plus a Western-trained pharmacist, a family of traditional Chinese herbalists, acupuncture treatments, and tui na massage; (209-211 Grand St., NY; 212 966-6370; www.kamwo.com; B, D, Q train to Grand St.).

Lin Sisters Herb Shop Inc. A bright, modern setting, friendly staff, and large selection of Chinese herbal medicines for sale and mail order, plus acupuncture upstairs. Proprietor Susan Lin has been treating women's and children's problems with Chinese herbs for many years, and has special formulas for building immunity, easing depression, and correcting beauty problems. (4 Bowery, NY; 212 962-5417; 4, 5, 6, N, R train to City Hall).

Siu Cheong Meat Market. Chinese butcher shop, with unusual health foods like sliced eels, frozen pigs' ears, and black chickens (89 Mulberry St., NY; 212 267-0350; A, C, E, N, R, J, M, Z, 6 train to Canal St.).

Tan Ai Hoa Supermarket. Large Vietnamese supermarket with Chinese foods and spices. Check out the Thai coffee (with corn and soy added to improve health) and the Japanese shiritaki noodles in the refrigerated noodle case. An island by the entrance features seasonal herbs and gooey sweets; no herbal doctor on premises (81½ Bowery, NY; 212 219-0893; A, C, E, N, R, J, M, Z, 6 train to Canal St.)

Indian

Butala Emporium, Inc. A book and magazine shop with a fine selection of Ayurvedic herbal pills for sale and mail order—wholesale and retail. Check out their catalogs for health books and herbs (37-46 74th St., Jackson Heights, Queens; 718 899-5590; E, F, G, R train to Roosevelt Ave.).

Foods of India. Offering a wide variety of Indian foods and cooking supplies, loose and bottled Ayurvedic herbs, and Ayurvedic beauty products. The exceptionally friendly staff has been serving New York for over 20 years (121 Lexington Ave., NY; 212 683-4419; 6 train to 28th St.).

Little India. Behind the checkout counter is a fine selection of top-quality bottled Ayurvedic herbals made by Shiriji, a Bombay company. Elsewhere in the store you'll find a wide selection of incense, teas, bulk spices, and Indian cooking equipment(128 E. 28th St., NY; 212 683-1691; 6 train to 28th St.).

Patel Brothers Market. A huge selection of quality fresh fruits and vegetables, nuts, spices, and Ayurvedic herbal products (37-27 74th St., Jackson Heights, Queens; 718 898-3445; E, F, G, R train to Roosevelt Ave.).

Japanese

Katagiri. This eclectic supermarket sells all types of Japanese health foods. Ask for their mail-order catalog; they will ship orders of any size to anywhere in the world (224 E. 59th St., NY; 212 755-3566; www.katagiri.com; 6, N, R train to 59th St./Lexington Ave.).

Sunrise Mart. Groovy East Village Japanese supermarket. A great resource for Japanese cooking ingredients, utensils, and videos; not to mention healthy daikon radishes, fresh lotus root, bamboo shoots, Japanese eggplant, prepared dishes, fresh meats and fish, and shiso, that tasty leaf that decorates the sushi platters (4 Stuyvesant St., 2nd floor, NY; 212 598-3040; 6 train to Astor Pl.).

Mitsuwa (formerly **Yaohan**). A Japanese health-food store in northern New Jersey, featuring raw seaweed, shiritaki, and natto (595 River Rd.,

Edgewater, NJ; 201 941-9113; a shuttle bus leaves from Gate 51 in the south building at Port Authority every hour; or take the ferry from South Street Seaport—it's a half-hour ride to Edgewater).

More Information on Asian Herbs and Health

Flavor & Fortune. This magazine is an excellent source of information on Chinese teas and traditional foods from the Institute for the Advancement of the Science and Art of Chinese Cuisine (718 997-4153).

www.eastearthtrade.com. This website sells Chinese herbs, patent remedies, teas, essential oils, and books covering Chinese health practices.

www.herbwalk.com. This website offers informative and entertaining information on Chinese herbs used to enhance health, beauty, and sexuality—as well as Chinese herbs used in cooking, gardening, and current research information. Their "virtual herb walks" are a trip!

www.winghopfung.com. This informative website offers a weekly herbal Q & A column and a resource for ordering Chinese herbs, teas, gifts, and books on traditional Chinese medicine.

Acupuncturists, Herbalists, and Other Health Practitioners

Dr. Shide An. A Chinese professor of neurology, Dr. An treats stroke, paralysis, migraine, Bell's palsy, TMJ, diabetes, impotence, addictions, and allergies (336 Bay Ridge Pky., Brooklyn; 718 921-4769).

Henry Buck. Originally from Hong Kong, Buck combines craniosacral adjustments and acupuncture. His work is aimed at facilitating emotional release. Treatments can be given in conjunction with other forms of psychotherapy, but it's not recommended to have both on the same day (260 Riverside Dr., NY; 212 662-7460; 1, 2, 3, 9 train to 96th St.).

Chelsea Healing. Located next to the kitschy Chelsea Hotel, with a New-Age atmosphere and soft music wafting through the air. Open daily, the center has two acupuncturists, Ildar Gadol and Jennifer Hoang (216 W. 23rd St., NY; 212 645-6447; 1, 9 train to 23rd St.).

Chinese Holistic Center. Acupressure, tui na massage, and acupuncture sessions all at extremely reasonable rates. Brisk and no-nonsense, with limited English. Dr. Yang is available for acupuncture three days a week (143-40 38th Ave., Flushing, Queens; 718 762-1127; 7 train to Flushing/Main St.).

Dr. Ai Ja Lee. This skilled Chinese herbalist and acupuncturist is also a Western-trained pharmacist. She specializes in women's health problems and will barter for her fee (38 W. 32nd St.; 212 239-5559; B, D, F, Q, N, R train to 34th St.).

Dr. Lucy Liu. Dr. Liu has offices at Columbia Hospital uptown and at Health Town, Inc. in Chinatown. Her Chinese herbal prescriptions usually cost about $6 for a pack of herbs—the usual recommendation is 5 to 6 packs per week (59 Mott St., NY; 212 406-1188; www.health world-us.com; A, C, E, N, R, J, M, Z, 6 train to Canal St.).

Dr. Nan Lu. Known for its integrated program for prevention and treatment of breast cancer using foods, herbs, and qi gong exercises (American Taoist Healing Center; 396 Broadway, Suite 502, NY; 212 274-0999; www.breastcancer.com; A, C, E, N, R, J, M, Z, 6 train to Canal St.).

The Office of Tibet (241 E. 32nd St.; 212 213-5010; www.tibet.com; 6 train to 33rd St.) and **Tibet House** (22 W. 15th St.; 212 807-0563; www.tibethouse.org; N, R, L, 4, 5, 6, F train to 14th St./Union Sq.) are sources of information on Tibetan doctors visiting from north India.

Dr. Qin and Dr. Zhang. Located in Brooklyn, these licensed acupuncturists and herbalists have successfully treated chronic pain, arthritis, allergies, asthma, stroke, weight loss, migraines, and sexual complaints for over 20 years. Call ahead for an appointment (1906 Kings Hwy., Brooklyn; 718 627-6812; D, Q train to Kings Highway).

Dr. Tashi Rabten. This traditional Tibetan doctor has an office at Wainwright House in Rye, New York (40 minutes from Grand Central on Metro North). He uses traditional Tibetan diagnosis (observation of the pulse and tongue, urine analysis, and careful questioning) and often prescribes Tibetan "precious pills"—made from as many as 100 rare plants, gems, and minerals, and prepared using many chanted prayers (914 967-6080 x1465).

Eliot Tokar. An American native, Eliot has studied for 17 years with highly respected Tibetan doctors in India and the United States. He has also studied Chinese medicine and acupuncture and offers advice on macrobiotic diet and herbs. Check out his website for information on Tibetan medicine and his publications (151-31 88th St., Howard Beach, Brooklyn; 718 641-7323; www.tibetanmedicine.com).

Dr. Huynh Van O. A Vietnamese doctor with over 40 years' experience in acupuncture, herbs, and osteopathy (125 Elizabeth St., NY; 212 334-5690; B, D, Q train to Grand St.).

Dr. Yuan Wan. Located in the Empire State Building, Wan received her medical training at the Shanghai University of Traditional Chinese Medicine and has taught acupuncture at the Beijing and Shanghai Uni-

versities of TCM. She has reasonable prices and offers senior citizen discounts (350 Fifth Ave., Suite 1122; 212 594-4811; 6 train to 33rd St.).
Dr. Lili Wu. Offers skilled acupuncture, often with a short back massage. She has two locations—the Brooklyn office is also an herb shop. Her prices are very fair though somewhat higher in her Manhattan office (20 W. 24 St., 1D, NY; 212 741-6674; E train to 23rd. St.; 6811 Ft. Hamilton Pkwy., Brooklyn; 718 439-8805; N train to Ft. Hamilton Pkwy.).

Acupuncture Schools: Student Treatments for Nominal Fees
New York College for Wholistic Health Education & Research. This school offers treatments for pain and a variety of illnesses. They also have a one-time acupuncture treatment for people who want to stop smoking—which they claim is effective more than 80 percent of the time (6801 Jericho Turnpike, Syosset, Long Island; 800 922-7337)
Pacific College of Oriental Medicine. The college has an intern and professional clinic, where you can get acupuncture, Chinese herb treatments, and tui na massage (915 Broadway, 3rd floor, NY; 212 982-4600, 212 982-3456; www.ormed.edu; N, R train to 23rd St.).
Tri-State College of Acupuncture. Begun some 20 years ago by Mark Seem, an author of several books on acupuncture. Unlike other Chinese medicine colleges, Tri-State teaches integrated degree programs that include French meridian acupuncture, Japanese and Classical Chinese acupuncture, and TCM. Special classes are also taught by America's preeminent Japanese educator, Kiiko Matsumato (80 Eighth Ave., NY; 212 242-2254, clinic 212 242-2254; 4, 5, 6, N, R, L train to Union Sq.).

Veterinary Acupuncturists
Animal Natural Healing Center. Marcie Fallek, DVM, offers acupuncture, homeopathy, vitamins, and herbal and other remedies for pets (247 W. 11th St., NY; 212 216-9177; 1, 2, 3, 9 train to 14th St.).
Heart of Chelsea Animal Hospital. The office is organized and caring, and they even do weekly follow-up phone calls to see how Pussy and Rex are doing! Marc Siebert, DVM (257 W. 18 St., NY; 212 924-6116; 1, 9 train to 18th St.).

Bodywork
(see also Spas and Other Beauty Treatments in Shopping, Fashion, & Beauty)
The Best Chinese Back Rub and Integrated Body Work. The two walk-in Manhattan locations are not listed in the phone book, but

they're among the city's best health secrets for those in the know: a relaxing qi gong massage from the highly skilled therapist of your choice at truly reasonable rates for a half hour or for a full hour (145 Grand St., basement, NY; 212 925-1276; 179 Grand St., NY; 212 334-3909; B, D, Q train to Grand St.).

Do-In Shiatsu Center. A massage school in midtown Manhattan, offering evening and weekend courses in shiatsu (605 Fifth Ave., 5th floor, NY; 212 644-9232; E, F train to Fifth Ave.).

International Chun Do Sun Bup Institute. Korean healing center in Manhattan specializes in ridding the body, mind, and spirit of toxins and offers individual massage treatments (15 W. 30th St., 5th floor, NY; 212 695-5656; www.cdsb.org).

The New York Open Center. Offering a wide array of bodywork and other classes (83 Spring St., NY; 212 219-2527; www.opencenter.org; N, R train to Prince St.).

The Ohashi Institute. The institute's founder, Wataru Ohashi, teaches a unique form of bodywork called Ohashiatsu. The hour-long session can include stretching and deep pressure massage with the hands, elbows, and knees. Call to find out about classes, free demonstrations, and treatments (147 W. 25th St., NY; 646 486-1187, 800 810-4190; www.ohashishiatsu.org; 1, 9, F, C, E train to 23rd St.).

Osaka. Two Manhattan locations, each offering sports and medical massage, body wraps and facials, and Japanese hot baths (50 W. 56th St., NY; 212 956-3422; B, Q train to 57th St.; 37 W. 46th St., NY; 212 575-1303; B, D, F, Q to 47–50th sts./Rockefeller Ctr.).

Dr. Qin. Walk-in massage service at Grand Meridian on Grand Street in Manhattan. Dr. Qin combines internal qi gong with massage to build vitality and reduce pain. (209-211 Grand St., NY; 212 965-1503; A, C, E, N, R, J, M, Z, 6 train to Canal St.).

Dr. Vittoria Repetto. A chiropractor who also employs kinesiology, muscle balancing, cranial work, acupressure, Chinese herbs, and homeopathic remedies (285 West Broadway, NY; 212 431-3724; A, C, E, 1, 9 train to Canal St.).

Wai Hai Herb Trading Company. Located in Sunset Park, Brooklyn's Chinatown. Mrs. Leung gives an incredible one-hour massage at an extremely reasonable rate. Her husband, Yu Chun Leung, teaches tai chi, offering two 90-minute classes weekly. Private lessons available (5304 8th Ave., Brooklyn; 718 435-4972; N train to 62nd St.).

Ayurvedic Skin Care

Ayurveda Center. Herbal wraps, massage, teas, and beauty treatments (204 W. 96th St., NY; 212 280-1000; 1, 2, 3, 9 train to 96th St.).

Tej Ayurvedic Skin Care. Herbal facials, detox treatments, and an out-of-this-world scalp massage (162 W. 56th St., Room 204, NY; 212 581-8136; N, R train to 57th St.).

Movement, Meditation, and Exercise

Qi Gong

American Taoist Healing Center. Offers *wu ming qi gong*, designed to promote relaxation with a few simple movements (396 Broadway, Suite 502, NY; 212 274-0999; A, C, E, N, R, J, M, Z, 6 train to Canal St.).

Qi Gong Center. Masters Shen Rong-Er and Wu Yi teach several styles of *qi gong* designed to improve health, mental clarity, and overall well-being. The 90-minute classes meet three times weekly (146 E. 55th St., 3rd floor, NY; 212 752-0792; 4, 5, 6, N, R train to 59th St./Lexington Ave.).

Yoga

Atmananda Yoga Center. Offers 35 weekly classes in yoga and *qi gong*; also Ayurvedic herbal and wax beauty wraps (552 Broadway, NY; 212 625-1511; N, R train to Prince St.).

Integral Yoga Institute. Offers hatha and specialized instruction, breathing and meditation, teacher training and classes for HIV care and vegetarian cooking (227 W. 13th St., NY; 212 929-0586; www.integral yogaofnewyork.org; 1, 2, 3, 9 train to 14th St.).

Jivamukti Yoga Center. The largest yoga center in New York. Near Cooper Square in the Village—look for the neon Sanskrit OM—Jivamukti offers athletically challenging yoga classes as well as massage services, music events, and *kirtan* (devotional singing) and *satsang* (gathering of like minds) evenings. The yoga studio of choice for models, rock stars, and other glitterati (404 Lafayette St., NY; 212 353-0214; www.jivamuktiyoga.com; 6 train to Astor Pl., N, R train to 8th St.).

Sat Nam Yoga Garden. Offers "withdrawal technique, radiant health, Sehaj Bliss, hatha and japa yoga" (236 W. 75th St., NY; 212 874-8701; 1, 2, 3, 9 train to 72nd St.).

Sivananda Yoga Vedanta Center. Learn asanas (yoga postures), meditation, pranayama (breathing practices), philosophy, and chanting (243 W. 24th St., NY; 212 255-4560; 1, 9, train to 23rd St.).

Yoga Zone. Hatha yoga classes, plus yoga clothes and health items (138 Fifth Ave., NY; 212 647-9642; N, R train to 23rd St./160 E. 56th St.; 212 935-9642; 4, 5, 6, N, R train to 59th St./Lexington Ave.).

Tai Chi

William C. C. Chen Tai Chi Chuan. One of the great tai chi teachers (12 W. 23rd St., 2nd floor, NY; 212 675-2816; F, N, R train to 23rd St.).

Martial Arts

Bond Street DoJo for Aikido. Features aikido classes in a Noho location (49 Bond St., NY; 212 477-0899; www.bondstreet.org; B, D, F train to Broadway-Lafayette).

Chau's Wu Mei Kung Fu. Considered the deadliest of martial art forms (159 W. 25th St., NY; 212 633-8865; 1, 9 train to 23rd St.).

Laughing River Jujitsu (Dino Blanche). His three-hour jujitsu classes meet twice weekly (266 Bleecker St., Brooklyn; 718 418-1337; www.kuntu.com; M train to Knickerbocker Ave.).

NY Martial Arts and Health Center. Classes in Thai kick boxing, tae kwon do, and hapkido. Located in Manhattan's Soho (598 Broadway, NY; 212 431-1100; N, R train to Prince St.).

Peridance. Studio offers tae kwon do, Thai kick boxing, or hatha yoga in addition to ordinary dance classes (132 Fourth Ave., NY; 212 505-0886; L, N, R, 4, 5, 6 train to 14th St./Union Sq.).

Seido Karate. Traditional Zen-based Japanese karate in a community atmosphere that's unusually supportive of women and their training: The ratio is roughly half, and both genders kick butt. Point fighting for green belt and higher, no full contact (61 W. 23rd St., NY; 212 924-0511; www.seido.com; F, N, R train to 23rd St.).

Shaolin Temple Overseas Headquarters This Buddhist Temple combines the strengthing of mind with the conditioning of the body. Both prayer and the art of kung-fu are practiced at this Flushing location (132-11 41st Ave., Flushing, NY; 718 539-0872; www.shaolin-over seas.org; 7 train to Flushing/Main St.)

chinatown

They started coming nearly 200 years ago, a tiny trickle of Chinese men, some sailors having jumped ship, some escapees from brutal lives of near-slavery on Caribbean plantations, a Cantonese opera troupe stranded when their American manager absconded with their funds. For decades they existed almost unnoticed, 75 or so single men, biding their time in a cluster of boardinghouses hard by the East River docks. Then in 1869, the Transcontinental Railroad was completed, turning the trickle into a stream as Chinese from California sought a home free of the rampant discrimination found there. Lower Mott Street became Chinatown, swelling with hundreds of new immigrants, almost entirely single men—most expected to return home to their wives after they had made their fortune— from the Toishan district south of Canton. That is, until 1882, when the federal government clamped down on Chinese immigration so tightly that Chinese populations plummeted everywhere in America. It was only with the easing of restrictions during World War II, and then again in 1965, that New York's Chinatown exploded, suddenly overwhelming the haunts of Italians, Irish, and Jews alike. In 1910, Chinatown boasted a population of less than 4,000. Ninety years later, this sprawling, chaotic neighborhood is home to a population estimated to number at least 100,000, speaking dialects ranging from Fujianese to Mandarin, and Cantonese to Toishan, making it the largest Chinatown in the nation. And still it grows.

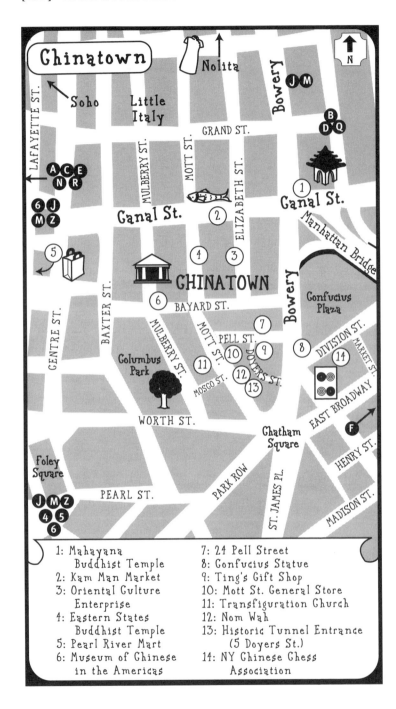

Chinatown

Nolita

Soho

Bowery

Little Italy

GRAND ST.

LAFAYETTE ST.

MULBERRY ST.

MOTT ST.

ELIZABETH ST.

Canal St.

Manhattan Bridge

Canal St.

CHINATOWN

BAXTER ST.

Columbus Park

MULBERRY ST.

BAYARD ST.

MOTT ST.

PELL ST.

DOYERS ST.

MOSCO ST.

Bowery

Confucius Plaza

DIVISION ST.

MARKET ST.

EAST BROADWAY

HENRY ST.

CENTRE ST.

WORTH ST.

Chatham Square

Foley Square

PEARL ST.

PARK ROW

ST. JAMES PL.

MADISON ST.

1: Mahayana
   Buddhist Temple
2: Kam Man Market
3: Oriental Culture
   Enterprise
4: Eastern States
   Buddhist Temple
5: Pearl River Mart
6: Museum of Chinese
   in the Americas

7: 24 Pell Street
8: Confucius Statue
9: Ting's Gift Shop
10: Mott St. General Store
11: Transfiguration Church
12: Nom Wah
13: Historic Tunnel Entrance
    (5 Doyers St.)
14: NY Chinese Chess
    Association

public transportation

SUBWAY: J, M, Z, N, R, 6 to Canal St.; B, D, Q to Grand St.; F to East Broadway. BUS: M15 south on 2nd Ave. to Chatham Sq.; M15 north from Battery Park.

Located on the lower east side of Manhattan, Chinatown's borders are somewhat amorphous, loosely defined by Grand Street on the north, Sarah Roosevelt Park (Chrystie Street) on the east, Broadway on the west, and East Broadway on the south. A good place to start exploring is at the corner of Mott and Canal streets, the gateway to "Old Chinatown." The bulk of the restaurants—Cantonese, Shanghainese, Sichuan (as well as Thai, Vietnamese, Malaysian)—and tourist shopping begins here. Restaurants upstairs and down crowd the narrow little streets, too many to name here. Suffice it to say that it has long been a New York maxim that the only really good Chinese food in the city is to be found south of Canal Street—at prices a third less than those uptown. As for shopping, there is the usual plethora of gimcracks and gewgaws, but here one can also buy gourmet tea, figured red silk for Chinese wedding gowns, fine China lamps,

Outside a Chinatown clothing shop, a selection of dresses—including variations on traditional styles, like the short *cheongsam* on the far right—are set out to attract the attention of passers-by.

and interesting little antique purses. There are Chinese supermarkets with huge kitchenware departments, so you can cook your favorite delicacies at home. Traditional pharmacies offer herbal remedies, if your cooking and your stomach do not agree.

On the southwest corner of Mott and Canal streets looms the pagoda-roofed former headquarters of the On Leong Tong. It was once the most imposing building in Chinatown, illuminated with orange neon at night and host to many a grandiose celebration. The On Leong gained fortune and notoriety as the keepers of the illicit gambling and opium dens that once peppered the neighborhood, as one of the more powerful "Tongs," or associations that were formed to "protect" these particular Chinese interests of the day, along with other "private indulgences." The opium is long-gone, however, and state-run OTB parlors have taken the edge off the remaining gambling operations found in dingy back rooms and basements. The building, like its aging membership, is also a bit faded these days, but the Tong remains a force to be reckoned with, even if they have adopted a lower profile and prefer to be known as the "Chinese Merchants Association."

Moving south along Mott Street, the next seat of power in old Chinatown can be found at 62 Mott. From the time of its founding in 1884, the CCBA (Chinese Consolidated Benevolent Association) was considered the unofficial government of Chinatown, and for those speaking the Toishan dialect, it still is. Inside this 1960s building, the venerable "Mayor of Chinatown" and his officers dole out charity, regulate commerce, referee domestic disputes, and dictate relations with the outside world. They also run a Chinese school, in which many a Chinatown resident has spent long, grueling hours memorizing characters.

Crossing Mott, Bayard Street is home to many, cheap, hole-in-the-wall restaurants, where a plate of rice-and-whatever can be had for three or four dollars. Bayard was once known as "Chin Street," for the ornate 1927 home of the Chin Family Association, to be seen to the left at 62-64 Bayard Street. This is just one of dozens of family and village associations that form the glue of Chinatown society. Through them, people find jobs, apartments, a bowl of noodles when times are lean, and companions with whom to gamble away the lonely nights over dominoes or mah jongg.

To the east, at 13 Elizabeth Street, the biggest Chinese-language bookstore in New York can be found on the second floor of the **Oriental Culture Enterprise.** And to the west, on the corner of Mulberry and Bayard streets, is the old **P.S. 23,** the school where, until the 1970s, Chinatown's children were educated. Today it is home to various civic organizations, like a senior center and a Chinese opera orchestra, whose music can be heard wafting through an open window as one walks by, past the street vendors hawking shoe repair, fortunes, and cheap jade.

On the second floor is the not-to-be missed **Museum of Chinese in the Americas.** Here, a permanent exhibition beautifully illustrates the Chinese American experience, while changing shows celebrate Chinese American artists and historians. The museum's overflowing archive is a mecca for those researching the story of Chinese in the United States.

This part of Mulberry Street was for decades firmly Italian,

Lively exhibits at the Museum of Chinese in the Americas tell the story of Chinese in the U.S. from the earliest days of immigration.

only to see a gradual influx of Chinese businesses—in particular, funeral parlors. Today, Chinese American funerals have evolved into a creature unique in the world. While Chinese tradition calls for long processions replete with firecrackers and gongs to frighten evil spirits, New York City authorities have long frowned on such practices. So, for nearly a hundred years, Italian bands from neighboring Little Italy have provided the pomp and noise, adding to the long processions of mourners (professional and otherwise) who wind their way throughout Chinatown, allowing the souls of the deceased to pay one last visit to the landmarks of their lives.

Across the street, Columbus Park—on the site of the old "Five Points," the most notorious slum in 19th-century North America—has been totally overwhelmed by Chinese residents playing basketball, Chinese chess, poker, and the ever-fascinating game of gossip over neighborhood scandals.

As Mott Street winds farther south, the neighborhood seems to travel back in time. 34 Mott Street was the site of the first Chinese retail presence on the street. Established in 1872, Wah Kee's import/export store (now the Pong Lai Gift Shop) soon became ground zero for New York's Chinese community, which then numbered fewer than 200 men (Chinese women would not arrive for another ten years). Seemingly overnight, Mott Street between Pell Street and Chatham Square became home to numerous Chinese boardinghouses and shops and New York's first Chinese restaurant, probably at Number 20. In the next two decades, China Town, as it was then known, became a tourist destination. Its riot of brightly colored balconies hung with a jumble of banners, lanterns, and Chinese signs gave the tiny enclave an exotic look and feel.

A little of that look can still be seen at **Quong Yuen Shing** (or, the **Mott Street General Store**), at 32 Mott. Inside, it is still 1899, the year that the store moved here from its original location across the street. The same portraits of Chinese ladies still hang high near the ceiling, the same clock still ticks on the wall, and the same gloriously carved arch still spans what used to be

Quong Yuen Shing (the Mott Street General Store) with its intricate carvings and antique decor, is a thriving reminder of days past.

the herbal counter in back. Every store and restaurant in China-town once had carvings like this, valued not just for their beauty but for their ability to confound straight-flying evil spirits with twisting likenesses of peacocks and lucky fish. But bottom-line development has taken its toll, today leaving Quong Yuen Shing with the only such antique decor in public view.

On the corner of Mott and Park (now Mosco) streets the **Transfiguration Catholic Church** still stands. Back in its early days, the clergy were horrified by the influx of the "heathen Chinee," who one priest claimed made the neighborhood "a perfect hell." It would not be until the 1920s that Chinese finally started to be accepted in the congregation. Today, with its school and various outreach programs, it is one of the busiest of many Chinese churches in New York, joining the ranks of Lutherans, Baptists, Presbyterians, and others that have long made China-town their home. Around the corner at 24 Pell Street, old Chi-natown can also be vividly seen in the facade of the Sun Wui Village Association (now a dim sum restaurant). The painted and carved exterior remains decked out in red, gold, and green, the colors of prosperity. The curving eaves and the carvings in its cornice still protect against those pesky evil spirits, ever looking for mischief.

In the 1880s, Pell Street also became home to the On Leong's greatest rivals, the Hip Sing Tong, which is still headquartered at 16 Pell Street. From the 1890s until the 1930s, the Hip Sing and the On Leong would periodically clash in battles over gambling turf that became known in legend as the "Tong Wars." Periodic shootings, stabbings, and near riots would erupt largely on Pell and on tiny, twisting Doyers Street, which doglegs to the right off Pell.

One remnant of the Tong Wars can be found at 5 Doyers Street. It's the site of the old **Chinese Opera House,** the scene, in 1906, of a bloody massacre by Hip Sing members firing point-blank into a crowd of On Leongers enjoying a play. The assailants were nowhere to be found, however, because they had escaped into Chinatown's network of secret tunnels. If you go through the door at 5 Doyers Street today, you will find a stairway leading down into one of these tunnels, snaking around until it suddenly spews out on Chatham Square, right next to the OTB parlor. The **Chinatown Tunnel** is also a more benign place these days, home to businesses like a travel agency, a feng shui practice, and a coin dealer. But those with good imaginations can still envision screaming and bloody Tong warriors, battling away in its dark confines.

As Doyers was also home to a number of low-life saloons where Bowery thugs (and a singing waiter named Irving Berlin) would hang out, the bend in Doyers became known in the press as the "Bloody Angle." These days, Doyers is known more benignly as "Cutting Hair Street," because of its myriad barber shops. But don't miss **Nom Wah** at 15 Doyers Street, New York's oldest dim sum parlor. It remains little changed since it first opened in 1920. While not necessarily the tastiest place for dumplings, it is definitely the best restaurant for atmosphere—unhurried, comfy, and old-fashioned.

A symbol of the rivalry between old and new Chinatown is

An eye-catching display of characters leads customers to the steep, narrow entrances that are often found at Chinatown shops. Mei Dick, one of the many barber shops that are in and around Doyers Street, is a good example.

found at Chatham Square. Facing Mott Street, a hulking statue of
Confucius speaks of the traditional values of the Cantonese and
Toishan elders. Nearby, haughtily placed with its back to the ven-
erated philosopher, stands the grandiose image of **Commis-
sioner Lin,** a great Fujianese general, with his face toward East
Broadway, or "Little Fouzhou." For it is the Fujianese who have
flooded Chinatown in the last 20 years or so, outnumbering the
Cantonese-speakers and relegating the old "Mayor of Chinatown" to the second-best seat at festive banquets.

Long, straight, and broad, East Broadway has its share of
souvenir shops and restaurants, many of which are gargantuan
banquet halls, presided over by uniformed hostesses wielding
walkie-talkies. Midway down the block, amid crowds of produce
vendors, is a huge wedding mill, supplying elaborate dresses,
hairdressers, photographers, and white stretch limos with little
wedding dolls strapped to the grills—everything, in short, for
the modern, over-the-top Chinese version of American nuptials.

Street vendors—this one is on East Broadway—are a significant part of
Chinatown's bustling life.

Farther down, built into the arches of the Manhattan Bridge, is a little shopping mall with community-oriented stores selling things like clothing and videos. But on the second level is the huge dim sum restaurant with the lucky name of **Triple Eight Palace** (as eight is considered to be the luckiest number), packed to the gills on weekends with Chinese families shouting, eating, and happily tossing chicken bones over their shoulders as they hungrily reach for more.

East Broadway is also home to a small branch of the New York Public Library, the busiest in the city library system. Naturally, there is a generous selection of books and videos on all aspects of Chinese life, except that at any given time, much of it will be checked out.

And then there is Chinatown north of Canal Street, home to countless vegetable stalls, fish stores, butchers, and one live poultry market, for those who like their fowl *really* fresh. On the northeast corner of Canal and Broadway is the delightfully quirky **Pearl River Mart** department store, packed with everything recent Chinese arrivals miss from home. Traditional Chinese clothes, cookware, videos, packaged foods, dishes, and an amazing assortment of *tchotchkes* fill its three floors.

New Hong Kong money has left its mark on Canal Street, with the north side of the street lined with merchants selling gold and diamonds. Sleek-suited businessmen conduct power dim sum lunches at the Holiday Inn on Lafayette Street. Banks are everywhere, some even open on Sundays to handle the ever-growing torrents of cash. At least one, the stunningly beautiful landmark Greenpoint (formerly Bowery) Bank on the corner of Grand and the Bowery, is a veritable palace of commerce.

For those seeking a respite from the hustle, a stop at the **Eastern States Buddhist Temple,** at 64 Mott Street, or the **Mahayana Buddhist Temple** would be in order. The Mahayana temple is the largest Buddhist temple in New York, and its taxicab yellow facade can be seen just off Bowery at the corner of Canal, north of the Manhattan Bridge. Inside, a big, golden Buddha is surrounded by neon symbols and electric candles. A

The door is open at the Eastern States Buddhist Temple on Mott Street to dedicated observers as well as the occasional visitor.

shrine to the dead is up front. And, as always, visitors are invited to donate a dollar to take a fortune from the big bowl. But be warned, this is not some fortune-cookie platitude. On a recent visit, the selected message read, "Chances for success: Poor. He who you call your best friend will betray you, and steal something of great value."

So much for a respite from the world.

·4·

religion & spirituality

E mbedded within the concrete and bricks, the getting and spending, the dizzying array of cultures with all they have to offer and absorb while in pursuit of a better life—in short, everything that makes New York New York—are places celebrating the nonmaterial and the spiritual, pockets of serenity where people draw strength and wisdom from ancient traditions that have bound together families and communities for generations. In the past 30 years—in concert with the influx of immigrants from Asia into the city and the West's fascination with the intuitive, meditative religious practices of the East—Asian spirituality has grown into a formidable and influential presence in New York.

Of course, in actuality, there's nothing new about the West adopting Eastern spiritual practices (Christianity, for example?). And continuing that tradition, New Yorkers of varying backgrounds are finding new truths in old systems of belief and practice from the East, and adapting them to their own lives and needs by universalizing the basic tenets and dropping some of the strictures. At the forefront in popularity are Buddhism and yoga, which are taught, practiced, and celebrated in scores of establishments throughout the city. New York is a center of the

Overleaf: Immense Buddha sits with offerings before him, and a much smaller Buddha near his right shoulder, in a Buddhist temple near Canal Street. (Photo © Corky Lee)

Outside the Queens Public Library in Flushing, young observers take part in closing ceremonies following the annual parade—usually in May—in honor of Buddha's birthday. (Photo © Corky Lee)

"spiritual supermarket," and the menu of options ranges from taking a class in ashtanga yoga (hatha yoga practiced at aerobic speed) to embarking on years of textual study in a school of Tibetan Buddhism.

But Asian religions are also alive and well in institutions that are less about universalizing and more about serving as religious, ethnic, and cultural touchstones for the immigrant populations they serve. These institutions help to instill a knowledge of the deep spiritual and religious underpinnings of the home culture in the young, as well as being comforting reminders of home for those not born here.

Recently, I went in search of the ancient traditions of the East, curious to see how they had adapted to their new home in the West.

ch'an Buddhism

My exploration into Asian religion and spirituality in New York began one afternoon when I went in search of Hindu temples in Jackson Heights, Queens, home to perhaps the city's largest Indian community. A 40-minute subway ride from Times Square brought me to an elevated concrete platform with a view of Manhattan's skyline in the distance. I descended, got my bearings on the bustling street, and struck out north, weaving through the thick Sunday crowds that milled in front of sari shops and glitzy stores selling gold jewelry.

I picked up a copy of *News India-Times* and scanned it over a lunch of curried lamb. The newspaper covered commerce and politics—life's practicalities, not spirituality. After lunch, I wandered the neighborhood, remembering my trip to India some time ago, where temples abounded and religion seemed to be at the center of life. Here, the temples appeared to be few and far between, and no *sadhu* with begging bowls and staffs walked the pavements on pilgrimage to holy places.

I crossed at the light, under the thundering tracks and through the salsa music flaring from cars jockeying along the strip. I passed brick tenements and single-family homes, some with small plots of lawn and daffodils blooming in the cool spring day. The afternoon was overcast, with puffs of wind. The neighborhood was a melange of Thai, Korean, Vietnamese, and Hispanic faces and businesses. I veered north along Corona Avenue toward Flushing and Forest Hills. As I crossed the street in Elmhurst. I noticed a door with Chinese characters on its side. Inside, a little girl, perhaps four years old, was doing full-body prostrations before a gold Buddha. As I looked around, I realized that I had stumbled upon the center of Ch'an Buddhist Master Sheng-yen, well-known in the Buddhist community as a superb teacher.

Indeed, "our teacher has a very high social status in China," said Guo-jin, the grave and diminutive woman who led me through the **Dharma Drum Mountain Buddhist Association Ch'an Meditation Center,** Sheng-yen's New York City home. The building was modest and functional, reflecting the utilitarian Chinese aesthetic I had encountered before in Ch'an—which was strikingly different from the clean, formidable simplicity and elegance of Zen, its Japanese counterpart. Master Sheng-yen's base is in Taiwan, where he fled with the Nationalist Army from Shanghai after Mao seized power on the mainland in 1949. Ch'an is the original Chinese form of Zen, its Japanese cousin, and is not as well known in the West. Both Ch'an and Zen emphasize silent sitting meditation, and in the Elmhurst center I was told by Guo-jin that practitioners sit facing the meditation hall's walls, following the lead of the first Ch'an master, Bodhidharma. Legend has it that this fifth-century master achieved enlightenment after nine years of meditating in front of a blank wall.

The center has a Sunday open house, tai chi classes, beginning meditation classes, a Tuesday evening sitting, and a Saturday sitting. It also has one- and two-day retreats open to experienced meditators; longer retreats are held at the rural Dharma Drum Retreat Center in Pine Bush, New York. In the Elmhurst center, a selection of the over 80 books Sheng-yen has authored are for sale.

Hinduism

A couple of blocks farther along Corona Avenue was the doorway to the **Geeta Temple Ashram,** or Geeta Mandir, a long, low concrete building nestled in the industrial smokestacks of northern Queens.

Geeta Mandir has large, carpeted space with low lights. Behind a rail at the front of the room are life-size statues of Hindu deities—Vishnu, Shiva, Ganesh, Krishna Radha, Naryan Laxmi, Hanuman—surrounded by fruit and flowers, enthroned like royalty. On the day I was there, large beautifully carved dark wooden statues of elephants had been placed in either corner of

Shiva represented as Lord of the Dance, from about 970 A.D., by an Indian sculptor working in copper alloy. (Photo © Lynton Gardiner)

the room. A flow of devotees rang the entrance bell and moved purposefully forward to the rail, where they consumed *prasad*, small bits of dried fruit and nuts, and touched their foreheads with *tilack*, a smear of purple paste placed in the position of the third eye, which believers say aids spiritual insight and helps astral beings identify the devout.

To outsiders, the prayer and obeisance paid to the florid statues, or *murti*, might seem like idolatry. To the participants, the worship is a consecration of the invisible and ineffable infinite, which can manifest in any container. The *murti* allow the worshiper to form a personal relationship with the divine. The flowers and food are consumed by the *murti* in the astral realm, and the *prasad* offered to the worshipers are the leftovers from this sacred feast.

A side room houses a statue of Shiva, the destroyer or transformer, the third principal in the Hindu trinity of Brahma, the creator, and Vishnu, the preserver. Opposite the statue, set close to the floor, is a Shiva lingam, a smooth phallic plinth of brown stone in a shallow grooved stone basin. The lingam symbolizes a phallus, consciousness without movement, the male principal. The lingam is bathed in coconut milk, or shakti: energy, juice, movement, the female principal. Bathing the lingam symbolizes the cleansing of the mind.

Visitors are allowed into the temple at any time of the year, but the best time to visit temples may be during one of the annual festivals, when the pageantry and public presence of the Hindu community is strongest. Particularly powerful is the all-night Shivaratra, a lunar holiday that takes place when the new moon is farthest away from the earth, in February or March. The religion identifies Shiva with the new moon, and Krishna, the lover, with nights when the moon is full. During the Shivaratra, priests chant the Vedas, the most ancient sacred texts of India, and food is served late into the night—until 2 or 3 a.m. People come and go as they please.

Another branch of the Geeta Temple is in Woodside, Queens, a short walk from the commercial strip of Jackson Heights. Housed in a graffiti-covered warehouse building, the outside of this temple gives few clues to the wonders inside. The temple is affectionately known as **Divya Dham,** or "holy place." Like most Hindu temples in the United States, Divya Dham hosts the entire pantheon of Hindu deities together under the same roof to try to accommodate as many Hindu families as possible, instead of specializing in a single deity or family of deities as most temples in India are able to do. What sets Divya Dham apart, though, are their recreations of some of Hinduism's most sacred pilgrimage sites, created so that Hindus living in the U.S. wouldn't have to travel all the way to India to go on pilgrimage. The temple houses a papier-mâché replica of the Himalayas, complete with a cave-like tunnel and a recreation of a Vaisno-Devi goddess shrine in Kashmir. Construction has recently begun to build a replica of the Ganges, Hinduism's most sacred river, inside the sprawling temple complex. Complete with water imported from the sacred river, this Ganges re-creation promises to make Divya Dham a major temple in the years to come.

Back in Corona, past the Latino beauty parlors, Laundromats, and restaurants serving grilled chicken, was the locked entrance to the **Shiv Shakti Peeth.** As I stood there contemplating what to do, other arriving visitors located the doorbell, and the door was buzzed open. I followed them into a small vestibule where we shed our shoes, and a garrulous and friendly swami led us into the small but very bright and clean temple, where the now-familiar statues of deities stood behind a rail at the front of the room, and plush carpet covered the floor. The swami, whose name is Harishchander Puri, said the Corona temple was affiliated with Kurukshetre Gita, a temple near New Delhi. Puri had come to America "for religious purposes, to serve the expatriate community" and "because the children born here don't understand Hindi. We teach language classes and we maintain the traditions." The swami added that he welcomed visitors who "come in peace," but not those that cause him "headaches."

As I left, he said, "God bless you," and urged me to take *prasad,* a banana and apple, and a handful of dried fruit and nuts.

"If you eat this food you will go to heaven," said one of the worshipers.

zen Buddhism

"Deep down, the American spirit is Buddhist," says Seigan, a resident monk at the **Zen Studies Society.** "The transcendentalist spirit of Whitman, Thoreau, and Emerson is Zen spirit. Freedom, independence, a great love of nature—all these are the hallmarks of Zen."

Seigan pours green tea, carefully half-filling the cups first to warm them and then dumping the tea back into the pot. The center inhabits a brownstone on the Upper East Side of Manhattan. It is quiet on Monday morning. Seigan's head is shaved. Wrapped in gray robes, the 35-year-old American-born former art student has been immersed in Zen for the past 15 years. From 1995 to 1998, Seigan went to study Zen at the Shogen-ji Monastery in Gifu-Ken, Japan. He has related that it was a remarkable place to live, but being there also proved to be a personal trial.

Seigan's new home is nothing like the Japanese monastery where he suffered from bitter cold and sometimes fearsome cruelty. It is an oasis of calm, simplicity, and austere beauty in the midst of the bustling city. The building was converted from a carriage house to a zendo in 1968. The zendo, or main downstairs meditation room, has stained oak parquet floors, authentic Japanese tatami mats, and meditation cushions for over 40 people. A smaller adjacent zendo looks out over a Japanese rock garden, which Seigan cleans every other day. The wooden Buddha statue standing on the main altar is from the Ryutaku-ji monastery in Mishima City, where Eido Roshi trained as a monk. Other Buddha statues include a bronze Kannon Bosatsu, and a huge seated bodhisattva in meditation posture. Japanese scrolls adorn the zendo, along with beautiful flower arrangements.

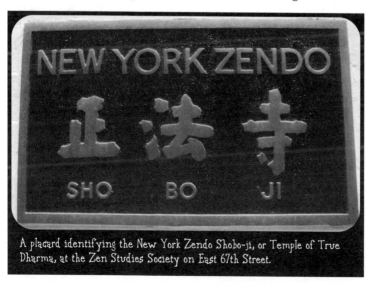

A placard identifying the New York Zendo Shobo-ji, or Temple of True Dharma, at the Zen Studies Society on East 67th Street.

I asked Seigan about his Shogen-ji experience. It was my impression, I said, that he believed that true Zen, the real thing, is back in Japan, and that a lot of the Zen that goes on in America is somehow diluted.

"Wrong! Bad assumption!" Seigan said, smiling. "The Zen masters came to America because of our purity of spirit. Zen in Japan is a formalized facade. Very few Zen students in Japan really want to be monks. They're in monasteries because they want to take over their fathers' temples. There, Zen has become a livelihood and a filial obligation. In America, Zen appeals to our pioneer spirit. It's an adventure. We're living in rugged untouched territory."

soka gakkai international

Downtown, while crossing 15th Street on my way to Tibet House, I noticed the letters SGI on a handsome building. Crossing the street, I entered a quiet lobby with a gleaming marble floor and lush plants. The place was clean, and bright. A receptionist sat behind a large desk. It suddenly occurred to me that I was standing in the New York headquarters of the lay Buddhist group Soka Gakkai (Value Creating Organization) USA.

The Soka Gakkai practices the teachings of Nichiren Daishonin. Contrary to other forms of Buddhism popular in the West, the Daishonin taught that you do not have to practice austerities and give up your desires in order to find enlightenment in this lifetime. Although many people are originally attracted to the Soka Gakkai and its teachings for material reasons, they soon find that the real benefit of chanting nam myoho renge kyo is the inner transformation (which SGI members call their Human Revolution) they experience. The goal of the Soka Gakkai is world peace through individual happiness. With ties to the UN as an NGO (non-governmental organization), they are particularly concerned with helping refugees, fighting for disarmament, and advancing the cause of world peace.

Tibetan Buddhism

Across Fifth Avenue on West 15th Street is **Tibet House,** the brainchild of its president, Robert A. F. Thurman, the scholar, author, former Tibetan Buddhist monk, translator, friend of the Dalai Lama, and, perhaps most famously, father of actress Uma Thurman. Tibet House was formed in 1987 at the request of the Dalai Lama to help ensure the long-term survival of Tibet's rich culture and its amazing Buddhist tradition, regardless of the fate of Tibet itself, which was invaded by the Chinese in 1949 and has been victimized by the regime ever since. Tibet House has attracted celebrities like Harrison Ford, Richard Gere, Patti Smith, Natalie Merchant, and David Byrne, who have appeared at fundraising events. The Dalai Lama's imprimatur, Thurman's towering scholarship, and the aura of celebrity lurking in the wings are a potent combination: Tibet House has done much to raise consciousness in the West about the plight of the Tibetan people and the richness and beauty of Tibetan Buddhism.

The beautiful galleries of Tibet House include an exhibit of tanka paintings by the modern master Pema Namdol Thaye. Particularly captivating is his portrayal of arhats, or saints, who have conquered the enemy, or dissonant emotions. Other enlightened beings appear riding tigers and holding vipers.

Every Tuesday evening from 6:15 to 7:30, Tibet House sponsors informal gatherings open to the public where people can learn about meditation techniques from an eclectic range of Buddhist teachers. Nancy Braxton, development coordinator, says Tibet House has "no missionary zeal. No particular agenda. We want people to incorporate whatever they find useful, beneficial, into their lives." On Wednesday evenings, Tibet House has classes in Tibetan Buddhist philosophy.

The classes in philosophy and meditation are held in the gallery, facing Tibet House's traditional Lhakang Shrine. People can come and meditate in this small, brightly colored room, which has, at its center, a Buddha statue. Each morning there are offerings made to Buddha of bowls of water for his mouth and

Buddha statue in New York's Tibet House presides in this room for meditation and classes in the ways of Tibetan Buddhism.

feet, perfumed water for his chest, and incense, flowers, candles, music, and food. The sense offerings are transmuted into a more subtle form, says Braxton. To either side of the Buddha, traditional shelves are lined with sacred texts. The Shrine incorporates a three-dimensional Green Tara mandala, and other sacred Tibetan paintings. A chair in which his holiness the Dalai Lama sat is now draped with a traditional white offering scarf. A lending library holds over 700 volumes.

As sacred as these rooms feel, the guardians of Tibet House stress that it is not a temple. "Temples are for monks," Ganden Thurman, one of Robert Thurman's sons, emphasized.

My next Tibetan venue in the city was nearby, on West 22nd Street. It was late in the day by the time I took the elevator up to the sixth floor of a dark old building in Chelsea. I emerged into a light airy space with people bustling about. I had entered the **N.Y. Shambhala Center**, which had been started by the late Trungpa Rinpoche, the revered and rather infamous Tibetan tulku (a reincarnated lama) who had brought his own particular form of "crazy wisdom," as he liked to call it, to the West.

I'd become familiar with Trungpa in Boulder, Colorado,

where he had resided for years, drawing students like poets Allen Ginsberg and Anne Waldman, who helped found the Naropa Institute, Shambhala's affiliated university of Buddhist studies. Although I had never met Trungpa, I had heard much about him. Photos of him were up on the walls of the 22nd Street space, and looking at them I was again struck by his slightly ominous quality. He looked like a big cat, a lion or tiger, perhaps—a brilliant author and poet, he was a controversial teacher of undisputed power.

In the Chelsea Shambhala, a tall elderly man with a flowing white beard—whose name was Ric Lavin, a self-described "junior student" of Tibetan Buddhism—explained that this was in fact the anniversary eve of the venerable teacher's death, or *parinirvana*, in 1987. Lavin, now retired, and an actor in his former life, showed me around the center's offices, meditation rooms, kitchen, and room for Kyudo, or Zen archery. The Kyudo room smelled of hay; targets mounted on poles were stuffed with it. Kyudo is taught at Shambhala each Monday night. Unlike traditional archery, Kyudo, Lavin said, is not about being a perfect marksman. "Marksmanship is meditation in action—a synchronization of body and mind."

Like many before him, Lavin came to Shambhala on the advice of his psychotherapist, who believed meditation might benefit him. He took meditation instruction, the same training that the center now offers free of charge to the public twice a week. What he found was "a place to learn to focus the mind without having to become Buddhist or denounce anything." The style of meditation meshed with Lavin's philosophy. "The kind of meditation taught at Shambhala has a particular nonaggressive way of dealing with thoughts," Lavin says. "The focus is on breath, bringing attention back to the breath. The mind is racing, faster than we realize. Meditation slows it down, so we can observe it, work with it."

Before I left I noticed the side-by-side photos of Trungpa and his son, Sakyong Mipham Rinpoche, 37, who now heads Shambhala International, which has branches all over the world,

with its headquarters in Halifax, Nova Scotia. I had naively
assumed that Trungpa's group would disband after he died.

But the followers of the teachings of Shambhala (named after
the Buddhist Atlantis, a mythical city that some say was buried
under the sands of the Gobi Desert) were still going strong. Eric
Spiegel, a senior student and teacher at Shambhala New York, said
that Trungpa's followers did indeed go through hard times after
their master's death, but that they have found a new footing. "In
the last ten years of his life," Spiegel said, "Trungpa taught the
Shambhala teachings, which were ecumenical. They were about
how to live, not about beliefs in this god or that god. We've tried
to continue that at Shambhala, to distill the essence of the Buddhist teachings without all the trappings."

islam

My first impression of the Imam, the prayer leader of the
Islamic Cultural Center in New York, the enormous new
mosque located on 96th Street and Third Avenue in Manhattan,
was of a small man with a trimmed beard, warm smile, and cor-
dial manner. "You are welcome! You are welcome," he said,
greeting me and taking my hand. The Imam's name was
Mohamad Mostafa. He was dressed in a blue robe that extended
to the floor and a cap with a red top and white rim.

A group was gathering for the dzuhr, the early afternoon
prayer, in a large room with tiles on its walls and carpet on its
floor, located on the ground level of the center. I removed my
shoes and sat with my back against the partitions that divided
the area marked "sisters" and the library from the main area for
prayer. A man called the muezzin stood at the front of the room,
before the mihrab, an empty, tile-lined alcove, and sang the Arabic
call for prayer into a microphone. Its hauntingly mournful
melody sounded throughout the mosque. (The Imam would
later translate the call, which repeats the phrases, "I bear witness,
there is no God but Allah . . . Come to prayer, come to prayer . . .
Come to success, come to success.") The dzuhr is one of five

The Islamic Cultural Center serves a diverse community of Muslims from all corners of the globe.

prayers recited each day by Muslims all over the world. Men gathered and bowed in unison, touching their foreheads to the floor, all facing east, toward Mecca. The men and women gathered together for prayer came from a number of ethnic backgrounds, reflecting the history of the mosque. The mosque's construction was financed by a number of predominantly Muslim countries. The largest contribution was made by Kuwaiti benefactors, and the Malaysian government contributed over $10,000 to the project. The Pakistani government donated the mosque's carpets, and the Indonesian government donated the mosque's *minbar*, or stage. The result is a diverse religious center that incorporates artistic traditions from all over the Islamic world. Similarly, the mosque's constituents include new immigrants from Bangladesh and Indonesia, diplomats from the Middle East, refugees from the former Yugoslavia, and African Americans from East Harlem, all praying alongside one another in an amazing display of both the unity and diversity of Islam.

After the service, I toured the mosque upstairs. Used for special services and gatherings, it's a soaring room of green marble with a high, domed ceiling. I spoke briefly again to the Imam, thanked him, and said good-bye.

Lower down on the East Side, the **Medina Masjid,** located behind a converted storefront in the East Village, greets visitors with signs announcing the basic tenets of Islam in three different languages: English, Arabic, and Bengali, which is the native tongue of most of the mosque's members. The mosque's signs declare, "Islam is the way. Read the Holy Quran, the final revelation. There is no God but Allah, Muhammad is his messenger." While the neighborhood's newest breed of hipsters walk by, Bangladeshi men in silk *kurtas* and skullcaps rush inside the mosque's doors, which are wide open during prayer time. In the back of the mosque's brick façade, a built-on minaret, or tower, is painted bright blue and green and decorated with Arabic calligraphy. From speakers inside this minaret, the call to prayer resounds through the streets of the Village as it does in countless faraway Muslim communities throughout South and Southeast Asia.

Yoga New York

I took the train downtown from 96th Street to Union Square, slurped down a bowl of roast duck wonton soup at a Chinese noodle shop, and then walked crosstown to the **Integral Yoga Institute (IYI)** on West 13th Street. I wished, when I arrived, that I had saved my appetite for the tempting juice bar and deli counter at the IYI's health food store. Next door was a small bookstore, where yoga students registered for classes.

IYI's winding townhouse stairs led to several floors of serene spacious rooms, where the yoga classes were held. The place had a relaxed, homey atmosphere. The term yoga comes from the Sanskrit word yuj, meaning "to yoke, join, or bind"—a path to union of mind and body with the divine. What distinguishes the IYI's yoga from other types taught around the city is its meditative aspect. "We let postures flow," says Boris Pisman, IYI's administrative director. "We are continuously aware of movement that not only strengthens and relaxes the body but helps us become more fully aware. A big component of the yoga we do is its meditative attitude."

Founded by Swami Satchidananda in 1967, IYI now serves close to 6,000 students a month and holds 100 classes each week. Anyone can walk in off the street and take a class for $7 to $12 (depending on the class's duration). IYI is one of 40 centers all over the world founded by Satchidananda, who was brought to New York City in 1966 by the artist Peter Max. According to Pisman, Satchidananda's guru Shivananda practiced many different types of yoga, which Satchidananda adopted, expanded, and made his own. Satchinananda is a recipient of the Albert Schweitzer Humanitarian Award and today lives in a place with the sprightly name of Yogaville, IYI's retreat center in rural Virginia.

Across town, opposite the Public Theater on Lafayette Street, is the **Jivamukti Yoga Center.** As at IYI, people can walk in off the street and take a yoga class (cost $15), which includes chanting and meditation. The center also offers massage and has a small meditation room that is open to the public.

Jivamukti was started in 1984 by David Life and Sharon Gannon on the principal, according to Life, of "living liberation. We don't have to wait to die to go to heaven. Our body is not an impediment but a tool." Life said he was using the term "heaven" as a "generic representation of freedom, happiness, love, none of which are entirely appropriate. Jivamukti, the yogic term in Samadhi, bridges the gap between ancient teaching and modern life."

At five o'clock on a Monday afternoon, the place was buzzing with activity. People hurried in, registered at the front desk, quickly hung their coats opposite the small boutique and bookstore, and entered the changing rooms, emerging in yoga garb—tights, leotards, loose pants. The vibe was very hip, downtown: models, actors, the beautiful people.

Life said the yoga the center teaches is "vigorous, forceful, almost gymnastic. The first yoga teachers in this country were sponsored by little old ladies in church groups. We've tried to reincorporate the extremity of practice."

Jivamukti has a small meditation room, accessed through a door that looks as if it might lead into a secret garden. Inside the door, I pushed aside heavy velvet drapes. The light in the room was low, the ceiling domed. It was warm inside, very peaceful, an oasis of calm. The activity of the center beyond the room's walls echoed somewhere faintly in the distance; the clang and scuffle of the city's streets was little more than a dreamy purr. I sat for a while, breathing slowly and deeply, keeping the focus on my breath and inside myself, far, far away from the brassy, restless rhythms of the streets.

religion & spirituality
THE LISTINGS

Buddhist Centers

Brooklyn Buddhist Association Sogen/International Zen Dojo of Brooklyn Kai. Daily classes offered in Aikido (a martial art developed in Japan) and Zazen (group silent sitting meditation) (211 Smith St., Brooklyn; 718 488-9511; www.directmind.com/bba.html; F, G train to Smith-9th sts.).

Dharma Drum Mountain Buddhist Association Ch'an Meditation Center. Home of Master Sheng-yen, one of the foremost teachers of Ch'an (the Chinese form of Zen) in the world today. Saturday and Tuesday evening sitting meditation practice and Sunday open house with group meditation and dharma talks by Master Sheng-yen when he is in residence, or his senior students, a vegetarian lunch, and afternoon devotional chanting (90-56 Corona Ave., Elmhurst, Queens; 718 592-6593; www.chan1.org; R, G train to Grand Ave./Newtown).

Eastern States Buddhist Temple. This Buddhist temple in Chinatown is realtively small but offers a peaceful space for prayer, meditation, and to ponder your future from a selection of traditional fortune indicators (64 Mott St., NY; 212 966-6229; A, C, E, N, R, J, M, Z, 6 to Canal St.).

Mahayana Buddhist Temple. Located at the base of the Manhattan Bridge, a bright yellow facade greets visitors to the largest Buddhist temple in New York (131–133 Canal St., NY; 212 925-8787; A, C, E, N, R, J, M, Z, 6 to Canal St.).

Nechung Foundation. Meditation classes Wednesday and Saturday evening, Sunday afternoon Tibetan language classes, Thursday evening art class, call for special programs listing. Lama Pema Dorjee (110 First Ave., 5th floor, NY; 212 388-9784; L train to First Ave.).

New York Buddhist Church and American Buddhist Academy. A bronze statue of Shinran-Shonin guards this Buddhist Church and social center on Riverside Drive (331–332 Riverside Dr., NY; 212 678-9213; 1, 9 train to 103rd St.).

New York Insight Meditation Center. Meditation and yoga classes, retreats, community events around the city. Call for listing and information about current programs (P.O. Box 1790, Murray Hill Station, NY 10156; 917 441-0915; www.nyimc.org.).

New York Shambhala Center & Dharmadhatu of New York. Practice and study center dedicated to the practice of Buddhadharma, the Shambhala Training path, and the practice of contemplative arts, after the vision of Chögyam Trungpa Rinpoche (118 W. 22nd St., 6th floor, NY; 212 675-6544; www.shambhala.org; 1, 9, F, N, R train to 23rd St.).

Palden Sakya Centers. Centers for traditonal Tibetan Buddhist meditation and learning. The Sakya tradition is one of the four traditional schools of Tibetan Buddhism. Lama Pema Wangdak (4-10 W. 101st St., Suite. 63, NY; 212 866-4339; www.vikramasila.org; B, C train to 103rd St.; 289 Brookside Ave., Cresskill, NJ; 201 541-0007; 234 Mead Mountain Rd., Woodstock, NY; 914 679-4024).

Soka Gakkai International New York. Founded in Japan in 1930, an American Buddhist Association with worldwide centers based on the philosophy of Nichiren Daishonin, who lived in 13th-century Japan. Stresses Buddhist practice in daily life. A nongovernmental organization with the United Nations that works toward world peace. Members chant *nam myoho renge kyo* (7 E. 15th St., NY; 212 727-7715; www.sgiusa.org; 4, 5, 6, N, R, L train to 14th St./Union Sq.).

The Tibet Center. Oldest Tibetan Buddhist center in New York City, founded in 1975. Evening classes in Buddhist teachings and meditation. Open to the public during the day for sitting meditation. Classes and admission are free. Rato Khyongla Rinpoche (107 E. 31st St., 5th floor, NY; 212 779-1841; www.thetibetcenter.org; 6 train to 33rd St.).

Tibet House. Exhibitions in Tibetan art, performances, group meditation in the Tibetan Buddhist tradition, beautiful shrine room, a reading room and lending library (22 W. 15th St., NY; 212 807-0563; www.tibethouse.org; 4, 5, 6, N, R, L train to 14th St./Union Sq.).

Zen Studies Society/New York Zendo Shobo-ji. The society emphasizes the practice of *zazen* (sitting Zen meditation). An orientation class is open to the public; also offered are *zazen* meetings throughout the week, retreats, and Dharma talks. (223 E. 67th St., NY; 212 861-3333; www.zenstudies.org; 6 train to 68th St.).

Hindu Centers

Ganesh Temple Society of North America (Sri Maha Vallabha Gana-pati Devasthanam). Dedicated to the Hindu spirit of tolerance and Ganesh—the elephant-headed deity—spectacular stone-carvings of the creatures greet you at the entrance. Visitors are welcome for holiday and festival celebrations as well as daily prayer and worship. (45-57 Bowne St., Flushing, Queens; 718 460-8484, 1-800-99 HINDU; 7 train to Flushing/Main St., then Q27 bus to Bowne St.).

Geeta Temple Ashram (Geeta Mandir). Hindu meditation center, replete with statues of Hindu gods and goddesses, celebrating all major holidays with prayers and gatherings. Call for information and a schedule of events (92-09 Corona Ave., Elmhurst, Queens; 718 592-2925; G, R train to Grand Ave./Newtown).

Geeta Temple/Divya Dham. A branch of the Geeta Temple Ashram in Elmhurst. Open every day until 10:00 p.m. Celebrates all major holidays. Houses all major Hindu deities, including the nine forms of Durga and a few important Gujarati saints. All house a replica of a Kashmiri Vaisno-Devi (goddess) shrine. Extremely friendly staff (34-63 56th St., Woodside, Queens; 718 429-5615; G, R train to Northern Blvd.).

International Society for Krishna Consciousness. Every morning a public discussion at 8 a.m. on the Vedic scripture Srinad Dhacavatan; Wednesday 7 p.m. public class on the Bhagavad-Gita, followed by a vegetarian dinner; Sunday 5:30 p.m., a public program: dancing, chanting, temple ceremony, sometimes a performance, and always a vegetarian feast. Donation (305 Schermerhorn St., Brooklyn, NY; 718 855-6714; www. iskcon.com; A, C, G train to Hoyt-Schermerhorn, 2,3,4,5 train to Nevins St., D, M, Q, N, R, train to DeKalb Avenue).

Satya Narayan Mandir. Large Hindu temple celebrating all holidays. Open to the public daily for prayer and worship. Hindu statues of the gods and goddesses (75-15 Woodside Ave., Elmhurst, Queens; 718 899-8863; G, R train to Elmhurst Ave.).

Shiv Shakti Peeth. Newish, small, and snazzy Hindu temple with friendly swami. Hindu gods and goddesses. All holidays and festivals celebrated (97-26 Corona Ave., Corona, Queens; 718 393-0873; G, R train to Grand Ave./Newtown).

Sikh Cultural Society of New York, Gurdwara Sahib. Sikhs hold religious services and dine here while children study the Punjabi language and study Indian musical instruments. Visitors who remove

their shoes and cover their heads are welcome (95-30 118th St.,
Richmond Hill, Queens; 718 441-5581; A train to Lefferts Blvd.).
Vedanta Society. Society affiliated with the Ramakrishna Order
founded in 1894 by the first teacher of Vedanta to come to the West,
Swami Vivekananda (34 W. 71st St., NY; 212 877-9197; www.vedanta
newyork.org; B, C, 1, 2, 3, 9 train to 72nd St.).

Muslim Centers

Astoria Islamic Foundation. Daily prayers. Holiday celebrations.
Quran classes (25-67 31st St., Astoria, Queens; 718 726-7172; N train
to Astoria Blvd.).
His Highness Prince Aga Khan Shia Imami Ismaili Council for USA.
Ismailis are a unique Shia sect of Islam with strong cultural ties to
South and Central Asia. Daily prayers. Cultural center. Festivals (Two
Grand Central Tower, 140 E. 45th St., NY; 4, 5, 6, 7, S train to 42nd
St./Grand Central).
International Islamic Community. This mosque serves Muslim diplo-
mats from all over the world, including Malaysia, Indonesia and Pak-
istan. Daily prayers (Room 3351A, UN Secretariat, NY; 4, 5, 6, 7, S
train to 42nd St./Grand Central).
Islamic Cultural Center. Large mosque on the Upper East Side of
Manhattan, Muslim center, bookstore and gift shop, offering daily
prayers and religious activities around festivals and holy days (1711
Third Ave., NY; 212 722-5234; 6 train to 96th St.).
Jamaica Muslim Center. Daily prayers. Friday gatherings. Many South
Asian Muslims from the surrounding community pray here. Call for
more information (85-37 168th St., Jamaica, Queens; 718 739-3182;
F train to 169th St./Hillside Ave.).
Medina Masjid. The latest addition to the East Village religious scene,
this Bangladeshi mosque is housed in a converted storefront. The call
to prayer, broadcast through the mosque's built-on minaret, echoes
through the streets of the East Village. Daily prayer. Holiday celebrations
(401 E. 11th St., NY; 212 533-5060; L train to First Ave.).
Muslim Center of New York. A one-stop shop for Islam in New York.
Daily prayer. Quran classes. Book service. Daily elementary school.
Sunday school for children and adults. Matrimonial services. Counseling. Study sessions. Financial help (137-58 Geranium Ave.,
Flushing, Queens; 718 460-3000; www.muslimcenter.org; 7 train to
Main St./Flushing).

Muslim Majlis of Staten Island. Daily prayer. Sunday school for children (104 Rhine Ave., Staten Island; 718 816-8866; salam.muslimson line.com; Richmond Road Exit off Staten Island Expwy./I-278 West).

Sufi Books. Center for Sufism, Islam, and other traditions of religion and healing. Also offers lecture series on different sacred traditions, health and healing, and the creative arts. Call for schedule of events (227 West Broadway, NY; 212 334-5212; www.sufibooks.com; 1, 9 train to Franklin St.).

Yoga Schools
(see also Yoga listings in Health & Fitness)

Integral Yoga Institute. Well-established West Village center with a full roster of daily yoga classes at all levels which are open to the public without a reservation, as well as a bookstore and health food store (227 W. 13th St., NY; 212 929-0585; www.integralyogaofnewyork.org; 1, 2, 3, 9, A, C, E, L train to 14th St.).

Jivamukti Yoga Center. Sophisticated power yoga at Village locale. Meditation room. Massage by appointment. Bookstore, clothing store, incense and Indian sundries (404 Lafayette St., NY; 212 353-0214; www.jivamuktiyoga.com; 6 train to Astor Pl., N, R train to 8th St.).

Siddha Yoga Meditation Center of New York. Small ashram and Siddha Yoga center affliated with the sprawling and opulent South Falls-burg Siddha Yoga Ashram of Gurumayi Chidvilasananda, who inherited it from Swami Muktananda. Call for times the center is open and a schedule of activities (324 W. 86th St., NY; 212 873-8030; www. siddha.org; 1, 9 train to 86th St.).

india in
new york city

Outside the TKTS booth in Manhattan's Times Square, two visiting Indians, purchasing half-price tickets for a Broadway show, were gossiping loudly in Hindi. Suddenly, one of them turned around and saw another *desi*, or countryman, right behind her.

"You must have followed everything we have been saying," she said.

"I wouldn't be the only one," he said, a little amused. "Half of New York could follow Hindi, you know," he said, tongue firmly planted in cheek.

With well over 200,000 people from the Indian subcontinent living and working in New York City, it is nearly impossible to escape the influence of India in the Big Apple. There are more than 13,000 cabbies of Indian or Pakistani origin here, and hundreds of South Asian–born men who work at newsstands from around five in the morning until late into the evening. Want to check out a fantastic no-frills curry restaurant? Just ask a cabdriver.

Once upon a time, say as recently as fifteen or twenty years ago, when you thought of India in New York, you thought of a packed strip of Indian restaurants on East 6th Street and a concentration of Indian grocery stores and bakeries around 27th Street on Lexington Avenue—and a movie theater or two that showed overtly melodramatic and relentlessly romantic movies from India. The word "Bollywood"—denoting movies from Bombay, India's own Hollywood—was unknown here then.

Today, you will find India's presence everywhere in New York—more widespread now in Manhattan, and particularly more established in Queens. Indian businessmen, professionals, homemakers, and students in New York represent every Indian state and culture and speak in at least 26 languages and nearly 50 dialects.

Their contributions touch all areas of life in New York—the arts, academia, Silicon Alley, science and medicine, and publishing are just a few. If you are strolling near Columbus Avenue, you might bump into filmmaker Ismail Merchant, who has made New York his home for over four decades, planning such Oscar-nominated classics as *A Room with a View* and *Howard's End*. And Columbia University's distinguished Indian faculty is led by professors Jagdish Bhagwati, his wife, Padma Desai, and Sreenath Sreenivasan, one of the youngest journalism professors in America. Columbia also attracts scores of India's brightest students. New York is the home of Sonny Mehta, the distinguished editor-in-chief of the Alfred A. Knopf publishing house and his equally distinguished wife, the novelist Gita Mehta (*The River Sutra*). And New York is also the home of Madhur Jaffrey, who has, more than any other Indian, popularized Indian food through her books and cooking classes aired over PBS.

Lexington Avenue in the upper twenties still has a lot of Indian restaurants, and is still Manhattan's center for Indian breads, sweets, spices, and other condiments for the home cook. **Kalustyan's,** with its recent facelift, is bigger and better than ever; **Foods of India** is another good place to check out.

Here too, as in the East Village and Jackson Heights, the number of restaurants owned by Pakistani and Bangladeshi immigrants is increasing. Curry in a Hurry and Shaheen are among the non-Indian restaurants along Lexington Avenue, but they offer the same kind of food Indian restaurants would offer and are popular with Indian customers too.

Naghma House, a music and home appliances shop run by a Pakistani immigrant, is a popular neighborhood stop to buy music and movie videocassettes from the subcontinent. But since the Indian movie industry dominates the entertainment world in South Asia, it is natural that Naghma House has more in the way of Indian entertainment items. There are also several shops that offer newspapers and magazines from India.

Yet, waiting outside of Manhattan for students of Indian history, religion, culture, and traditions, even a casual walk through pockets of Queens such as Jackson Heights and Flushing offers tantalizing insights and raises hundreds of intriguing questions.

Want to watch Hindu festivals and rituals? Take the 7 train to Flushing and go to the **Ganesh Temple,** which for nearly three decades has welcomed Hindus not only from India but from a dozen other countries including Trinidad, Guyana, Malaysia, Mauritius, Fiji, and South Africa. Today, 30 years later, there are nearly a dozen Hindu temples in New York and Long Island. All of the priests are from India, but community leaders and trustees at the Ganesh Temple are hopeful that a priest from the second generation is forthcoming. Their logic is that if the Hare Krishnas have been able to attract large numbers of Americans to renounce their careers and become full-time devotees and priests, then traditional Indian temples should also succeed in drawing young Indian Americans.

India is alive in the *gurdwara* in Queens where Sikhs worship, and in mosques in Brooklyn and Queens where Indians join fellow Muslims from Pakistan and Bangladesh in weekly communion. Christian India is alive and well in more than ten churches that offer Holy Mass in such languages as Tamil, Telugu, Hindi, and Urdu. In some churches, heavily dressed priests with flourishing beards offer services using orthodox rituals that are centuries old. Given the fact that Christianity reached India 2,000 years ago—much before Ireland welcomed it—and that there are about three million Christians across India, Indian Christians are proud of their heritage. "Occasionally I worship in an American church," says an Indian businessman. "But I

At markets like Patel Brothers in Jackson Heights, you can find any vegetable you might need for preparing an Indian meal.

prefer our own churches because I feel at home—and I feel there is much more discipline in them. For one thing, we dress more respectfully in our churches and we take our services more seriously."

On the weekends, more than 100 shops and restaurants in Jackson Heights in Queens are packed with Indians (and people from neighboring countries) not only from other parts of New York, but from New Jersey and Connecticut as well. They come to buy colorful saris and other traditional Indian outfits; gold jewelry; newspapers and magazines in half a dozen languages; and religious books and materials used in prayer rooms. Some stop by to consult one of half a dozen astrologers, including one who claims to be India's first female astrologer. They also come for cigarettes. Indian cigarettes contain more nicotine than American cigarettes. Small, thin "bidis," known in India as "the poor man's cigarette," are sold singly at Indian bodegas and other stores; their potency and relatively low price have made them popular with many an American youth.

At such shops as **Patel Brothers,** one can choose from over 100 varieties of vegetables and fruits. Some vegetables, such as the thumb-size tindoora (which tastes something like a Brussels sprout) or the long snake gourd, would certainly seem exotic to

public transportation

EAST VILLAGE/NY (6th St. between 1st and 2nd aves.) SUBWAY: L to 1st Ave. BUS: M15 on 1st or 2nd Ave. to 6th St.

LEXINGTON AVENUE/NY (Lexington Ave. in the twenties.) SUBWAY: 6 to 28th St. BUS: M101, M102, M103 on Lexington Ave. to 28th St.

ELMHURST/QUEENS SUBWAY: 7 to 90th St.-Elmhurst Ave., G, R to Elmhurst Ave. BUS: Q32 to 82nd St. and Roosevelt Ave.

FLUSHING/QUEENS SUBWAY: 7 to Flushing/Main St. BUS: Q66 to Main St.

JACKSON HEIGHTS/QUEENS SUBWAY: E, F, G, R to Roosevelt Ave./Jackson Hts.; 7 to 74th St./Broadway BUS: Q32 to 74th St.

non-Indians. It is not unusual for a stranger to gingerly ask the workers at the shop how to cook the tindoora. "Fry onions in oil, add green chilies and black pepper and cook the cut tindoora on low flame, and add plenty of ghee (clarified butter) and fresh coconut," offers one.

People also go to Jackson Heights to eat in such landmark restaurants as the **Jackson Diner**. For many years a celebrated corner "desi" coffee shop, it is today one of the ritzier Indian restaurants in Queens. The lines here on Saturday nights are even longer than the ones for a hit Bollywood movie at the nearby **Eagle Theater**.

You can also go to Jackson Heights to enjoy spicy organ meats and trotters, or hilsa fish from Bengal—the kind of items other Indian restaurants are wary of offering. Trotters are shanks, as in lamb shanks, and are considered a delicacy in India. Hilsa fish, much loved by the people of Bengal, is not readily available here except in Bengali-run restaurants. Like the fresh Portuguese sardines flown to the city daily, hilsa fish can only be found in a few select spots. Fish-head curry, one of the delicacies of Bengal, has not yet surfaced in Indian restaurants in New York, though some Malay restaurants are offering the dish in Queens and Manhattan.

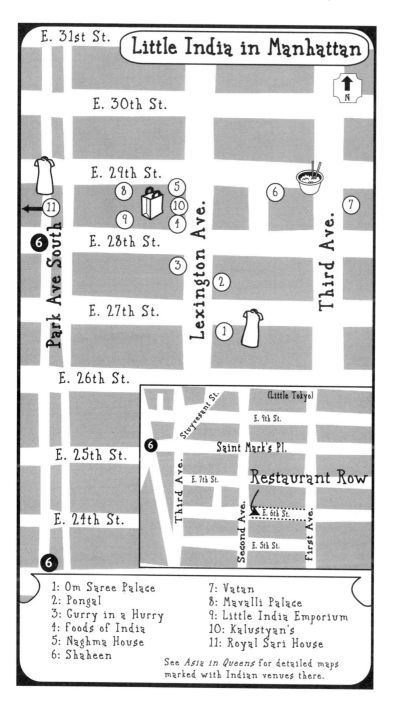

Little India in Manhattan

1: Om Saree Palace
2: Pongal
3: Curry in a Hurry
4: Foods of India
5: Naghma House
6: Shaheen
7: Vatan
8: Mavalli Palace
9: Little India Emporium
10: Kalustyan's
11: Royal Sari House

See *Asia in Queens* for detailed maps marked with Indian venues there.

Kalustyan's in Manhattan's Little India carries more spices—and many other fragrant ingredients—than most Westerners might imagine exist.

Which leads us to a larger issue: Just how Indian are the Indian restaurants of New York? Purists will not step into any restaurant that has a sign advertising Indian, Pakistani, and Bangladeshi cuisine. "No self-respecting Indian restaurant will add the names of the other two countries," says one diehard.

As for those neighborhood pockets of the city where wall-to-wall Indian restaurants attract visitors by the busload, many are no longer Indian at all. It is an open secret, for example, that, these days, the "Little India" restaurants on 6th Street in the East Village are run largely by Bangladeshis. Purists will insist that the food there is inferior to that cooked by Indian chefs. Fortunately, common sense and taste buds have a way of winning out over ideology—especially when you remember that Indians and Pakistanis live on both sides of the border, and that Indians and Bangladeshis eat very similar foods. The main difference is that Hindus shun cow and are often vegetarian, while Muslims eschew pork.

The festering politics of the subcontinent are largely forgotten in the three movie houses in Queens that show Hindustanilanguage movies from India throughout the week. The Eagle, one of the three theaters, used to show X-rated movies until a few years ago, when it was shut down by the city. Today, it shows first-run Bollywood movies, often subtitled for the benefit of Trinidadians and Guyanese of Indian origin—or the second-generation Indian kids who are coaxed by their parents to join them.

Indian films are banned in Pakistan and Bangladesh, ostensibly to protect their own struggling movie industries, though video piracy ensures that people in those countries often get to see the Indian movies even before they have been released in movie houses in India.

"But here we see them without any embarrassment or fear," says a Pakistani cabdriver. "And we see it on a big screen. We do not remember the border wars—or any other problems between India and Pakistan when we are here. For three hours, Indians, Pakistanis, and Bangladeshis all become one."

•5•

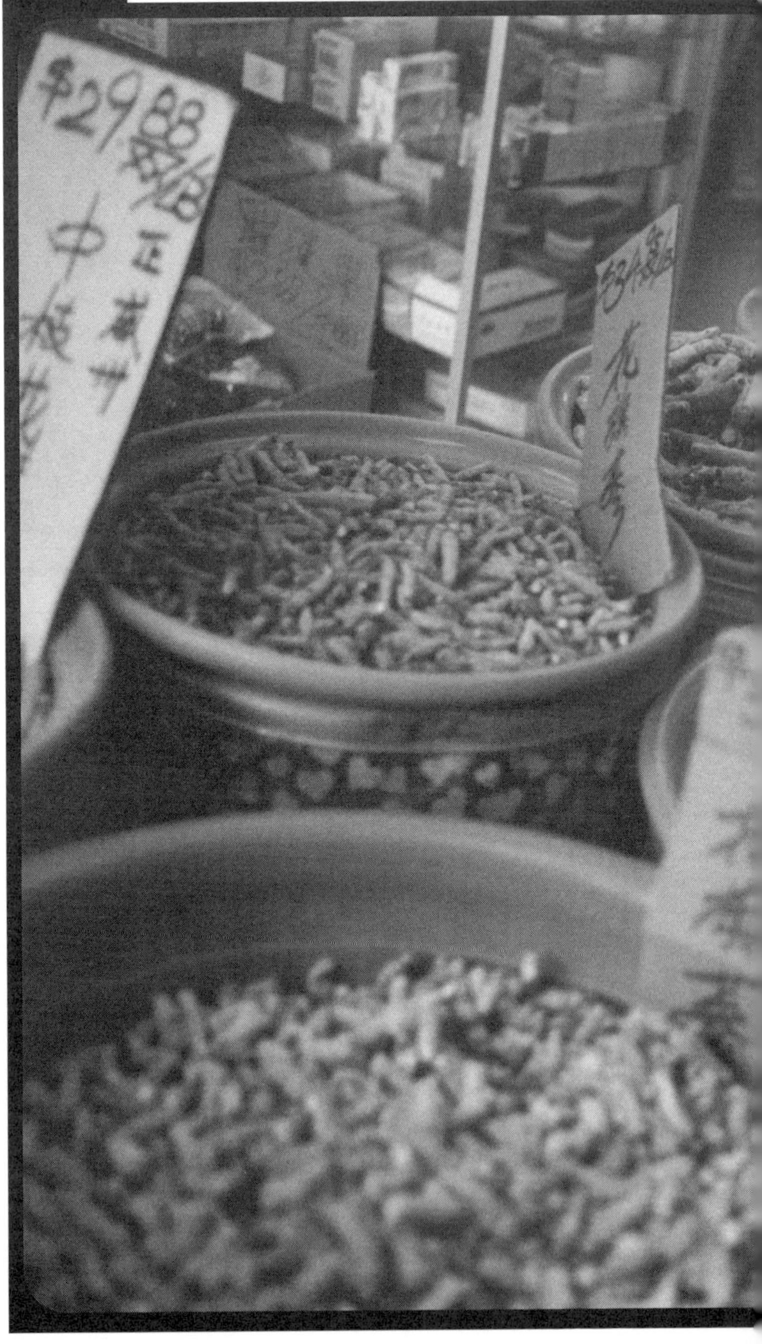

food & drink

Eating out at an Asian restaurant in New York City once meant ordering some version of "chop suey"—more often than not a plate of limp, pallid vegetables served over gummy white rice and topped off with crispy noodles from a freshly opened can. At the close of the '60s, the Big Apple's Chinese eateries, complemented by a smattering of American palate–friendly "Japanese" steakhouses and Indian curry houses, posed little threat to the French bistros, spaghetti joints, chophouses, delicatessens, and Automats that reigned over the city.

But in just 30 remarkable years, all that changed. The big shift started in the 1970s when Sichuan cuisine, with its fireworks of flavors, lured New Yorkers away from the Cantonese culinary tradition—an elegant, understated cuisine that had largely been diluted into tepid, Americanized comfort food. New Yorkers were dazzled by the fresh, explosive foods of southwestern China, fired by hot pepper sauces and chili oils. Unfortunately, that cuisine would also be done in by its own popularity—by the 1980s, there were simply too many

Overleaf: There seems to be no end to the variety of greens, gourds, tubers, herbs, and fruits that fill the racks and stalls of New York's Asian markets.

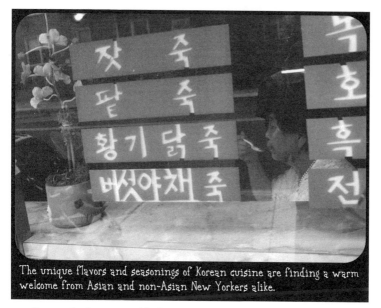

잣 죽

팥 죽

황기닭죽

버섯야채죽

녹

호

흑

전

The unique flavors and seasonings of Korean cuisine are finding a warm welcome from Asian and non-Asian New Yorkers alike.

mediocre Sichuan establishments, and the food's appeal began to wane.

Fortunately, new alternatives were already springing up all over the city. As immigration laws loosened in the '70s and '80s, Asian immigrants flooded New York, bringing with them their native foods and dishes. In every borough Asian restaurants thrived, offering food prepared at high levels of quality and innovation—and often served at shockingly reasonable prices. This explosion of Asian cuisines onto the New York food scene would, over the next two decades, change the way the city ate, cooked, and thought about food. Perhaps Manhattan's Chinatown benefited most: The malaise suffered by Cantonese restaurants in the '70s was reversed by an influx of creative Hong Kong chefs, and the neighborhood was further revitalized by the introduction of Thai, Vietnamese, Malaysian, and Fujianese restaurants.

Non-Asian New Yorkers found themselves entranced by the new flavors: Thai cuisine, with its deft blend of disparate ingredients, textures, colors, and aromatic herbs; Vietnamese food, with its fragrant melody of sweet and sour tastes; and Malaysian cuisine, with its delicate use of heat and fresh, colorful ingredients. At the same time, Korean "barbecues" sprang up between Fifth and Sixth avenues in the shadow of the Empire State Building, where customers cooked their own hearty dinners on tabletop grills. And inspired Indian, Pakistani, and Bangladeshi chefs opened innovative eateries all across the city, introducing New Yorkers to regional delicacies from places like Bengal, Sylhet, and the Punjab. Neighboorhoods specializing in a specific Asian cuisine sprouted up everywhere: a grouping of Filipino restaurants and bakeries now thrives around Roosevelt Ave. and 69th St. in Woodside, Queens.

These days, Asian food is no longer defined by that unhappy little bowl of chop suey. Serendipity, in the form of great Asian meals of every nationality, can be found in virtually any neighborhood. Getting a delicious meal of Tibetan spicy spareribs, refreshing Vietnamese summer rolls, or delicate Japanese noodles is simply a matter of turning a corner.

chinese fare:
hong kong to shanghai

In a city with no fewer than five Chinatowns, Chinese fare is New York's most varied. Every culinary region in China has its representatives in New York, from Chaozhou-style shrimp balls and Hangzhou soya duck to Hong Kong dim sum and Chengdu *mapo* tofu. New Yorkers follow their appetites to **New York Noodle Town,** in Manhattan's Chinatown, for roast duck in noodle soup, or to **Ping's** in Elmhurst, Queens, for Dungenness crabs.

The lines are long out in front of **Joe's Shanghai** on Manhattan Chinatown's narrow Pell Street. Inside, the hurried staff shuttle stacks of bamboo steamers to hungry diners. At the table, steamer lids are lifted to reveal steaming *xiao long bao,* or Shanghai soup dumplings, filled with pork and crab and a rich, fatty broth, served with a dip of dark vinegar and julienned ginger. A slice into one of the dumplings releases the intensely flavored "soup" inside. These are the dumplings that spurred the recent

dim sum and yum cha

Dim sum are the small snacks and appetizers that have been served in teahouses in southern China for centuries. **Yum cha** is "to drink tea." And to yum cha is, by tradition, to eat dim sum: little delicacies such as dumplings steamed or fried, shrimp-stuffed eggplant, sticky rice wrapped in bamboo leaves, sesame balls filled with lotus-seed paste, and bite-size custard tarts. These morsels can be enjoyed in a number of settings, from the grand restaurants that can seat as many as a thousand people (such as **Silver Palace,** the first of the ornate Hong Kong–style restaurants to open in Manhattan's Chinatown) to the more intimate environs of coffee shops (like **Hop Shing,** a good place for dim sum takeout).

Many Chinese restaurants serving dim sum do so seven days a week, starting as early as 7 a.m. and ending around 3 or 4 in the afternoon. The variety of dim sum (there are more than a hundred kinds) offered on weekends is usually much broader than that served on weekdays. Tea is one's first consideration: **bo nay,** a black tea; **lung jing,** a green tea; **guk fah,** chrysanthemum tea; or **moot lay,** jasmine tea. Those who don't state a preference often are served jasmine tea by default. Yum cha participants keep one another in tea and pour for each other as cups are emptied. To signify thanks when someone has poured for you, tap two fingers on the table next to your cup. If you've had enough tea, just leave your cup full. When the teapot needs to be refilled, an inverted lid signals the waiter.

As you settle in for tea, watch for the dim sum trolleys bearing stacks of covered steamers and dishes being pushed around by waiters who will call out in Cantonese the contents of their carts. They don't necessarily stop at every table, so flag them down if necessary to take a look at their offerings. You can point out what you would like, but you aren't at all obligated to order from a cart. Though some find it difficult to constantly monitor the carts while eating and socializing in larger restaurants, to ensure that you are getting the freshest dim sum, order from carts as they emerge from the kitchen, especially for such deep-fried delicacies as spring rolls and taro puffs.

proliferation of Shanghai restaurants, like **Shanghai Tang, New Green Bo, Goody's,** and **Shanghai Cuisine.**

Shanghai restaurants have been around for a long time (New York's first is said to have opened in 1949), and there has always been a cult of the soup dumpling, says restaurant consultant Ed

Schoenfeld, who has played a prominent role in opening many a Chinese restaurant in New York (most recently Our Place Shanghai Tea Garden). But that cult would see its membership explode when Joe Si and Peter Lam opened the first Joe's Shanghai in Flushing, Queens, in 1995. Capitalizing on the success of their soup dumplings, they have since opened Joe's Shanghai restaurants in three additional locations.

Meanwhile, restaurants such as **Grand Sichuan, Wu Liang Ye,** and **Golden Monkey** have revived diners' taste for spicy Sichuan specialties. Hong Kong–style palaces—**Jing Fong,** Silver Palace, Golden Unicorn—are venues for nine-course banquets or morning and weekend dim sum. The cooks at **Big Wong** carve barbecued *char siu* pork for customers crowded at the front counter and the tanks of fresh fish in the windows of **Oriental Garden** promise meals of soft-shell crabs, prawns, razor clams, and sea bass. Fujianese restaurants and markets have sprouted along East Broadway, in New York's Chinatown and east of Sara Delano Roosevelt Park off Grand Street.

Still, whether you're dining at a Sichuan, Cantonese, or Fujianese restaurant, don't be surprised by a little infusion of

The dim sum cart makes its rounds at Harmony Palace on Mott Street.

Behind the scenes at New York Noodle Town in Chinatown.

Shanghai—a sign hanging in the window that reads, "We have soup dumplings."

Kalbi on every corner

It's 2 a.m. in Sam Ship Iga, in midtown Manhattan's Koreatown, and late-night diners spoon into big bowls of *sul long tang*, a milky soup with rice and noodles and beef, flavored with long-simmered oxtails and served with coarse salt and lots of finely chopped scallions. The soup is a specialty at **Gam Mee Ok,** one of several Koreatown restaurants that stay open around the clock for late-shift workers or for the young crowds that frequent Koreatown's nightclubs. Two doors down at **Kum Gang San,** tabletop grills sizzle with *bulgogi* (marinated slices of steak) and *kalbi* (marinated short ribs). But as morning draws near and a night of revelry threatens to take its toll, orders mount for *haejang guk*, a moderately spicy soup with beef, bean sprouts, and cabbage that is said to be a hangover preventative.

Late at night or early in the afternoon, Koreatown is always

Korean side Dishes

One of the best things about sitting down to a meal in Koreatown is the panoply of side dishes, known as *banchan*, that automatically arrives at the table. A variety of small bowls and saucers cradle savory, briny, or sweet morsels, to be nibbled on leisurely throughout the meal—wild mountain vegetables such as *todok* (*lanceolata codonopsis*), dried anchovies, seasoned beef, or tofu. Such "side dishes" play a central role in traditional Korean meals: The lavishness of a Korean meal is measured by the number of *banchan*, and the expertise of a Korean cook is displayed in their seasoning and spiciness.

a source of satisfaction for cravings that range from *pajon* (scallion pancakes) and *nak-ji bokkum* (octopus stir-fried with vegetables and noodles) to *bibimbap* (rice, meat, vegetables, and egg served in a hot stone bowl and mixed with *kochujang* chili paste). **Cho Dang Gol** makes its own tofu and serves it in casseroles, in soups, or with noodles, while **Hangawi** offers elegant vegetarian fare. **Mandoo Bar** specializes in *mandoo*, dumplings filled with

Kalbi houses like this one in Koreatown, specialize in a variety of barbecue that grows rapidly on newcomers.

A glossary of *banchan*

muk: acorn-flour jelly served with soy sauce, scallions, and sesame oil

kosari namul: fiddlehead fern shoots, cooked with sesame oil, soy sauce, and chicken broth, and sprinkled with sesame seeds

shigim-chi muchim: spinach with soy sauce, sesame oil, garlic, and scallions

oi muchim: cucumber with salt, sesame, vinegar, and red pepper powder

sogogi jangjolim: shredded beef seasoned with soy sauce, sugar, and chilies

tubu choerim: tofu spiced with garlic, red chili powder, dried chili threads, and scallions

tubu gui: tofu stuffed with ground beef, garlic, ginger, and onion

doraji: seasoned root of Chinese bellflower

kimchi: pickled vegetables (*see more on kimchi below*)

The Kimchi story: For fresh, fresh kimchi, watch the red pepper powder fly at Korean grocery **Han Ah Reum** in Flushing, Queens, where kimchi is made in big bowls right there. A Korean staple for more than 1,600 years, kimchi comes in hundreds of varieties; almost anything can be preserved in kimchi fashion—watermelon, pine nuts, even abalone. Ingredients and seasonings vary from region to region in Korea; the spiciest kimchi is made in the Cholla and Kyongsang provinces of the south, where more salt and red pepper is used. A few blocks west of Han Ah Reum on Northern Boulevard is **Jahnchi Jahnchi,** a small store with rows of not only kimchi but also namul, lightly steamed or stir-fried vegetable salads. **Assi Plaza,** at the end of 39th Avenue, stocks the fresh salted shrimp and anchovies used to make kimchi.

meat and vegetables. And North Korean restaurant Okryukwan offers the specialties of Pyongyang, North Korea's capital—big dumplings and neng myun, cold buckwheat noodles in beef broth.

Beyond Koreatown, a growing number of restaurants have spurred a movement to better acquaint the uninitiated with Korean food. "Korean food is incredible, a very sophisticated cuisine, but underexposed to the average New York diner," says Brad Kelley, owner of the trendy Thai restaurant **Kin Khao** and Daily Chow, which features a pan-Asian menu that includes Korean cuisine in the former location of Bop (now closed), his highly praised all-Korean eatery.

That underexposure is on its way to being remedied as Korean restaurants have opened in New York's various neighborhoods with increasing frequency: Clay in Nolita, **Do Hwa** in the West Village, **Woo Lae Oak** in Soho, Jin Dal Lae on the Upper West Side. "I don't see why there isn't *kalbi* on every corner," says Ruth Reichl, former *New York Times* restaurant critic and now editor-in-chief of *Gourmet* magazine. "I think we're going to be seeing a lot more Korean food."

india meets pakistan

When cooking authority and longtime New Yorker Madhur Jaffrey published her first cookbook, *An Invitation to Indian Cooking*, in 1973 (she has since published more than a dozen), she lamented New York's lack of good Indian restaurants. "Instead of specializing in food from a particular state or district, [restaurants] serve a generalized Indian food from no specific area whatsoever," she wrote.

tandoor tip If you're looking for a quick, cheap snack of excellent samosa, marinated and grilled meats, or stewed vegetables over rice, keep an eye out for a covey of yellow cabs at modest storefronts—the Pakistani cab drivers know the best spots in town for terrific, inexpensive tandoori treats.

New York's Indian restaurants have since blossomed. Indian specialties from almost any region of the subcontinent are available to New Yorkers, who have responded enthusiastically to the vegetarian fare of Hyderabad, the seafood dishes of Kerala, and the vindaloo cooking of Goa. At **Chola,** the menu includes dishes that originated in Calcutta's Jewish quarter—*bamia koota* (lamb with okra), and chicken makmura prepared in a sauce with nuts and raisins. The Mangalorean fish curry at **Tikka** is the chef's own mother's recipe, flavored with coconut, tamarind, cumin, red and green chilies, curry leaves, and mustard. **Salaam Bombay**'s *ringna batata nu shaak* (eggplant and potatoes cooked in a sweet and sour sauce) is a Gujarati specialty.

"There was a cry for authentic Indian food, and New York's

In true NYC fashion, this unassuming spot in Tribeca—offering a full range of Pakistani specialties—is tucked between a Mexican restaurant and a deli.

Indian restaurants have much improved. It has happened very slowly, but we're seeing authentic Indian food, we're seeing regional Indian food, we're seeing Indian fusion for the first time," Ms. Jaffrey now says, and points to a vitality in the cuisines of Bangladesh, Sri Lanka, and Pakistan as immigration from those areas has increased.

In Queens, a handful of restaurants in Jackson Heights' "Little India" boast Pakistani specialties along with Indian and Bangladeshi (and even halal Chinese). But **Tabaq 74** serves "only 100 percent Pakistani food," says owner Ijaz Zaman. He serves katakat meats, such as chicken or beef brains, cooked in the tawa (a large, rounded cast-iron skillet) and named after the "katakat" sounds of cooking utensils against the metal pan. The chapli kabab khyberi, patties of ground beef (since Pakistan's population is largely Muslim, the cow isn't sacred) fried "frontier style" with onion, scallions, cilantro, and a dash of chilies, peppercorns, and whole coriander seeds, are probably the best "Pakistani burgers" in New York.

What distinguishes Pakistani cuisine from Indian? It's the spicing, according to Mr. Zaman, who is from Lahore in northeast Pakistan. "Just enough is used to bring out the flavor of the food. Beef should taste like beef. Chicken should taste like chicken. And lamb should taste like lamb."

of *katsu* and *kaiseki*

In a second-floor soba restaurant in the heart of Soho, trained experts turn buckwheat flour into skeins of fresh noodles. The cooks at **Honmura An** continue a Japanese tradition that dates back to the early 17th century, rolling out buckwheat dough and slicing it by hand to produce strands of perfect soba. The soba is served hot or cold with homemade broth, plain or topped with slices of duck or giant prawns flown in from Tokyo's Tsukiji fish market.

Whether soba, *tonkatsu*, yakitori, or sushi, Japanese menus often focus on one or two dishes that are prepared with a deeply honed expertise. In Japan, there are restaurants singly dedicated to such specialities as *unagi* (grilled eel), tempura, or *oden* (vegetables, eggs, fish cake, and other delicacies simmered in broth). In New York, the same custom of such focused attention is more loosely practiced but still characteristic of very good Japanese restaurants. *Shabu-shabu*, thinly sliced beef quickly immersed in boiling water in a pot at the table and then dipped in *ponzu* or *gomadare* sauce, is the particular province of restaurants like

When it comes to sushi, presentation is everything. Along with the freshest of fish you'll always find a beautiful presentation.

sushi talk   A sushi bar in every neighborhood attests to New Yorkers' love of sushi, but connoisseurs seek the freshest fish prepared with the highest standards.

Like specialty sushi restaurants in Japan, traditional **Kuruma Zushi** serves only sushi and no cooked foods. Toshihiro Uezu, a sushi chef for 38 years, opened Kuruma Zushi in 1972, attracted to New York by its "challenging spirit." Adept at making perfectly molded sushi, Mr. Uezu is also a charming host. He describes the elements of excellent sushi: "The size of the rice and size of the fish should be matched perfectly. The size of sushi should not be too big or too small. Also, sushi should look nice, and it should not be too soft or too hard. Needless to say, fish should be fresh and only the best part of the fish should be used."

Nigiri zushi, the hand-formed sushi that originated in Tokyo in the early 19th century, is a deceptively simple delicacy—vinegared rice topped with slices of raw fish and shellfish. But to perfectly mold the tiny ingots of rice is no easy task. In his cookbook *Japanese Cooking: A Simple Art*, Shizuo Tsuji reveals the difficulty: "They say when done properly, all the rice grains face the same way."

"The rice must be cooked properly, with the right amount of water during cooking," says Takako Yoneyama. She stands behind the counter of her tiny West Village sushi bar, **Taka**. Behind her are the shelves that hold teacups inscribed with the names of her regular customers, teacups that she herself has made. "I have a picture in my mind of what the sushi should look like."

Her comments on etiquette: "I want my customers to be comfortable, but with regulars I will mention that too much soy sauce in the dish is not a good idea. Use just a little bit at a time. For eel [which already is cooked with sauce], soy sauce isn't necessary." Nigiri zushi can be picked up with the fingers, the fish side dipped into the soy sauce, and eaten in one or two bites. Ms. Yoneyama does notice and is impressed by customers who eat neatly.

Shabu-Tatsu and **Lan**. At **Katsuhama,** the focus is on *katsu*, breaded, deep-fried cutlets of pork or chicken. The *aka-chochin* red paper lantern in front of Yakitori Taisho advertises its yakitori, skewers of flavorful grilled meat and vegetables. Otafuku (named after the puffy, happy-faced Japanese masks that adorn the timbers framing the restaurant's doorway) serves only *takoyaki*, tasty griddled balls of batter with chopped octopus, and *okonomiyaki*, "your choice" pancake filled with whatever you like—beef, pork, shrimp, or squid, with cabbage, scallions, and egg.

Although the distinctions between Tokyo cuisine (Tokyo ryori) and Kyoto cuisine (Kyoto ryori) are largely unproclaimed in New York, restaurants such as **Sugiyama** and **Nadaman Hakubai** produce elaborate, formal kaiseki meals, a refined Kyoto tradition intended to appeal to all the senses. Kaiseki meals are served in several courses on lacquerware and ceramics chosen to suit each dish. The chef orchestrates the meal, using only the freshest ingredients and only what is in season. Each succeeding taste serves as a counterpoint to the last: sweet followed by sour, a simmered course followed by a fried course, one surprise after the next. Only the merest seasonings are used, in the Kyoto manner. One of kaiseki chef Nao Sugiyama's meals might include apricot suspended in aspic, sashimi tinged with gold leaf, scallops grilled on a hot stone right at the table. "Umami ga arimasu"— meaning, roughly: "Here is the height of tastiness."

southeast asia on baxter street

Baxter Street isn't an especially long stretch of road. It runs a few blocks north-south from Grand Street to Park Row on the edge of Manhattan's Chinatown. On the west side of Baxter between Walker and Leonard streets looms the Criminal Courts Building, a foreboding Art Moderne structure built in 1939 that houses the Manhattan Detention Center, also known as "The Tombs," where alleged criminals await arraignment. Frequent Baxter Street often enough, and you're bound to witness an occasional "perp walk."

It seems an unlikely spot to have fostered a microcosm of Southeast Asia. But right in the shadow of The Tombs, brightly lit signs and colorful awnings welcome those seeking big bowls of pho noodle soups, grilled pork chops, and spring rolls on rice vermicelli at one of the three Vietnamese restaurants tucked between a tiny parking lot and American Liberty Bail Bonds. **Thai So'n, Nha Trang,** and **New Pasteur** were among a wave of

Vietnamese restaurants that first sprouted in Chinatown in the early '80s (the first was **Viet Huong,** which opened a block over, on Mulberry Street, in 1981).

More recently, Malaysian restaurants have made their presence known in Chinatown: **Penang** on Elizabeth Street, **Nyonya** on Grand, **Baba** on Bayard. In the arcade between Bowery and Elizabeth streets, the takeout window at New Malaysia Restaurant is a nice place to stop in the summertime for shaved ice flavored with pineapple or coconut or red beans. Jaya Malaysian restaurant is Baxter Street's most recent addition; owner Hann Low opened Jaya in 1998 next to Marco Polo Noodle Shop Inc. The Malaysian menu is an amalgam of Malay, Chinese, and Indian cuisines. Roti canai pancakes served with chicken curry, Indian mee goreng noodles, and Hainanese chicken are crowd pleasers.

At the corner of Baxter and Bayard is **Pongsri Thailand Restaurant.** Manager Jerry Tang (Tang is his abbreviated version of a 15-letter Thai name) says his brother Jimmy Tang and Jimmy's wife, Pongsri, opened the restaurant in 1974, when there were no other restaurants along Baxter Street. The Tangs serve central-Thailand dishes—tom ka gai, coconut soup with chicken; and grapow moo, pork with basil and chilies—first cooked by Pongsri in what used to be a coffee shop and a bar. The bar's wagon-wheel light fixtures still hang in what otherwise looks like a traditional wood-paneled Thai house. "A lot of cops, judges, attorneys come in," Mr. Tang says, referring to his courthouse clientele. "But we don't get many prisoners."

East Meets West Meets NYC

Sautéed foie gras with ginger and mango at Vong. Halibut with a coating of crisped rice in a lime and watermelon curry at Tabla. Kabocha cheesecake with a coconut and almond-flour crust at Sono. Some of New York's top chefs have long incorporated the flavors and cooking techniques of diverse cuisines into their repertoires, but the past decade has seen Asian cuisines come to the fore as chefs conceive increasingly venturesome offerings.

French chef Jean-Georges Vongerichten, who once worked at the Oriental Hotel in Bangkok, opened **Vong** in 1992, blending French and Thai tastes. Nobuyuki Matsuhisa caused a stir with the 1994 opening of **Nobu,** where the much-heralded Japanese cuisine is interspersed with Peruvian touches.

"I wrack my brain working on new dishes," says Linda Rodriguez, executive chef of the restaurant **Bond Street,** which opened its doors in 1998. She created a Japanese menu inflected with "a little Thai, a little Malaysian, a little Filipino." Her ponzu sauce, a Japanese soy-citrus sauce, might include the bay leaves and peppercorns more typical of a Philippine adobo. "I try to experiment a lot, without undermining what's essentially Japanese . . . You have to know what marries."

Squab with kaffir lime leaf paste. Filet mignon with red miso. Such are the marriages rendered by chef Tadashi Ono, who had worked at the French restaurant and New York institution La Caravelle for several years and who opened **Sono** in 1999, combining French techniques with a Japanese appreciation for the properties of individual ingredients. He folds tofu and soybeans into crab cakes and seasons them with ginger and soy sauce. He poaches lobster with a bouillon of lobster stock and chrysanthemum leaves and petals. "In the Japanese way, contrasting flavors make you recognize what lobster really tastes like," he explains. "And the sharp flavor of the leaves kicks through the taste of the lobster."

When restaurateur Danny Meyer opened **Tabla** in 1998, he tapped Floyd Cardoz of Lespinasse as executive chef. At Lespinasse, Mr. Cardoz had received the tutelage of chef Gray Kunz, renowned for his complex Asian-influenced innovations. Mr. Cardoz refers to his own cooking as "American food, Indian spices." To a city of gastronomes, the menu at Tabla offers dishes like lobster soup with pink lentils, Magret (duck) and potato samosa, and eggplant-stuffed Vidalia onion with a cumin-and-black-pepper curry. "New Yorkers are adventurous, and they are tough critics," Mr. Cardoz says. "But if you are good at what you do, then you want tough critics."

sweets and teas

Served with butter (traditionally yak butter) in Tibetan restaurants, mixed into rich ice cream at Japanese eateries, poured ad infinitum at Chinese dim sum palaces, tea—and tea culture—has its roots in Asia. But as its health benefits, particularly those of green tea, have captured much interest, U.S. tea consumption has nearly doubled during the past decade. A wide variety of teas is available at several New York tea shops and restaurants, from India's Darjeeling, oft prepared with cardamom and cloves, to China's Lapsang Souchong. Taiwanese Bao Jong oolong, served by a tea sommelier at Heartbeat restaurant in Manhattan, commands more than $10 a pot. At the **Urasenke Chanoyu Center** on the Upper East Side, Japanese tea ceremony demonstrations and lessons are offered. (Note: If you like your beverages a little stronger, see the sake sidebar in Diversions.)

If you love tea, you can now share your passion with friends at one of New York's newly chic tea bars. In the elegant **T Salon Emporium,** located on 20th Street between Fifth Avenue and Broadway, you'll find Oriental teas served with light snacks.

sweets & confections

Chinese: discover a treasure trove of fat, soft, sweet buns filled with buttercream and topped with flaked coconut, or golden brown buns filled with sweet roast pork. Of note, **Yi Mei Fung Bakery** makes its own moon cakes during the Moon Festival. Cecelia Tam makes delicious, tiny egg cakes (12 for $1) at **Hong Kong Cake Co.,** her stand at the corner of Mott and Mosco streets.

Korean: Korean baked goods feature breads with chestnut or red bean fillings, yellow sweet potato cakes, and airy sponge cakes.

Japanese: *Wagashi* are Japanese sweets such as bean-paste-filled buns, lightly baked cakes, and sugar wafers delicately shaped into flowers and tree leaves.

Indian: Enticing Indian confections include *Rasgullah* cream cheese balls, *jallebi* fritter swirls, *galub jamun* sweet dumplings, and *burfi* pistachio sweetmeats.

Come here to sip oolong tea in the late afternoon, or to attend one of the lectures on tea in a wonderfully relaxed atmosphere (the attractive salon offers book and poetry readings as well). You can also join the tea-of-the-month club.

Both Manhattan and Brooklyn now boast branches of the **Saint's Alp Teahouse,** a chain of more than 40 stores that has recently arrived from Taiwan. Here you'll find tea drinks whipped together with fruit or tapioca, and such concoctions as green barley with plum juice, mung bean shakes, and litchi tea with *nata de coco.* "[The drinks] taste good and are good for you," says the youthful staff at the Sunset Park, Brooklyn, branch. "Anything with green barley juice is especially good if you've been up all night." Teas are served with dainty fish, eel, rice, and noodle dishes. Their three brightly lit cafes now in the metropolitan area are invariably filled with young Chinese Americans, European tourists, and couples. In fact, these spots have become popular dating destinations. They're not quite as intimate as European-style tea shops—you can remain noncommittal and simply order lunch, if you wish—and the atmosphere is relaxed, young, and on the go.

Toward the end of Prince Street in Flushing, Queens, right before the street meets 40th Road, there is **Q Sweet House,** a teahouse in the Taiwanese style offering *bo ba nai cha,* or milk tea with dark tapioca pearls, aka bubble tea. Fresh fruit juices such as honeydew or kumquat-lemon are blended with crushed ice and sago—tiny, chewy globes of what looks like rice but is actually a tapioca of sago starch. (The starch is extracted from sago palm trees and pressed through sieves to form drops that are then allowed to fall onto hot, shaking plates and rolled into round grains. The dark tapioca pearls served in milk teas are made from the starch of sweet potatoes and cassava tubers, and brown sugar.)

Confections such as *yokan* (an azuki-bean paste) and *higashi* rice-flour cakes are served with the powdered green tea known as *matcha* at **Toraya** teahouse. Indian confectionery, such as the sweetmeats once prepared for Mogul kings in 16th-century India, fill the shelves at bakeries such as **Delhi Palace Sweets** in Queens. Samosa dumplings, also often available at Indian bakeries, are the perfect snack for a cup of *chai*. Duck into one of Chinatown's many bakeshops for soft, sweet coconut buns, fruit-filled cakes, and well, if not tea, then an iced coffee or lemon coke.

TO Market

The bazaar that is Manhattan's Chinatown proffers live birds, quail eggs, fresh tofu, dried beef snacks, delicacies such as bird's nests and shark fins, and staples like oyster sauce and Kadoya sesame oil. Chinatown's meat markets sell *lapchang* sausages and the Smithfield hams used in recipes as a substitute for Yunnan hams, as well as fresh white "Peking" ducks from Long Island. Fresh fish—whole prawns, salmon filets, lobsters—practically spills onto the sidewalks from Chinatown's numerous fish stands.

Lotus root, water chestnuts, winter melons, tamarind pods, pale green and bumpy bitter melons, pomelos that look like swollen grapefruits—there seems no end to the variety of greens, gourds, tubers, herbs, and fruits that fill the racks and stalls of New York's Asian markets.

Much of the Asian produce in New York's markets and restau-

A typical Flushing, Queens, market offers an astounding variety of produce—from the exotic to the mundane.

Well-known even beyond Chinatown, Kam Man is a market to explore for everything from tea and herbs to produce, meats, cookware, and even kitchen utensils.

rants is grown on farms on Long Island and in New Jersey. Long Island farmers Fred and Karen Lee grow Asian vegetables on Sang Lee Farm, started by Mr. Lee's father and uncles in 1947—vegetables including bok choi, *nyu choi sum* (flowering cabbage with small yellow flowers), *guy lon* (Chinese broccoli), *guy choi* (Chinese mustard greens), and Korean *moo* (white radish). Davie C.Y. Yen, of Hydro Garden Farm in Yaphank, New York, offers his own kimchi at his stand at the **Union Square Greenmarket,** along with baby bok choi, wasabi greens, soy beans, and edible Asian lilies. He says "Ten years ago, no one was eating *tai choi*" (a small, dark leafy green similar to mustard greens with a sharp taste), so he didn't sell it. His new estimate: "Now Americans across the country eat 5,000 pounds of *tai choi* a day . . . maybe more!"

food & drink

THE LISTINGS

Markets

Chinese

(*see also* **Health & Fitness listings**)

Bayard Meat Market. (57 Bayard St., NY; 212 619-6206; A, C, E, N, R, J, M, Z, 6 train to Canal St.)

Chinese American Trading Co. (91 Mulberry St., NY; 212 267-5224; A, C, E, N, R, J, M, Z, 6 train to Canal St.)

Chung Chou City. (39 Mott St., NY; 212 285-2288; A, C, E, N, R, J, M, Z, 6 train to Canal St.; 218 Grand St., NY; 212 274-9338; B, D, Q train to Grand St.)

Fong Inn Too. (46 Mott St., NY; 212 962-5196; A, C, E, N, R, J, M, Z, 6 train to Canal St.)

Golden Harvest Trading, Inc. (5315 Eighth Ave., Brooklyn; 718 633-0985; N train to Eighth Ave.)

Hong Kong Supermarket. (109 East Broadway, NY; 212 227-3388; F train to East Broadway; 6023 Eighth Ave., Brooklyn; 718 438-2288; N train to Eighth Ave.)

Kam Kuo. (7 Mott St., NY; 212 349-3097; A, C, E, N, R, J, M, Z, 6 train to Canal St.)

Kam Man. (200 Canal St., NY; 212 571-0330; A, C, E, N, R, J, M, Z, 6 train to Canal St.)

Siu Cheong Meat Market. Chinese butcher shop, with such unusual health foods as sliced eels, frozen pigs' ears, and black chickens (89 Mulberry St., NY; 212 267-0350; A, C, E, N, R, J, M, Z, 6 train to Canal St.).

Filipino

New Manila Food Mart. (351 E. 14th St., NY; 212 420-8182; L train to First Ave.)

Bulk rice imported from Thailand—a staple readily found in supermarkets in many Queens neighborhoods.

Indian and Middle Eastern

Foods of India. (121 Lexington Ave., NY; 212 683-4419; 6 train to 28th St.)

Kalustyan's. (123 Lexington Ave., NY; 212 685-3451; 6 train to 28th St.)

Little India. (128 E. 28th St., NY; 212 683-1691; 6 train to 28th St.)

Oriental Pastry & Grocery. (170-172 Atlantic Ave., Brooklyn; 718 875-7687; 2, 3, 4, 5 train to Borough Hall)

Patel Brothers Market. (37-27 74th St., Jackson Heights, Queens; E , F, G, R train to Roosevelt Ave.; 718 898-3445; 42-79 Main St., Flushing, Queens; 718 321-9847; 7 train to Main St./Flushing)

Sahadi. (187 Atlantic Ave., Brooklyn; 718 624-4550; 2, 3, 4, 5 train to Borough Hall)

Japanese

Fuji Grocery Store. (227 Sullivan St., NY; 212 674-5242; A, C, E, B, D, F, Q train to West 4th St.)

Katagiri. (224 E. 59th St., NY; 212 755-3566; 4, 5, 6, N, R train to 59th St./Lexington Ave.)

Mitsuwa (formerly **Yaohan**). (595 River Rd., Edgewater, NJ; 201 941-9113; shuttle from Port Authority; call for schedule.)

Sam Bok Groceries. (*see* Korean, below)

Sunrise Mart. (4 Stuyvesant St., 2nd floor, NY; 212 598-3040; 6 train to Astor Pl.)

Korean

Assi Plaza. (131-01 39th Ave., Flushing, Queens; no phone; 7 train to Main St./Flushing)

Han Ah Reum. (23 W. 32nd St., NY; 212 695-3283; B, D, F, Q, N, R train to 34th St.; 141-40 Northern Blvd., Flushing, Queens; 718 358-0700; 7 train to Main St./Flushing; 25 Lafayette Ave., Englewood, NJ; 201 568-7799; 260 Bergen Turnpike, Little Ferry, NJ; 201 871-8822).

Jahnchi Jahnchi. (138-28 Northern Blvd., Flushing, Queens; 718 461-3030; 7 train to Main St./Flushing)

Sam Bok Groceries. (127 W. 43rd St., NY; 212 582-4730; N, R, 1, 2, 3, 7, 9 train to 42nd St.)

Union Square Greenmarket. (Union Square, Broadway between 14th & 17th sts., NY; 4, 5, 6, N, R, L train to Union Sq.)

Thai and Vietnamese

Bangkok Center Market. (104 Mosco St., NY; 212 349-1979; A, C, E, N, R, J, M, Z, 6 train to Canal St.)

Tan Ai Hoa Supermarket. (81½ Bowery, NY; 212 219-0893; A, C, E, N, R, J, M, Z, 6 train to Canal St.)

Thai and Indonesia Grocery. (81 Bayard St., NY; no phone; A, C, E, N, R, J, M, Z, 6 train to Canal St.)

Bakeries, Sweets, and Confections

Chinese

Chiu Hong Bakery. (161 Mott St., NY; 212 966-7664; A, C, E, N, R, J, M, Z, 6 train to Canal St.)

Fay Da Bakery Corp. (83 Mott St.,NY; 212 791-3884; A, C, E, N, R, J, M, Z, 6 train to Canal St.; 41-60 Main St., Flushing; 718 886-4568; 7 train to Main St./Flushing)

Hong Kong Cake Co. (at the corner of Mott and Mosco sts., NY; A, C, E, N, R, J, M, Z, 6 train to Canal St.)

Maria's Bakery. (148 Lafayette St., NY; 212 219-8369; 125 Walker St., NY; 212 219-2012; 42 Mott St., NY; 212 732-3888; A, C, E, N, R, J, M, Z, 6 train to Canal St.)

Q Sweet House. (40-11 Prince St., Queens; 718 445-7737; 7 train to Main St./Flushing)

Sweet-n-Tart Cafe. (76 Mott St.; 212 334-8088; 20 Mott St., NY; 212 964-0380; A, C, E, N, R, J, M, Z, 6 train to Canal Street; 136-11 38th

Ave., Flushing, Queens; 718 661-3380; 7 train to Main St./Flushing)
Tai Pan Bakery. (194 Canal St., NY; 212 732-2222; A, C, E, N, R, J, M,
Z, 6 train to Canal St.; 135-20 Roosevelt Ave., Flushing, Queens; 718
461-8668; 7 to Main St./Flushing)
XO Kitchen. (148 Hester St., NY; 212 965-8652; B, D, Q train to
Grand St.)
Yi Mei Fung Bakery. (135-38 Roosevelt Ave., Flushing, Queens; 718
886-6820; 7 train to Main St./Flushing)

Indian
Aladdin Sweets & Restaurant. (37-14 73rd St., Jackson Heights, Queens;
718 424-6900; 7 train to 74th St., E, F, G, R train to Roosevelt Ave.)
Bombay Paan House Kulfi & Juice Center. (72-29 37th Ave., Jackson
Heights, Queens; 718 424-5700; 7 to 74th St.-Broadway, E, F, G, R
train to Roosevelt Ave.)
Delhi Palace Sweets. (37-07 74th St., Jackson Heights, Queens; 718
507-0666; 7 train to 74th St.-Broadway, E, F, G, R to Roosevelt Ave.)
Rajbhog Sweets. (72-27 37th Ave., Jackson Heights, Queens; 718 458-
8512; 7 to 74th St.-Broadway, E, F, G, R train to Roosevelt Ave.)
Shaheen Sweets. (130 E. 29th St., NY; 212 251-0202; 6 train to
28th St.)
Spice Corner. (135 Lexington Ave., NY; 212 689-5182; 6 train to
28th St.)

Japanese
Minamoto Kitchoan. (608 Fifth Ave., NY; 212 489-3747; E, F train to
Fifth Ave.)

Korean
Canaan Bakery. (40-30 Union St., Flushing, Queens; 718 359-6124;
7 train to Main St./Flushing)
Koryodang. (39-02 Union St., Flushing, Queens; 718 762-6557; 7
train to Main St./Flushing)
Pari Pari Ko. (43 W. 32nd St., NY; 212 967-1929; B, D, F, Q, N, R train
to 34th St./Herald Sq.)

Cafes
Chai Salon. Teas and samosas (475 Park Ave., NY; 212 838-1717; 4, 5,
6, N, R train to 59th St./Lexington Ave.).

Pan Ya. Green tea tiramisu, red bean–filled donuts, croquettes, and *yakisoba* sandwiches (10 Stuyvesant St., NY; 212 777-1930; 6 train to Astor Pl.).

Sake
(see sidebar in Diversions)

Teas and Teahouses

Felissimo Tea House. On the top floor of the Felissimo shop in a midtown townhouse, afternoon tea is served from black earthenware pots in a tranquil setting. Sandwiches, scones, and chocolates are accompaniments to tea here, as are the haiku poems (10 W. 56th St., NY; 212 247-5656; E, F train to Fifth Ave.).

Kamwo Herb & Tea Co. Find here a selection of hundreds of Chinese herbs, as well as liniments and texts on acupuncture. The variety of teas includes several varieties of jasmine teas, white teas, oolong teas, and such green teas as gunpowder green tea, snow sprout green tea and dragonwell (209-11 Grand St., NY; 212 966-6370; www.kamwo.com; B, D, Q train to Grand St.).

Saint's Alp Teahouse. (51 Mott St., NY; 212 766-9889; A, C, E, N, R, J, M, Z, 6 train to Canal St.; 5801 Eighth Ave., Brooklyn; 718 437-6622; N train to Eighth Ave.).

Takashimaya. The Tea Box, in the elegant Japanese department store, has a wide selection of quality teas (693 Fifth Ave., NY; 212 350-0100; E, F train to Fifth Ave.).

The T Salon Emporium. Oriental teas with light snacks, plus book and poetry readings (11 E. 20th St., NY; 212 358-0506; www.tsalon.com; 6 train to 23rd St.).

Ten Ren's Tea and Ginseng Co. This chain also has a wide selection of quality teas (135-18 Roosevelt Ave., Flushing, Queens; 718 461-9305; 7 train to Main St./Flushing).

Toraya. Macha green tea served in a serene setting (17 E. 71st St., NY; 212 861-1490; 6 train to 68th St.).

Urasenke Chanoyu Center/Urasenke Tea Ceremony Society. The center offers courses in "the way of tea." Monthly open houses afford the opportunity to participate in traditional Japanese tea ceremonies (153 E. 69th St., NY; 212 988-6161; 6 train to 68th St.).

Dim Sum
In Manhattan (A, C, E, N, R, J, M, Z, 6 train to Canal St.):
98 Mott Restaurant (94-98 Mott St.; 212 226-6603)
Golden Unicorn (18 East Broadway; 212 941-0911)
HSF (Hee Seung Fung) Restaurant (46 Bowery; 212 374-1319)
Harmony Palace (94 Mott St.; 212 226-6603)
Hop Shing Restaurant (9 Chatham Square; 212 267-0220)
Jing Fong (18 Elizabeth St.; 212 964-5256)
Lan Hong Kok Dim Sum House (31 Division St.; 212 431-9063)
Mandarin Court (61 Mott St.; 212 608-3838)
Nice Restaurant (35 East Broadway; 212 406-9510)
Nom Wah (15 Doyers St.; 212 962-6047)
New Silver Palace (52 Bowery; 212 964-1204/1205)
Triple Eight Palace (88 East Broadway; 212 941-8886)

---

dim sum sampler

har gow: dumplings of whole shrimp wrapped with thin, translucent dough; the litmus test of good dim sum

yerng kaehr: eggplant stuffed with chopped shrimp and covered with brown sauce

siu mai: pork and shrimp dumplings, steamed and shaped like tiny cups

gow choi bao: steamed or pan-fried chive dumplings

har to si: shrimp and pork fat on toast, and deep-fried

juk: congee rice porridge, often with pork, turnip, and ginger

lor bak go: pan-fried turnip squares with bits of pork and small shrimps

char siu bao: fluffy buns stuffed with sweet roast pork

jing pai gwut: spare ribs with black bean sauce

wu gok: deep-fried balls of mashed taro root

cheung fun: rice noodles filled with ground beef or other meats and vegetables

chow heen: clams in oyster sauce and black beans

nor mye gai: packages of sticky rice with chicken or sausage in lotus leaf

ji ma kow: deep-fried balls of rice dough filled with lotus-seed paste

dahn tot: egg custard tarts; always tasty but so delicious when warm.

In Flushing, Queens (7 train to Main St./Flushing):
East Lake (42-33 Main St.; 718 539-8532)
Gum Tong Gung (133-30 39th Ave.; 718 939-6018)
Jade Palace (136-14 38th Ave.; 718 353-3366)
KB Garden (136-28 39th Ave.; 718 961-9088)

In Sunset Park, Brooklyn (N train to Eighth Ave.):
Jade Plaza (6022 Eighth Ave.; 718 492-6888)
Ocean Palace (5423 Eighth Ave.; 718 871-8080; 1418 Ave. U; 718 376-3838)

Asian Restaurants by Cuisine

Afghan and Persian

Afghan Kebab House. The variety of inexpensive kebabs doesn't disappoint: spicy fish kebab, beef *tikka* kebab, ground lamb *kofta* kebab. The vegetable dishes include *palau* (rice) pumpkin with tomatoes, onions, and peppers (74-16 37th Ave. Jackson Heights, Queens; 718 565-0471; E, F, G, R train to Roosevelt Ave., 7 train to 74th St.-Broadway; 764 Ninth Ave., NY; 212 307-1612; C, E train to 50th St.; 155 W. 46th St., NY; 212 768-3875; B, D, F, Q train to 47–50th sts./Rockefeller Ctr.).

Balkh Shish Kebab House. Kebabs are the specialty, but the *aushak* dumplings filled with scallions and served with yogurt sauce and *manti* dumplings filled with beef steal the show (23-10 31st St., Astoria, Queens; 718 721-5020; 7 train to 33rd St.).

Colbeh. An extensive Persian menu includes delicious whitefish kebabs; season them with lemon and sumac. The *olivieh* salad combines chicken, potatoes, and egg with pickles and peas. For dessert, try Persian baklava (43 W. 39th St., NY; 212 354-8181; B, D, F, Q train to 42nd St.).

Kabul Cafe. This friendly West Side Afghan restaurant serves crispy *bulanee* turnovers filled with spiced potatoes. The kebabs, such as cornish hen and filet mignon, are both flavorful and tender. Good, moderately priced food offsets a homely interior (265 W. 54th St., NY; 212 757-2037; C, E train to 50th St.).

Khyber Pass. An East Village cafe offering *manti* dumplings and *kabuli palau* (lamb and basmati rice studded with carrots, almonds, and raisins), in addition to the selection of kebabs (34 St. Marks Pl., NY; 212 473-0989; 6 train to Astor Pl.).

Nader. Kebabs are served with grilled plum tomato, saffron rice, and parsleyed onions, along with a side of cool and creamy yogurt sauce. Persian stews, such as *gheimen*, with chunks of beef, yellow split peas, and baby eggplant, are savory and hearty (48 E. 29th St., NY; 212 683-4833; N, R, 6 train to 28th St.).

Pamir. The tasty fried turnovers at this Upper East Side Afghan restaurant are stuffed with spiced pumpkin and onions and served with yogurt dipping sauce. The kebab combo is tempting, but pay attention to fish specials (1437 Second Ave., NY; 212 734-3791; 6 train to 77th St.; 1065 First Ave.; 212 644-9258; 4, 5, 6, N, R train to 59th St./Lexington Ave.).

Persepolis. The salmon kebabs at this Persian restaurant are perfectly complemented by a dish of yogurt mixed with cucumber and mint. The hummus and tabouleh are familiar favorites, and the *sherazi*—tomato, cucumber, and onion salad—is refreshing (1423 Second Ave., NY; 212 535-1100; 6 train to 77th St.).

Ravagh. A pleasant Persian restaurant in the carpet district. *Mira ghazemi* combines eggplant with tomatoes and garlic. The best of the kebabs: *kobideh* kebabs of ground lamb and beef (11 E. 30th St., NY; 212 696-0300; 6 train to 28th St.).

Burmese

Village Mingala. An East Village spot for *mohinga*—rice noodles in fish broth with coriander, lemon grass, and minced fish. *Keema* pancakes are layered with curried beef and potatoes (21-23 E. 7th St., NY; 212 529-3656; 6 train to Astor Pl.; **Mingala Burmese.** (1393B Second Ave.; 212 744-8008; 6 train to 68th St.).

Cambodian

Cambodian Cuisine. May be the only Cambodian restaurant in New York. The flavors of lemon grass, kaffir lime, and *galangal* (a variety of ginger) are among the cuisine's characteristics. Offerings include soup with shrimp and pineapple, noodles with vegetables and egg, and spicy beef stew (87 S. Elliot Pl., Brooklyn; 718 858-3262; A, C train to Lafayette Ave., G to Fulton St.).

Chinese

Big Wong. The meat counter at the front forms the hub of this bustling hole-in-the-wall on Mott Street. Cheap rice and noodle dishes topped with duck or *char siu* pork and comforting congee rice porridge attract lunch time crowds (67 Mott St., NY; 212 964-0540; A, C, E, N, R, J, M, Z, 6 train to Canal St.).

Canton. A venerable Chinatown restaurant, though relatively expensive, serving flavorful Cantonese fare; squab with vegetables in a carapace of

---

A CHEF'S FAVORITES   Alex Lee, chef de cuisine at Daniel Boulud's restaurant Daniel, recommends a few of his favorite Asian restaurants:

Shun Lee Palace.
"Sometimes I'll order off the menu, but if I want something special, I'll give Michael Tong [the owner] a call and talk to the chefs. I once had an amazing saute of scallops and pigeon and squab. But they also do classic preparations—steamed black sea bass or flounder with black bean sauce, something like my grandmother would make."

Oriental Garden.
"I like the variety of seafood there; they offer a lot of seafood. I recommend the drunken prawns. They're really delicious. The seafood never disappoints."

Honmura An.
"I almost always order a tasting menu. It gives a nice variety of dishes, and it's not what you typically find at a Japanese restaurant. I like the aesthetic appeal, the way the food is presented. And I like the fact that the cuisine is based on *soba*. The staff is informative; if you've never experienced that kind of food before, they're very good at explaining what it is you're eating."

---

lettuce, for example, is a standout. Just as good: the deep-fried pork chops or the glazed and seared whitefish (45 Division St., NY; 212 226-4441; A, C, E, N, R, J, M, Z, 6 train to Canal Street, F train to East Broadway).

Chao Zhou Restaurant. A bright, inexpensive Flushing spot that serves such Chaozhou specialties as "country style soy sauce duck," stir-fried fish with noodles, and deep-fried crab balls. Also: sliced pork with mustard greens and pan-fried sliced conch (40-52 Main St., Flushing, Queens; 718 353-7683; 7 train to Main St.).

David's Taiwanese Gourmet. David's Taiwanese specialties include fermented pork, crispy fried scallops and clams with basil, and a chicken and ginseng soup. The food may be gourmet, but the prices aren't (84-02 Broadway, Elmhurst, Queens; 718 429-4818; G, R train to Elmhurst Ave.).

Dynasty Taste of China. The cheap, delicious Sichuan dishes here are labeled hot & spicy, extra hot & spicy, or very hot & spicy. If you like it really hot, try the cold appetizer beef orange, with thin slices of beef, stomach and capsicum chilies (seeds included) topped with fresh coriander (2836 Broadway, NY; 212 665-6455; 1, 9 train to 110th St.).

Evergreen Shanghai. Start by identifying the Eastern Chinese dishes from an almost overwhelming menu and order from there: crispy whole yellow fish, fresh bean curd with crab, Soochow duck, stir-fried eel, sauteed crab with egg (63 Mott St., NY; 212 571-3339; A, C, E, N, R, J, M, Z, 6 train to Canal St.).

Golden Monkey. The Sichuan dishes are the attraction here: shredded beef with hot peppers, twice-cooked pork, sliced beef with leeks in a peppercorn sauce, sliced tea-smoked duck served with pancakes (133-47 Roosevelt Ave., Flushing, Queens; 718 762-2664; 7 train to Main St.).

Goody's. The first dish on the menu is dried scallop, shrimp, and pork *xiao long bao*, or soup dumplings. It's tempting to fill up on soup dumplings alone, but don't pass up other Shanghai delicacies. The braised pork shoulder is sweet and meaty (1 East Broadway, NY; 212 577-2922/2662; F train to East Broadway; 83-84 Broadway, Elmhurst, Queens; 718 803-9484; G, R train to Elmhurst Ave.; 94-03B 63rd Dr., Rego Park, Queens; 718 896-7159; G, R, train to 63rd Dr.).

Grand Sichuan International. There is certainly something for everyone on the menu at Grand Sichuan, which is divided by region— Sichuan, Shanghai, "Mao's Home Cooking" (Mao was born in Hunan), plus Chinese American. The red-cooked pork is rich and succulent, but just one of more than 200 dishes (229 Ninth Ave., NY; 212 620-5200; C, E train to 23rd St; 745 Ninth Ave, 212 582-2288; C, E train to 50th St.; 125 Canal St., NY; 212 625-9212; A, C, E, N, R, J, M, Z, 6 train to Canal St.).

H.K. Seafood. A Hong Kong restaurant in the heart of Flushing. Among the seafood specials: fried clams with black bean sauce, salt-baked shrimp, deep-fried oysters, pan-fried flounder, and squid with ginger and scallion (135-32 40th Rd., Flushing, Queens; 718 539-2200; 7 train to Main St./Flushing).

Joe's Shanghai. Ground zero for the Shanghai soup dumpling craze.

Other East China dishes: drunken crabs (served raw), soya duck (a Hangzhou specialty many find tastier than Peking duck), and Shanghai noodles and fried yellow fish. Prepare to wait in line (9 Pell St., NY; 212 233-8888; A, C, E, N, R, J, M, Z, 6 train to Canal St.; 136-21 37th Ave., Flushing, Queens; 718 539-3838; 7 train to Main St./Flushing).

La Cascade. The hotel restaurant in the Sheraton La Guardia East Hotel serves banquets of Yunnan noodle soups, or "crossing the bridge" noodles. Pork, chicken, prawns, fish, vegetables, and noodles are stewed in broth in a tabletop pot (only for parties of six or more). Call ahead (135-20 39th Ave., Flushing, Queens; 718 460-6666; 7 train to Main St./Flushing).

New Green Bo. The decor is nondescript, but the Shanghai fare isn't. Try the braised beef with soy-ginger sauce appetizer, Shanghai dumplings—the pan-fried variety or filled with soup and steamed—or whole red snapper with a sweet and sour sauce. Also good: the tong po pork sandwiches (66 Bayard St., NY; 212 625-2359; A, C, E, N, R, J, M, Z, 6 train to Canal St.).

New York Noodle Town. It's more than the long list of cheap noodle and rice dishes that keeps throngs coming back to this unassuming Chinatown great; a rave review by former New York Times food critic Ruth Reichl didn't hurt, either. The roasted meats (duck, pork, baby pig) and seafood (baked softshell crabs) are transporting (28½ Bowery, NY; 212 349-0923/2690; A, C, E, N, R, J, M, Z, 6 train to Canal St.).

Oriental Garden. The Hong Kong–style aquariums at the front window provide fresh seafood for dishes using lobster, crab, razor clams, salt-baked shrimp, and steamed black bass (14 Elizabeth St., NY; 212 619-0085; A, C, E, N, R, J, M, Z, 6 train to Canal St.).

Ping's Seafood. The fish tanks at Ping's in Elmhurst are stocked with live shrimp of more than one variety, eels, lobsters, crabs, sea bass, and cod. Diners enjoy sucking snails out of their shells. The fried Dungeness crab and the shrimp rolls are simply delicious (83-02 Queens Blvd., Elmhurst, Queens; 718 396-1238; G, R train to Elmhurst Ave.; 20 East Broadway, NY; 212 965-0808; A, C, E, N, R, J, M, Z, 6 train to Canal St.).

Shanghai Cuisine. Using checkered tablecloths and vintage pinup posters from a Shanghai flea market, owner Josephine Feng has created a warm and pleasant ambience in NY's Chinatown to enjoy one's xiao lung bao (soup dumplings) at a very reasonable price (89 Bayard St., NY; 212 732-8988; A, C, E, N, R, J, M, Z, 6 train to Canal St.).

Shanghai Tang. A big, bright Flushing restaurant, Shanghai Tang offers excellent Shanghai fare: fried soup dumplings, yellow fish with scallions, shrimp with pea shoots. Hot pots, too. On the weekends, sweet treats: crullers and sesame balls (135-20 40th Rd., Flushing, Queens; 718 661-0900; 7 train to Main St./Flushing; 77 W. Houston, NY; 212 614-9550; N, R train to Prince St.).

Shun Lee. Get great Chinese fare and service at this West Side restaurant. For dim sum, try Shun Lee Cafe at the same location (43 West 65th St., NY; 212 769-3888; 1, 9 train to 66th St.).

Shun Lee Palace. Those who prefer New York Chinese fare served on fine china have been enjoying the highly rated food, Adam Tihany decor, and attentive service at Michael Tong's upscale flagship for decades. It's the banquet fare that's exceptional. Expect to pay dearly for the excellence (155 E. 55th St., NY; 212 371-8844; 4, 5, 6, N, R train to 59th St./Lexington Ave.).

Sweet-n-Tart Restaurant. Owner of Sweet-n-Tart Café Spencer Chan opened Sweet-n-Tart Restaurant in the bilevel space once occupied by restaurant 20 Mott Street, keeping the dinner menus and adding the inexpensive cafe selection of sweet and savory tong shui soups, noodle soups, rice dishes, fruit juices and shakes (20 Mott St., NY; 212 334-8088; A, C, E, N, R, J, M, Z, 6 train to Canal St.).

Tang Pavilion. A midtown Chinese restaurant with an upscale ambience, known for its Shanghai menu: pungent drunken chicken flavored with rice wine, crispy fried eel, chewy jellyfish, jumbo shrimp with seaweed (65 W. 55th St., NY; 212 956-6888; E, F train to Fifth Ave.).

Wu Liang Ye. Wu Liang Ye's spicy, peppery Sichuan dishes stimulate the palate and olfactory buds, from the sliced conch served with chili oil to the mapo tofu (literally, "pockmarked old woman's bean curd"—spicy tofu with ground pork, garlic, ginger, and scallions) (36 W. 48th St., NY; 212 398-2308; B, D, F, Q train to 47–50 sts./Rockefeller Ctr.; 215 E. 86th St., NY; 212 534-8899; 4, 5, 6 train to 86th St.; 338 Lexington Ave., NY; 212 370-9647; 4, 5, 6, 7 train to 42nd St.).

Yangtze on Hudson. Specializing in both Sichuan and Shanghai dishes, the chefs at Yangtze render excellent Chengdu eggplant, double-cooked pork with capsicum, and braised whole fish with chili miso paste. The Shanghai dishes are just as inspired, and service is polite. The restaurant is in Battery Park City, of all places, overlooking the Hudson (21 South End Ave., NY; 212 964-6933; 1, 9 train to Rector St.).

Yung Sun. Fuzhou is known for its soups. This bright restaurant on East Broadway serves dumpling soups, a soup with braised lamb, and bird's nest and butterfly shrimp soup (47 East Broadway, NY; 212 346-9888; F train to East Broadway).

Filipino

Cendrillon. A warm, pretty Soho restaurant serving creative fare such as Balinese lamb shanks with tomatillo and mango chutney; sweet potato noodles with grilled squid stuffed with black rice and water chestnuts; and salt-roasted duck with quince *sambal* (45 Mercer St., NY; 212 343-9012; N, R train to Prince St.).

Elvie's Turo Turo. The daily buffet features rotating specials such as Mama Pinay's breaded pork chops. Everyday items include pork and chicken *adobo* marinated in vinegar, garlic, pepper, bay leaves, and soy sauce (214 First Ave., NY; 212 473-7785; L train to First Ave.).

Indian, Pakistani, and Sri Lankan

Ayurveda Cafe. The 4,500-year-old tradition of Ayurvedic medicine emphasizes balance, as do the preset menus of vegetarian platters at this cafe. The selection changes daily (706 Amsterdam Ave., NY; 212 932-2400; 1, 9, B, C train to 86th St.).

Cafe Spice. A sibling of uptown Dawat, this attractive, contemporary "Indian bistro" serves both northern and southern fare, perfectly spiced: the fried grain patties known as *dosai, roomali roti* (a thin, soft bread), and vegetarian and seafood dishes (72 University Pl., NY; 212 253-6999; 4, 5, 6, N, R, L train to Union Sq.).

Chola. The menu is a culinary tour of India: Hyderabadi *korma* (vegetables with coconut milk and curry leaves); Kerala-style shrimp with coconut and mustard; Kashmiri *bakri rogani* (baby goat) (232 E. 58th St., NY; 212 688-4619; 4, 5, 6, N, R train to 59th St./Lexington Ave.).

Dawat. A pioneer of innovative Indian cuisine, 14-year-old Dawat maintains its reputation with such dishes as cornish hen with green chilies and tamarind and *konju pappaas* (shrimp in coconut curry) (210 E. 58th St., NY; 212 355-7555; 4, 5, 6, N, R train to 59th St./Lexington Ave.).

Delhi Palace. Inexpensive North Indian fare served in a pleasant atmosphere. Shrimp vindaloo comes in a dark, chocolatey sauce spiked with vinegar, and the lamb *jalfrazie* is covered in a rich sauce of tomatoes and onions (37-33 74th St., Jackson Heights, Queens; 718 507-0666; 7 train to 74th St., E, F, G, R train to Roosevelt Ave.).

Haveli. Around the corner from the row of largely indistinct Indian restaurants on East 6th Street (except perhaps Raga at 433 E. 6th St.), Haveli has established itself as a popular bright spot with good grilled and vegetarian dishes (100 Second Ave., NY; 212 982-0533; F train to Second Ave., 6 train to Astor Pl.).

Jackson Diner. The crowds line up for the northern and southern Indian fare at this Jackson Heights institution, especially for the weekend buffet. The menu includes *dosai*, lots of tandoori and vegetarian specials, and Lahori lamb chops (37-47 74th St., Jackson Heights, Queens; 718 672-1232; 7 train to 74th St.-Broadway, E, F, G, R train to Roosevelt Ave.).

Lakruwana. A Sri Lankan restaurant offering rice crêpe hoppers, *pittu* (steamed rice flour and chicken or beef curry), shrimp biriyani, lentil soup, and *watalappan* pudding, a sweet-and-spicy coconut-milk pudding (358 W. 44th St., NY; 212 957-4480; A, C, E train to 42nd St.).

Mavalli Palace. Exciting Indian vegetarian fare such as delicious *baingan bharta* eggplant and peas, *palak paneer* spinach with cheese, *dosai* crêpes with coconut chutney, and *uttapam* pancakes (46 E. 29th St., NY; 212 679-5535; 6 train to 28th St.).

Pakistan Tea House. A little gem, with just 18 seats but a big menu and a bustling takeout business. At least a dozen fresh vegetarian dishes every day and such meat and fish dishes as *balti gosht* beef and Goan fish curry. (All the meats are *halal*.) Generous portions, low prices (176 Church St., NY; 212 240-9800; A, C, 1, 2, 3, 9 train to Chambers St.).

Pongal. Kosher vegetarian Indian. The *thali* platters offer great variety, with as many as 10 delectable dishes. The *dosai* crêpes filled with potato masala are huge. The restaurant gets crowded (110 Lexington Ave., NY; 212 696-9458; 6 train to 28th St.).

Salaam Bombay. Chefs in the windowed kitchen that overlooks the lavish dining room create mostly North Indian dishes such as meats cooked in the tandoori oven, but also chicken vindaloo and *macchi malabar* (fish simmered in a coconut sauce), specialties of Goa and Kerala, respectively (319 Greenwich St., NY; 212 226-9400; 1, 2, 3, 9 train to Chambers St.).

Surya. The trendy atmosphere attracts a loud crowd. The mostly South Indian dishes are modernized with unexpected presentation; the *dosai* and vegetable dishes are highlights (302 Bleecker St.; 212 807-7770; 1, 9 train to Christopher St.).

Tabaq 74. A friendly Pakistani restaurant in the heart of Queens' "Little India," serving excellent *chapli kebab* (ground beef patties with fresh spices), grilled mutton leg, and ginger chicken (73-21 37th Rd., Jackson Heights, Queens; 718 898-2837; 7 train to 74th St.-Broadway, E, F, G, R train to Roosevelt Ave.).

Tabla. Indian American fusion of the highest quality, offering such inventive dishes as tandoori quail; softshell crabs with daikon, coconut, and tamarind curry; and mustard fettuccine with veal. The food speaks for itself (11 Madison Ave., NY; 212 889-0667; N, R, 6 train to 23rd St.).

Taprobane. Sri Lankan restaurants aren't commonplace, so it's worth sampling this restaurant's spicy fare. The "string hoppers" are fried noodles with a tart sauce. Crêpes are airy and light, fashioned with rice flour and coconut milk (234 W. 56th St., NY; 212 333-4203; A, C, B, D, 1, 9 train to 59th St.).

Tikka. A sibling of Tiffin in Tribeca and Thali in the West Village. Tikka's chefs render such unusual dishes as *panir*-stuffed portabello mushrooms and braised leg of lamb marinated in rum. For dessert, try Parsi custard (344 Lexington Ave., NY; 212 370-4054; 4, 5, 6, 7 train to 42nd St.).

Vatan. A Gujarati restaurant serving three-course prix fixe meals comprising dozens of regional vegetarian specialties—lentil cakes, exquisite samosas, spicy okra and chickpeas, and spinach and potatoes—and as many helpings as you want (409 Third Ave., NY; 212 689-5666; 6 train to 28th St.).

Indonesian and Malaysian

Bali Nasu Indah. A pretty Indonesian restaurant serving such specialties as an *otak otak* mousse of fish mixed with spices and steamed in banana leaves. Also: pan-fried whole snapper, and chicken in chili or coconut sauce (651 Ninth Ave., NY; 212 765-6500; A, C, E train to 42nd St.).

Baba. One of the newer Malaysian restaurants in Chinatown, serving Malaysian and Peranakan (Chinese/Malaysian) specialties such as skewers of satay, grilled telapia fish in banana leaf and *kari ayam* (chicken in coconut curry) (53 Bayard St., NY; 212 766-1318; A, C, E, N, R, J, M, Z, 6 train to Canal St.).

Eastanah. An Indonesian and Malaysian menu with favorites from both cuisines: roti, a tofu satay, *otak otak*, and *pohpiah* spring rolls. The *ayam goreng nenas* is spicy chicken with chunks of pineapple, mint leaves, and yellow peppers (212 Lafayette St., NY; 212 625-9633; B, D, Q train to Grand St.).

Franklin Station Cafe. Malaysian noodles and curries in a cozy Malaysian-French cafe in Tribeca that also serves tasty sandwiches, salads, and fruit tarts (222 West Broadway, NY; 212 274-8525; 1, 9 train to Franklin St.).

Nyonya. This cheap, pleasant and popular Little Italy joint serves plenty of Malaysian seafood dishes, including fish head curry and stingray. Baba (above) has a similar menu (194 Grand St., NY; 212 334-3669; B, D, Q train to Grand St.).

Penang. The Chinatown locations (in Queens and Manhattan) of this chain of Malaysian restaurants are standouts, serving *ayam rendang* (chicken cooked with lemon grass and chili paste, in a coconut curry) and *bobo cha cha* dessert (sweet potato with coconut milk) (41-43 Elizabeth St., NY; 212 431-8722; A, C, E, N, R, J, M, Z, 6 train to Canal; 109 Spring St., NY; 212 274-8333; 6 train to Spring St.; 38-04 Prince St., Queens; 718 321-2078; 7 train to Main St.).

Rasa Sayang. Now with branches in Jackson Heights and the West Village. Rasa Sayang's *rojak* fruit salad is crunchy and sweet with jicama, pineapple, mango, and cucumber, flavored with *blacan*. The prawns *asam* are tangy with tamarind (47 Seventh Ave. S., NY; 212 255-2848; 1, 9 train to Christopher St.; 75-19 Broadway, Jackson Heights, Queens; 718 424-9054; 7 train to 74th St., E, F, G, R train to Roosevelt Ave.).

Sentosa Malaysian. The eastern edge of Manhattan's Chinatown on Allen Street is now home to a couple of Malaysian restaurants (Proton Saga is a few doors away at 11 Allen St.). The house specials, sautéed eggplant and sautéed shrimp, are spiked with *blacan*, Malaysia's trademark dried shrimp paste (3 Allen St.; 212 925-8018; F train to East Broadway).

Japanese

Blue Ribbon Sushi. Ultrafresh sushi served in a Soho setting where the chefs are known for their willingness to break from tradition to create spectacular combinations featuring daily specials (119 Sullivan St., NY; 212 343-0404; C, E train to Spring St.).

Bond Street. With an ambience that caters to glitterati, Bond Street serves innovative Japanese cuisine—lobster tempura, for example, or steamed rainbow trout with ginger-scallion broth. Sushi chef Hiroshi Nakahara turns out an impressive—and expensive—selection of sushi (6 Bond St., NY; 212 777-2500; B, D, F, Q train to Broadway-Lafayette, 6 train to Bleecker St.).

Hasaki. An attractive East Village establishment that serves consistently good, fresh sushi. Arrive early to avoid the inevitable line and to take advantage of twilight specials (210 E. 9th St., NY; 212 473-3327; 6 train to Astor Pl.).

Honmura An. Fresh, delicious soba and udon are made on the premises at this serene Soho restaurant. A cook rolls out the buckwheat dough in a booth next to the kitchen. *Kaiseki* meals—traditional, often formal, meals made up of small seasonal dishes—may be requested in

---

A critic's favorites Jeffrey Steingarten, *Vogue* food critic and author of *The Man Who Ate Everything* (Knopf, 1997), on some of his:

Kuruma Zushi.

"One of the three best [sushi bars] in the country. I always go there. I just went there, and [Mr. Uezu] had three different grades of *otoro*."

Nobu.

"The biggest success of any Asian restaurant in New York. If I had to go to one restaurant and only one restaurant over and over again, it would probably be Nobu. There's an informality about the restaurant that makes it very easy to go to and very pleasant. And the food is consistently good."

---

advance (170 Mercer St., NY; 212 334-5253; B, D, F, Q train to Broadway-Lafayette, N, R train to Prince St.).

Inagiku. An expensive Japanese restaurant in the Waldorf-Astoria Hotel, where the diminutive courses of sashimi, grilled black cod, *oshitashi* (seasoned spinach), and *chawanmushi* (savory custard) are complemented by seasonal offerings. Also: steak *ishikaya* and *anago* tempura (111 E. 49th St., NY; 212 355-0440; E, F train to Lexington Ave., 6 train to 51st St.).

Katsuhama. Cutlets of pork tenderloin, chicken, and prawns are breaded and deep-fried, but never greasy. Cheese *katsu* and cream croquettes also are served, as well as *kushiage*—skewered and fried meats and vegetables (11 E. 47th St., NY; 212 758-5909; B, D, F, Q train to Rockefeller Center).

Kuruma Zushi. An oasis of sushi one floor up and a world away from the bustle of midtown. Ask to be served *omakase*, or "chef's choice," and be delighted by chef and proprietor Toshihiro Uezu's skills and charms.

Even the wasabi is fresh (7 E. 47th St., NY; 212 317-2802; 4, 5, 6, 7 train to 42nd St.).

Lan. A popular place for *shabu-shabu* and sukiyaki. *Shabu-shabu* meats and vegetables are served on a huge platter and cooked in a pot at the table. A great spot for groups (56 Third Ave., NY; 212 254-1959; 4, 5, 6 train to Astor Pl.).

Nadaman Hakubai. Multicourse *kaiseki* meals are served in quiet, private tatami rooms in the Kitano Hotel. The beautifully presented offerings change from day to day and season to season (66 Park Ave., NY; 212 885-7111; 4, 5, 6, 7 train to 42nd St.).

Natori. Try this plain and cheap hole-in-the-wall on St. Marks Pl. for such Japanese staples as teriyaki and *katsudon* and tempura (58 St. Marks Pl., NY; 212 533-7711; 6 train to Astor Pl.).

Nobu. A place of highly coveted luxuries, including the much-copied miso-marinated black cod, yellowtail sashimi with jalapeño, and a seat in the back. You'll want to try it all, so order lots of appetizers instead of entrees. Very expensive. **Next Door Nobu** is the no-reservations annex with later hours (105 Hudson St., NY; 212 219-0500; 1, 9 train to Franklin St.).

Omen. A taste of Kyoto in Soho. Tranquil and rustic, Omen highlights the cuisine of Kyoto, serving such delicate treats as *shira ae* (sesame tofu puree), as well as noodles and sashimi (113 Thompson St., NY; 212 925-8923; C, E train to Spring St.).

Seryna. Luscious Kobe steaks are cooked on a heated stone right at the table. The *shabu-shabu* and sushi are just as appealing, if not quite so dramatically served (11 E. 53rd St., NY; 212 980-9393; E, F train to Fifth Ave., 6 train to 51st St.).

Sobaya. Freshly made buckwheat noodles are served in this East Village *soba* shop. Cold *soba* with *tsuyu* dipping sauce is a refreshing summer treat, while the chicken curry *udon* is especially hearty (229 E. 9th St., NY, 212 533-6966, 6 train to Astor Pl.).

Sono. The space once occupied by Le Chantilly now houses Sono, where chef Tadashi Ono offers such innovative, expert creations as tempura eel with shrimp consommé and foie gras with Hosui pears (106 E. 57th St., NY; 212 752-4411; 4, 5, 6, N, R train to 59th St./Lexington Ave.).

Sugiyama. Chef Nao Sugiyama prepares modern *kaiseki* meals, a parade of seasonal dishes artfully presented—sashimi, soups, grilled seafood. The staff explains each of the dishes as they are presented (251 W. 55th St., NY; 212 956-0670; A, C, B, D, 1, 9 train to 59th St.).

Sushi Hatsu. A seat anywhere other than at the sushi bar is too far from the sushi chefs and their recommendations. Put yourself in their hands for fresh and beautiful sushi (1143 First Ave., NY; 212 371-0238; 4, 5, 6, N, R train to 59th St./Lexington Ave.).

Sushi of Gari. The sushi selection changes daily, and the chefs turn excellent cuts of fish into dreamy *maki* rolls and sushi. (*Gari* is the pink, sliced, vinegared ginger that cleanses the palate.) (402 E. 78th St., NY; 212 517-5340; 6 train to 77th St.).

Sushisay. The descendant of Tokyo's Sushisei Honzen, a late-19th-century *sushiya* located in the Tsukiji fish market, Sushisay offers beautifully presented, fresh sushi in a minimalist setting. Its website (www.sushisei.com) lists which fish are in season (38 E. 51st St., NY; 212 755-1780; E, F to Fifth Ave.).

Sushi Yasuda. A comely sushi restaurant, in an airy space with bamboo wood from floor to ceiling. The variety of sushi is impressive—several kinds of yellowtail and eel and *toro* tuna. Eating the fatty *toro*, soft and pink and buttery, is a dreamlike experience (204 E. 43rd St., NY; 212 972-1001; 4, 5, 6, 7 train to 42nd St.).

Taka. Takako Yoneyama is sushi chef and proprietor at this tiny 10-table spot in the West Village. Her sushi creations are imaginative and her restaurant intimate (61 Grove St., NY; 212 242-3699; 1, 9 train to Christopher St.).

Tomoe Sushi. Expect to wait (and wait and wait) for a seat at this tiny sushi spot whose reasonably priced and superfresh sushi has established a cult following. After the deluxe sushi platter, try the coffee jelly for dessert (172 Thompson St., NY; 212 777-9346; C, E train to Spring St.).

Toraya. A charming space with charming owners, not to be confused with the Toraya tea room on 71st Street. Toraya's sushi bar seats only a handful of customers, who receive genial service and great food (300½ E. 52nd St., NY; 212 838-4351; E, F, 6 train to Lexington Ave./51st St.).

Yajirobei. The *sakana* drinking snacks at this busy *izakaya* are posted on the walls: bonito *tataki*, blowfish skin with *kimchi*, sashimi. The set menu includes yakitori and *kushiage*, as well as *chawanmushi* (a savory custard with seafood) and *agedofu* (thick, deep-fried tofu in broth) (8 Stuyvesant St., NY, 2nd floor; 212 598-3041; 6 train to Astor Pl.).

Korean

Cho Dang Gol. The fresh-made tofu is served in a dozen ways: in *doo boo kam ja jun* (potato pancakes) and with *doo boo doo ro chi gi* (pan-fried kimchi and pork on a sizzling platter) (55 W. 35th St., NY; 212 695-8222; B, D, F, Q, N, R train to 34th St./Herald Sq.).

Choga. A quaint second-floor Korean restaurant near NYU. The staples are soups and stews, and there's also sushi. Open till the wee hours (145 Bleecker St., NY; 212 598-5946; A, C, E, B, D, F, Q train to W. 4th St.).

Do Hwa. The stylish and loud younger sibling of East Village institution Dok Suni (see below). Do Hwa, in the West Village, attempts to maintain the traditional Korean table setting, with plenty of banchan side dishes accompanying each meal. The menu, divided by region, includes beef and kimchi (a spicy relish) dumplings, spicy squid, and a variety of meats for the grill tables (55 Carmine St., NY; 212 414-1224; 1, 9 train to Houston St.).

Dok Suni. *See* **Do Hwa,** *above* (119 First Ave., NY; 212 477-9506; 6 train to Astor Pl., L train to First Ave.).

Gam Mee Ok. A narrow restaurant with an open kitchen, where the chefs prepare sul long tang—soup with a simmered oxtail broth—and platters of grilled meats (43 W. 32nd St., NY; 212 695-4113; B, D, F, Q, N, R train to 34th St./Herald Sq.).

Han Bat. A popular 24-hour restaurant specializing in country food of Southern Korea such as the beef soup sul long tang. Also serves delicious bibimbap and pajun (53 W. 35th St., NY; 212 629-5588; B, D, F, N, Q, R train to 34th St./Herald Sq.).

Hangawi. Diners take off their shoes and settle in at low tables to enjoy elegant, delicious vegetarian fare of greens and mountain roots: pumpkin porridge, pancakes with leeks, stuffed tofu, seasoned mushrooms (12 E. 32nd St., NY; 212 213-0077; B, D, F, Q, N, R train to 34th St./Herald Sq.).

Kang Suh. A Koreatown barbecue emporium that also has a sushi bar. Other dishes: hae mool pa jun seafood pancakes and hae mool jap tang, a spicy broth with seafood and vegetables (1250 Broadway, NY; 212 564-6846; B, D, F, Q, N, R train to 34th St./Herald Sq.)

Kum Gang San. A sprawl of tables outfitted with grills for cooking kalbi (short ribs), cha dol baki (brisket) and jae yook gui (pork tenderloin). A waterfall and a piano player make Kum Gang San a favorite spot for barbecue (49 W. 32nd St., NY; 212 967-0909; B, D, F, Q, N, R train to 34th St./Herald Sq.; 138-28 Northern Blvd., Flushing, Queens; 718 461-0909; 7 train to Main St./Flushing).

Mandoo Bar. Fresh Korean dumplings are the specialty here: fried dumplings, meat dumplings, vegetarian dumplings, even baby dumplings. Watch them being made through the window at the front of the shop.

Bags of frozen mandoo dumplings are also sold (2 W. 32nd St., NY; 212 279-3075; B, D, F, Q, N, R train to 34th St./Herald Sq.).

Mill Korean Restaurant. Located way uptown in what was for several generations a greasy-spoon luncheonette, this attractive restaurant is appointed with Korean paintings and serves such favorites as tangy ribs and pancakes with squid, pork, and shrimp (2895 Broadway, NY; 212 666-7653; 1, 9 train to 110th St.).

Royal Garden. Rustic and pleasant, with dark wood tables and a menu of hearty soups and stews: duk man doo guk (dumpling soup with rice cake) and daegoo muritang (cod fish head and vegetable soup). Barbecue too (142-34 Roosevelt Ave., Flushing, Queens; 718 886-9292; 7 train to Main St./Flushing).

Woo Chon. Lots of banchan and barbecue at this "cow village." The wang kalbi are jumbo meaty short ribs. It's all served up in a pleasant setting with helpful service (8 W. 36th St., NY; 212 695-0676; B, D, F, Q, N, R train to 34th St.; 41-19 Kissena Blvd., Flushing, Queens; 718 463-0803; 7 train to Main St./Flushing).

Woo Lae Oak. A spare, sleek restaurant that suits its Soho setting. The Korean fare, like the space, evokes a sense of newness: try beef carpaccio wrapped in soybean pancakes or black cod in a spicy-sweet sauce. The variety of meats for grilling is impressive: beef, ostrich, oyster, shrimp, scallops (148 Mercer St., NY; 212 925-8200; B, D, F, Q train to Broadway-Lafayette, N, R train to Prince St.).

Thai

Amarin Cafe. A no-frills Thai cafe in Greenpoint, a sort of antidote to the noise and crowds of Williamsburg's more-popular Plan-Eat Thai. Squid pad thai, shrimp glass-noodle salad, tasty fish cakes. Plenty spicy. Look for the quail specials (617 Manhattan Ave., Brooklyn; 718 349-2788; G train to Metropolitan Ave., L train to Lorimer St.).

East Village Thai Restaurant. A tiny Thai takeout counter, with a few seats. Tom yum spicy and tangy soup with chicken, pad kee mao (broad noodles sautéed in a spicy basil sauce with vegetables and/or meat) and plenty of curries, including a red curry with pineapple and pork. Highest marks for the charcoal-grilled prawns in chili sauce (32 E. 7th St.; 212 673-4610; 6 train to Astor Pl.).

The Elephant. Diners at this small, colorful, and oft-crowded Asian/French bistro sip cocktails mixed with litchi juice and eat such tasty, inventive fare as Thai beef salad, which arrives as spires of layered sliced steak, mint, and cilantro atop jasmine rice. If you're looking for a scene, albeit a cool and mellow one, you might find it here (58 E. 1st St., NY; 212 505-7739; F train to Second Ave.).

Kai Kai. A matchbox-size Thai cafe with just a handful of tables and a small menu of Thai dishes, such as curries, that change daily. Try the rich *mussaman* curry with peanuts and potatoes, or *gang keow wan* green curry with vegetables and coconut milk (131 Ave. A, NY; 212 420-5909; 6 train to Astor Pl.).

Kin Khao. Soho's Kin Khao attracts a crowd, especially on weekends. The Thai food is fine: fresh *som tum* papaya salad, duck curry in a sweet and spicy curry, passable pad Thai. For dessert, try sticky rice with mango (171 Spring St., NY; 212 966-3939; C, E, 6 train to Spring St., N, R train to Prince St.).

Kway Tiow Thai Kitchen. The name means "noodles." And the noodles here are a bargain, but you might also try Kway Tiow's *larb* (chicken or pork with mint, chili, and lemon juice), a minced meat salad, or *mussaman* curry (with beef, coconut milk, potatoes, onions, and peanuts) (83-47 Dongan Ave., Elmhurst, Queens; 718 476-6743; G, R train to Elmhurst Ave.).

Little Basil. Delicious Thai cuisine pleasingly presented. The *pet kaprow* duck is fried crispy and sweetened with basil. *Yum nuer* beef salad, made with lime juice and tomatoes and spiked with chilies, is refreshing (39 Greenwich Ave., NY; 212 645-8965; 1, 2, 3, 9 train to 14th St.; *also* **Holy Basil:** 149 Second Ave.; 212 460-5557; 6 train to Astor Pl.).

Plan Eat Thailand. The relocated Plan Eat Thailand is huge and raucous, and although the move may have cost it its small-restaurant charm, it has gained a sushi bar and hibachi grill. The Thai dishes are still appealing (141 N. 7th St., Brooklyn; 718 599-5758; L train to Bedford Ave.).

Pongsri Thailand Restaurant. Casual and comfortable, the Chinatown Pongsri offers delicious *kai yud saie* and basil pork, especially good when the pork is minced ("*kaw sup*, please") (106 Bayard St.; 212 349-3132, 212 766-0939; A, C, E, N, R, J, M, Z, 6 train to Canal St.).

Rungsit Thai Food and Noodles. The restaurant might not be much to look at, but you can get a good pad Thai here—the noodles nice and crispy, not overcooked. The pumpkin custard is a satisfying dessert (161 E. 23rd St., NY; 212 260-0704; 6 train to 23rd St.).

Sripraphai. *Kao soy!* Not easy to come by this side of Chiang Mai. Egg noodles are served in a rich curry–coconut milk broth with pieces of chicken, beef, or pork and topped with crispy-fried noodles. So many delicious Thai dishes (64-13 39th Ave., Woodside, Queens; 718 899-9599; 7 train to 61st St.).

Takrai Thai. Situated in the same Elmhurst strip mall as Penang and Joe's Shanghai, Takrai serves up fried fish ball appetizers and durian ice cream dessert. In between, try *pad prik sod* (beef with chili and onion). (82-80 Broadway, Elmhurst, Queens; 718 898-7996; G, R train to Elmhurst Ave.).

Thai Cafe. Predecessor of Plan Eat Thailand (*see above*) (923 Manhattan Ave., Brooklyn; (718) 383-3562 ; G train to Greenpoint Ave.).

Thai House Cafe. Consistently good, cheap Thai food in unassuming Tribeca quarters. The menu includes plenty of vegetarian dishes, and the flavors of *galangal*, lemon grass, and chilies are fresh and vibrant (151 Hudson St., NY; 212 334-1085; A, C, E, 1, 9 train to Canal St.).

Ubol's Kitchen. This kitchen doesn't stint on spiciness, and its curry pastes are freshly made. The fresh flavors of green papaya salad include tangy lemon juice and pungent fish sauce (24-42 Steinway St., Astoria, Queens; 718 545-2874; N train to Astoria Blvd.).

Vong. Jean-Georges Vongerichten's Thai-French cuisine includes such masterful combinations as Muscovy duck breast with tamarind-sesame sauce, squab with egg-noodle pancake, and seared black sea bass in a mushroom broth (200 E. 54th St., NY; 212 486-9592; E, F train to Lexington Ave.; 6 train to 51st St.).

Tibetan

Lhasa. A tranquil spot with a friendly staff and pretty patio, and named after Tibet's capital. The *momo* dumplings would be hard to beat anywhere on earth. Here, they are filled with chicken and steamed or fried, and make a nice accompaniment for *la phing* bean jelly and *bhoja*, tea with butter and salt and cream (96 Second Ave., NY; 212 674-5870; F train to Second Ave.).

Tibet on Houston. The stewed spare ribs are spicy and tender, and the fried chunks of chicken are infused with the flavor of curry. A welcoming and popular Tibetan spot (136 W. Houston, NY; 212 995-5884; A, C, E, B, D, F, Q train to W. 4th St., 1, 9 train to Houston St.).

Tsampa. "Tsampa" refers to the roasted barley flour that is a Tibetan staple. This restaurant is an attractive and pleasant addition to a street lined with Japanese eateries. Try crispy pancakes with mushrooms and scallions; *nya tapa* grilled whole trout; or udon noodles with vegetables, onion, and ginger. (212 E. 9th St.; 212 614-3226; 6 train to Astor Pl.).

Vietnamese

Banh Mi So 1. This spot specializes in banh mi sandwiches layered with Vietnamese charcuterie on crispy-soft baguettes. Layers of barbecued pork and xa xiu pressed ham are topped with fresh coriander, marinated carrots, cucumber, and hot sauce (85 Bowery, NY; 212 219-8341; A, C, E, N, R, J, M, Z, 6 train to Canal St.).

Bo Ky. An eatery that suits the frenetic pace of Chinatown, Bo Ky is all about quick bowls of pho, and lots and lots of pho, none costing more than five bucks: curry chicken, fish dumpling, wonton, mustard greens, or Cambodian rice noodle soup (80 Bayard St., NY; 212 406-2292; A, C, E, N, R, J, M, Z, 6 train to Canal St.).

Café Asean. Enjoy Southeast Asian cuisine, with an emphasis on Vietnam, at this hip West Village local (117 West 10th St., NY; 212 633-0348; B, D, F, Q, A, C, E train to W. 4th St.).

Cyclo. An attractive East Village Vietnamese restaurant that offers excellent cha gio (spring rolls), to be wrapped in lettuce with fresh mint and carrot and dipped in nuac cham sauce. You'll recognize the restaurant by the cyclo parked in front (203 First Ave., NY; 212 673-3957; L train to First Ave., 6 train to Astor Pl.).

Gia Lam II. On Eighth Avenue in Sunset Park's Chinatown, Gia Lam II offers such favorites as grilled beef on rice vermicelli, lots of seafood—stir-fried eel, shrimp with tomatoes—and quail and pigeon specials (5606 Eighth Ave., Brooklyn; 718 567-0800; N, R train to Eighth Ave.).

La Soirée d'Asie. The setting in a two-story East Side townhouse may outshine the food but makes the restaurant worth a visit. The "special rice" served in a clay pot with shrimp, chicken, and black mushrooms is satisfying, and the shrimp paste on sugar cane is a treat (156 E. 64th St., NY; 212 421-7899; 4, 5, 6, N, R train to 59th St./Lexington Ave.).

Le Colonial. Ceiling fans, potted palms, and shuttered windows conjure up a movie-set Saigon. The menu features delicious, carefully turned-out Vietnamese dishes. Banh cuon rice crêpes are filled with chicken, shrimp, and mushrooms; the grilled eggplant is tangy with lime. Whole red snapper is crispy and flavorful (149 E. 57th St., NY; 212 752-0808; 4, 5, 6, N, R train to 59th St./Lexington Ave.).

Mekong. A comfortable, good-looking Vietnamese restaurant in the popular Nolita neighborhood. Delicious summer rolls, plus grilled pork and filet mignon (44 Prince St., NY; 212 343-8169; N, R train to Prince St.).

Nem. A Vietnamese take-out counter in a far corner of the dining concourse at Grand Central. Vietnamese sandwiches are the specialty. Fresh baguettes are smeared with butter and pâté, then filled with cucumbers, carrots, cilantro, and a choice of pork, sirloin, shrimp, chicken, or vegetables. (Grand Central Terminal dining concourse, NY; 212 223-8777; 4, 5, 6, 7, S train to Grand Central/42nd St.)

New Pasteur. New Pasteur on Baxter Street is the one with the bright pink awning. This Chinatown Vietnamese serves delicious fare, including perhaps this block's best barbecued pork with rice vermicelli (85 Baxter St., NY; 212 608-3656; A, C, E, N, R, J, M, Z, 6 train to Canal St.).

Nha Trang. This popular spot attracts weekend-night crowds with *pho* noodle soups, *bun* vermicelli dishes, spring rolls, curry chicken, and *suon nuong* grilled pork chops (87 Baxter St., NY; 212 233-5948; A, C, E, N, R, J, M, Z, 6 train to Canal St.).

Pho Bang. A chain of usually crowded *pho* shops, with more than 20 varieties of *pho* noodle soups (157 Mott St., NY; 212 966-3797; A, C, E, N, R, J, M, Z, 6 train to Canal St.; 6 Chatham Square, NY; 212 587-0870; 4, 5, 6 train to Brooklyn Bridge/City Hall; 3 Pike St., NY; 212 233-3947; F train to East Broadway; 41-07 Kissena Blvd., Flushing, Queens; 718 939-5520; 7 train to Main St./Flushing; 82-90 Broadway, Elmhurst, Queens; 718 205-1500; G, R train to Elmhurst Ave.).

Pho Hoai. Try the house special *banh hoi thit heo nuong*—grilled pork on rice stick noodles served with fresh lettuce, cucumber, and mint. Wrap them all together and enjoy (1906 Ave. U, Brooklyn; 718 616-1233; D train to Ave. U).

Pho Tu Do. The fried chicken is spiced with lemon grass and chili, and the table-grilled beef and shrimp are "perfectly marinated," just as the menu says. There's a set five-course family dinner that serves six people for less than $30 (119 Bowery, NY; 212 966-2666; B, D, Q train to Grand St.).

Pho Viet Huong. One of the tastiest specials here is the salt-and-pepper squid. If you dare to eat durian—the much-loved fruit of Southeast Asia that smells stinky (to put it mildly)—Pho Viet Huong serves durian shakes (73 Mulberry St., NY; 212 233-8988; A, C, E, N, R, J, M, Z, 6 train to Canal St.).

Thai So'n. With a list of more than 150 dishes and a grilled pork chop for just four dollars, it's hard to go wrong here. The "seven colors rainbow" dessert with shaved ice, sweet mung bean, coconut milk, and green gelatin is a refreshing summertime treat (89 Baxter St., NY; 212 732-2822; A, C, E, N, R, J, M, Z, 6 train to Canal St.).

Vietnam Restaurant. Find Vietnam right in the crook of curved Doyers Street and down a set of stairs. The long, long menu is almost overwhelming, but there are treasures to be discovered: shrimp paste grilled on lengths of sugarcane, for example, or grilled lemon grass chicken, Hue-style pho (11 Doyers St., NY; 212 693-0725; A, C, E, N, R, J, M, Z, 6 train to Canal St.).

koreatown

I t was Ruth Reichl, several years ago, who gave the neighborhood its nickname. The then–*New York Times* food critic affectionately dubbed Koreatown "Kimchi Alley." Kimchi is, of course, the spicy, pungent cabbage pickled in red chili pepper that accompanies nearly every Korean meal—it is so ubiquitous, it is used in everything from stews to dumplings. And Korean culture is equally ubiquitous in an area that is located around West 32nd Street, roughly enclosed to the east by Fifth Avenue and to the west by Broadway, Greeley Square (a small, pleasant green triangle in the middle of a very busy shopping district), and Herald Square. In fact, the Korean presence is so strong and vibrant here that the street sign at Broadway and 32nd Street reads KOREA WAY.

Of course, Korean American assilmilation is in evidence elsewhere in the city—specifically in the way New Yorkers have accepted and even embraced Korean cuisine. A handful of hip, nouveau Korean restaurants have recently popped up all over downtown Manhattan: geographically speaking, the arbiter of cool. Still, it is Koreatown that contains perhaps the largest concentration of Korean restaurants in the city; and the concentration there is highest on 32nd Street. For non-Koreans, these restaurants are the area's focal point. But a closer inspection reveals a tightly packed vertical city. At street level, the area is like any other block in multiethnic New York. There are restaurants, bars, coffee

All signs point toward Manhattan's Koreatown.

shops, clothing stores, a supermarket, bookstores, banks, and little malls where you can buy lingerie, cosmetics, and electronics. The difference here is the heavy presence of signs in distinctively geometrical Korean script, as well as the store offerings: At the supermarket **Han Ah Reum,** for example, at 25 West 32nd Street, Korean and Japanese food products and a large variety of premade Korean food and kimchi fill store shelves.

But it is vertically that Koreatown has seen much of its growth. Look up on narrow 32nd Street, and you will see an odd assemblage of restaurants, beauty salons, martial arts centers, pool halls, acupuncture clinics, law offices, karaoke clubs (or song rooms, with Korean, American, and sometimes, Japanese songbooks), and even a church—all stacked one on top of the other. Here also are several mid-priced hotels, most noticeably the Stanford Hotel, which is Korean-owned.

Walking along 32nd and 33rd streets, look for neon signs in restaurant windows that read OPEN 24 HOURS. Restaurants are open all day and night because many Koreans do not work regular hours. The area feels safe and cosmopolitan, especially on 32nd Street. At any given time in the day you will see university students, visitors from Korea, East Asian businessmen, shopkeepers, and livery cab drivers. Hanging out on the streets are Korean American youth, boys in comically loose hip-hop pants and reed-thin girls in tight clothes, calling each other on colorful blinking cell phones as they wait to shoot pool or rent a song room for the night. It's also not uncommon to see groups of non-Korean New Yorkers eating *bulgogi*—marinated beef barbecued on a table grill—and drinking bottles of potent *sujo*—Korean potato vodka—before or after hitting a nightclub or bar. One typical spot, **Gam Mee Ok,** at 43 West 32nd Street, is a traditional Korean restaurant with under a dozen specialty dishes. Its milky-white oxtail soup is delicious, and the kimchi is cut at the table.

Unlike Chinatown, Koreatown is strictly a business district. Koreans, who number around 250,000 in the New York metropolitan area, mostly live around the Queens neighborhoods of Flushing, Jackson Heights, Woodside, and Sunnyside; as well as in Fort Lee and Palisades Park in Bergen County, New Jersey, where a large number of middle-class Koreans have left New York City to form a suburban enclave. During the 1980s Japanese businessmen and their families moved into the area, which is close to Manhattan and to the many companies headquartered in New Jersey. Since then, northern New Jersey has seen a significant increase in the number of Asian Americans, with Koreans in the majority.

The Korean community is tightly organized around its churches, both Protestant and Catholic (which number around 180), and small business associations. Three daily newspapers, two television stations, and two radio stations serve the community. "The greater New York area has the second-largest Korean American population in the United States, after Los Angeles," says Chung-wha Hong, executive director of the **National Korean-American Service and Education Consortium (NKASEC).**

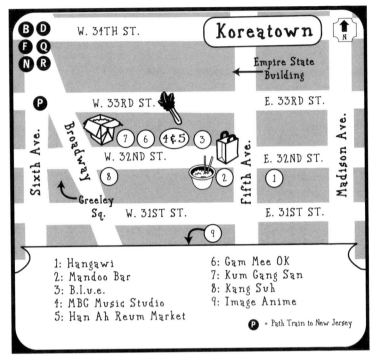

"Korean Americans have established a strong presence in New York through small businesses, cultural activities, increasing political activities, community activism, and the emergence of the growing second-generation Korean American population."

Most Korean immigration to New York City took place after the 1965 Immigration Act eased the quota system that was imposed on nations outside the Western Hemisphere. The change in the law brought into the country family members of those already residing here, students who stayed after graduation, wives of American soldiers, and skilled professionals who found work as the American economy expanded and boomed. During the period between the early '70s and the '80s, mostly well-educated, urban Koreans emigrated here, pushed out of their country by an unstable economy, a volatile political situation, and an explosion in population. Still, for most, it wasn't an easy transition. Upon arrival, they found that the language barrier and local prejudices and suspicions impeded smooth integration into the

public transportation

KOREATOWN (32nd St. between Broadway/6th Ave. and 5th Ave.)
SUBWAY: B, D, Q, F, N, R to 34th St./Herald Sq. BUS: M6 on 6th
Ave. and Broadway to Herald Sq.; M2, M3, M5 on 5th Ave.
FLUSHING, QUEENS SUBWAY: 7 to Flushing/Main St.; BUS: Q66 to
Main St.

American workforce. The Koreans simply responded the way
many other immigrant groups had before them—they started
their own small businesses. Those without capital joined *gae*, or
lending cooperatives, and opened bright and clean produce
stores that met the rising demand for greater freshness and
variety; discount stores; dry cleaners; seafood shops; nail salons;
and wholesale markets selling goods from Korea.

During the economic recession of the early '70s, Korean
merchants moved as a group into what is now Koreatown. Because
the area was considered somewhat dangerous due to its then-
seedy state, it was affordable. The first to pioneer the area were
wig importers; at the time, wigs were fashionable in the West.
Korea, earlier a big supplier of human hair for use in wigs, turned
its cheap and dexterous labor force to wig production using
improved synthetic hair, and Korean wig importers/wholesalers
set up shop in the neighborhood. Retailers came to restock their
merchandise, with business meetings taking place in the restaurants that grew up around the wholesalers. When the demand for
wigs decreased, the attention turned to hair accessories, scarves,
gloves, sunglasses, and handbags. Koreans entered the garment
trade as well; today clothing wholesalers and sweatshops stretch
above 32nd Street and the outlying area.

When the Korean economy burgeoned in the '80s, Koreatown grew accordingly (there are four Korean banks in the
immediate area). As it expanded, other businesses and services
that cater to native Koreans, like bookstores and travel agencies,
opened. The result of all this growth and success is that today,

Newspapers in almost any Asian language may be found in New York City. Here, a reader enjoys a moment in the sun with a Korean-language paper in Greeley Square.

Koreans enjoy the reputation of being one of the most highly productive ethnic groups in the city—not to mention, the country. However, Chung-wha Hong of the NKASEC cautions: "Korean New Yorkers face complex challenges of intergenerational issues, relationships, and tension with other ethnic and racial minorities, and the need to respond to barriers that prevent the full participation of Korean Americans in our society. To fully appreciate the successes, contributions, and hardships of the Korean American community, one must move away from the simplistic 'model minority success' myth and start to look at the complexity that characterizes the Korean American community as a vibrant, dynamic, and constantly transforming ethnic minority community."

film & performing arts

"New York City is a jam session of all people and languages. Within this urban crucible, I am striving to create my own sound, an expression of the Asian American experience."

—JASON KAO HWANG,
renowned composer and violinist;
and leader of his ensemble, the Far East Band

I f the proverbial melting pot—everyone melding discreetly into one identity—was America's 20th-century design for living, the 21st-century model has immigrants to America holding fast to their root cultures while also reveling in the American lifestyle. And nowhere is this more evident than in New York's performing arts world, where Asian American artists develop their work in a lively stew of traditional, multicultural, and intergenerational influences. But even if more and more Asian American artists are coming in to their own, this is a scene broken into many separate worlds, all struggling to define themselves aesthetically and culturally. An adventurous, even fearless, spirit may be the closest thing to a common defining attribute.

One thing is a given: This is a most opportune time to witness the artistic rumblings of future greats and the phenomenon of an Asian and Asian American art and film world working to define itself as it helps to bring the New York arts scene to its next level.

Overleaf: Qurban Fakirs of Shah-Jo-Raga performed in the Asia Society's Festival of Vocal Music of India and Pakistan. (Photo © Rachel Cooper)

fILM

If an Asian immigrant of 50 years ago was suddenly transported to the New York of today, one of the first things he would be struck by is the absence of ethnic movie theaters. In fact, recent years have seen dramatic changes in theater attendance and the movie-watching habits of the city's Asian immigrant population. The main culprits behind these changes are the hot home video market, the growing number of ethnic television stations, and the assimilation of Asian groups into American society and their involvement in mainstream American activities.

In the 1970s, there were still a stalwart handful of ethnic movie theaters in Manhattan's Chinatown devoted to screening the latest fare from Hong Kong. These theaters were the remnants of a string of popular Cantonese-language filmhouses that had sprung up in the 1930s to entertain the neighborhood's mostly

Caught at a moment between marquee updates, the Eagle theater in Jackson Heights is dedicated to screening the films of India's "Bollywood."

bachelor population of immigrant workers. The names of the
theaters are legendarily lyrical—the Sun Sing, the Rosemary,
the Pagoda—and legend they are, for all ten are now gone. The
Pagoda was the first to vanish, demolished in 1992 and
replaced by an office tower. The Rosemary, the last, was turned
into a Buddhist shrine in 1996. Just a year ago, its West Coast
counterpart, the Great Star Theater, the last of San Francisco's
Chinatown theaters, also died in a whisper, to laments from
many who remembered passing pleasant hours in Chinese-
language movie houses during their formative years. When the
Great Star passed, writer Edward Liu eulogized it, calling the
old Chinatown theaters "cultural lampposts which remind us
of who we are and where we came from."

Other ethnic filmhouses in New York fared little better. An
early-'60s showcase for Japanese films was the Toho Studio,
which leased the 55th Street Playhouse across from City Center.
It subsequently underwent several metamorphoses, including a
period as a porn theater, until it was torn down. By the '80s,
attempts to sustain a showcase for East Indian cinema succeeded
when the Gramercy Theater became an Indian movie theater.
But it too failed to ignite, and has since been converted to a
legitimate off-Broadway theater. Fortunately, one classic Indian
movie house still exists in Queens. The **Eagle Theater,** in Jackson
Heights, may be the last theater in New York catering to an
ethnic audience. It retains some of the atmosphere of the specialty movie house, with Indian sweets for sale and audiences
consisting of families who consider the moviegoing experience
a real event. For that—as well as for the singing-dancing pleasures afforded by a Bombay talkie—a trip to the Eagle is highly
recommended.

The closing of the ethnic movie theaters was a clear sign of
the changes in the way Asian Americans in New York experience
film. It seems the immediacy of seeing movies from their homeland in the comfort of home has superseded the theatrical experience. Home video outlets have become the dominant mode of
distribution for Asian films in the United States. You can witness

this phenomenon by walking through the city's ethnic neighborhoods and browsing through the local video stores.

Asia on video

The Indian population is spread out all over New York City, and so are its sources of the latest videos from Bollywood, the nickname for the Indian film industry—which remains the largest in the world, a humongous conglomerate churning out melodramas, musical romances, and farces with musical interludes that must be seen to be believed. You'll find video stores tucked among the row of Indian restaurants that line Sixth Street in the East Village, amid the spice shops and Indian-food buffets in Manhattan's East 20s—**Naghma House,** on Lexington Avenue has a particularly broad selection—and throughout Jackson Heights.

Asia on the Tube Although the home video market has become one of the major sources of distribution for many Asian films, there is also leased-time programming from Asia on the public access channels in New York City. Included is the **Filipino Channel,** shown over Time Warner's Manhattan Cable on Saturday afternoons; on Sunday afternoons, the same channel shows television from Taiwan. **NHK,** the major television station in Japan, will lease time off and on from the smaller public television stations in the area. Asian American programming sometimes can also be found on the cable station of the **City University of New York.** (Turn to Media in Services for additional listings.)

In the East Village you'll find **Anime Crash,** a specialty store, dealing with the Japanese animated film (anime). Japanese titles on video make up a large part of the stock of **HQ Video;** there is an emphasis on anime titles, as well as exploitation titles (the softcore "pink" films, some of which are subtitled). **Sunrise Mart,** one of the main components of the East Villlage's Little Tokyo, carries a wide variety of Japanese videos for rent, as does **TIC Akean,** in the same neighborhood. In the Rockefeller Center area the place for Japanese videos is **Kinokuniya Bookstore;**

there, you can browse through a stock of classic Japanese films on video (for sale only), an anime section, and Japanese comic books and film magazines.

These days "Chinatown" is almost a misnomer, with the recent influx into the neighborhood of immigrant populations from Vietnam, Malaysia, and Cambodia. In both of the city's Chinatowns—in Flushing and lower Manhattan—you'll find not only the popular Hong Kong action releases and other exports but shops that stock movies in Vietnamese as well. The Chinese population, once comprised largely of Cantonese emigres, has also changed, with people settling in from many other Chinese provinces. If you walk across Canal Street in lower Manhattan, you'll find sidewalk vendors selling movies on videocassette, and hole-in-the-wall shops that stock Hong Kong martial arts movies. Be warned, however: There's no way to vouch for the goods sold by Canal Street vendors; there's a good chance you may be purchasing something entirely defective.

High-end video stores throughout Manhattan offer a wide range of Asian film. **Kim's Video,** a small chain of music and video stores in lower Manhattan, is known for stocking hard-to-find foreign videos, and has an extensive anime stock (complete with accompanying toys and dolls), in addition to a large stock of Hong Kong action films. **World of Video** in the West Village is another good source.

going to the movies

New York's vintage movie theaters are largely history, and video stores may be the main source for ethnic movies, but there are still plenty of places in Manhattan where you can actually see screenings of Asian or Asian American films, both new and old. Several organizations, national film commissions, and consulates provide screenings, film events, and a wealth of information on Asian cinema. **Asia Society** has been the major institution devoted to showcasing the arts and cultures of Asia in New York City. The organization has a history of extensive cultural programming, including many film series and premieres, often in conjunction with exhibitions of art and photography. Asia Society's programs have been designed with the aim of cultural exchange, presenting the full range of the arts from Asia and the Pacific region.

Another renowned bastion of cultural exchange is the **Japan Society,** housed in a building constructed in the 1960s near the United Nations. The Society's film series (which usually runs on the weekends) has been a popular city staple for over two decades. Programming covers thematic shows—a series featuring "sword-play classics" was held in the last few years—retrospectives of classic directors (Ozu, Mizoguchi, Kurosawa, and many more), as well as an annual series of recent films from Japan (usually held in the fall). Kyoko Hirano, the dedicated director of the film program, does an admirable job of keeping this program active and relevant, adding guest speakers and seminars to the screenings.

Asian Cinevision (ACV), which founded the annual Asian American International Film Festival over twenty years ago, is the leading Asian American media organization in New York City. The festival takes place in the summer. Over the years, ACV has also sponsored a children's film festival, a video festival, and media production workshops. The organization started out as a news outlet over cable access, producing a daily news program in Chinese in 1975 out of a tenement building on East Broadway. One of the founders of ACV was Tsui Hark, a film student who would return to Hong Kong to become the highly acclaimed director of such films as *Peking Opera Blues* (1984). Vivian Huang, the program director, has started bimonthly screenings of recent Asian and Asian American films at Anthology Film Archives, in addition to the annual film festival.

The **Korean Consulate** sponsors film screenings; in the fall of 1999, the consulate put on a three-month series covering the history of Korean cinema at the Hammerstein Auditorium of Columbia University. Beginning in 2000, it started a monthly screening of new films from South Korea in the conference room of the **Korean Cultural Service,** also home to Gallery Korea.

In order to promote cultural exchange, the Taiwanese government leases a theater in the Rockefeller Center area. The **Taipei Theater** has shown a variety of performing arts, as well as art exhibitions and film series. Cultural activities have been somewhat curtailed of late, but you might contact them at the **Chinese Information and Culture Center** to find out what programs are currently available.

The **Philippine Center** has been a lively site for exhibitions and events, collaborating with other organizations and film venues to showcase Filipino films: An example would be the recent summer festivals of Filipino films presented in conjunction with the Film Society of Lincoln Center at the Walter Reade Theater.

Several cinematheques and museums in New York City have programmed and continue to program Asian films; among these are the **Museum of Modern Art,** the **Brooklyn Museum of Art,** the **American Museum of the Moving Image** in Astoria, Queens, and the **Brooklyn Academy of Music's Rose Cinemas (BAM Cinemathek)**. Asian and Asian American films and filmmakers have been presented at two major centers for experimental film, **Anthology Film Archives** and **Millennium Film Workshop**. The **Pioneer Theater** opened in 1999, promising an eclectic mix of independent and experimental film programming. Three other film showcases in New York City, the **Walter Reade Theater, Film Forum,** and the **Screening Room,** have programmed Asian films. (Film Forum was one of the first non-Chinatown venues to play a Hong Kong film, when it showed *Peking Opera Blues* in 1985; the Screening Room recently showcased a series called "Japanese Outlaw Masters.")

The **Solomon R. Guggenheim Museum** has been developing a media program under the direction of John Hanhardt: from February to April 2000, the museum held a retrospective of the pioneering video artist Nam June Paik, complete with a series of film screenings related to his work. The **Whitney Museum of American Art** has a media program dedicated to experimental film and video; over the years, there have been Asian American talents featured, beginning with the experimental feature films of the Japanese artist Arakawa, shown during the first season of film screenings in 1970.

Some of the more adventurous independent theaters in New York have eclectic programming, and include Asian films; these theaters include the **Angelika Film Center,** the **Quad,** and **Cinema Village**. Cinema Village, for example, provides a screen for small-distribution Asian-theme films such as 1999's *Genghis Blues,* but no longer has its summer festival of action films from Hong Kong. The audience for these films remains, as can be seen in the avidity of the video market, but the Hong Kong film industry has changed, and the action films of Hong Kong are no longer a commodity. The changeover from British rule to Chinese rule in Hong Kong saw many of the major talents (such as the director John Woo, and the actors Chow Yun-Fat, Jackie Chan, and Jet Li) accepting offers from Hollywood.

The film-school connection

The creative collusion and fusion of Asian American filmmaking is alive and well in New York. Asian cinema is a popular subject of study in New York's schools—and many Asian American filmmakers learned their craft under the guidance of non-Asian teachers in New York's famed film schools.

In terms of academic resources, **New School University** (formerly The New School for Social Research) has rotating courses on a wide range of cinema subjects, including Japanese cinema. The **Asian/Pacific/American Studies Institute**, now at **New York University** offers courses in Asian American art and Asian American film. As mentioned, Asian Cinevision offered workshops in media production during the '70s; other minority media organizations that still offer media production workshops include **Third World Newsreel** and **Downtown Community Television**.

The acclaimed programs at the **New School, NYU, Columbia University,** and the **School of Visual Arts** have led many Asian and Asian American students into filmmaking careers.

Playwright David Henry Wang (left) and film director Ang Lee (right) with Ismail Merchant as he is presented with the annual Media Award at the Asian American International Film Festival in New York. (Photo © Corky Lee)

For many years, the NYU Film Department was run by Christine Choy, the Korean American documentary filmmaker whose films include the Academy Award–nominated *Who Killed Vincent Chin?*

In 1989, the Hong Kong director Stanley Kwan shot his feature film *Full Moon in New York* in New York City; though financed by a Hong Kong production company, most of the crew had been recruited from the Asian professionals who had been involved with many of the media organizations cited above. Ang Lee, who graduated from NYU, began his feature film career with *Pushing Hands*, financed by Central Motion Picture, a Taiwanese production company, but shot in New York City in 1991. Two years later, Lee would direct *The Wedding Banquet*—also financed by Central Motion Picture, but one of the first Taiwanese-financed films to go into commercial distribution in the United States; this movie would prove to be one of the most successful "independent" productions of the year, and is certainly the most popular Chinese-language movie released in the United States to date.

A Lengthy Assimilation

The history of Asian film in New York City is surprisingly long and complex. During the earliest days of film (from the 1890s through the period just prior to World War I), there was a great deal of film activity in what is now the greater metropolitan area. Thomas Alva Edison had his Black Maria studios—the first film studios in the United States—across the river in New Jersey. Many of those who worked for the Edison company during this preliminary period of film production were people from Asia. Even skills honed in Edison's studios, however, could not keep Asian film workers from facing discrimination in the American entertainment industries. Without a place to work in America, many Asian filmmakers (even those who had been born in this country) returned to Asia, where they could do their work without encountering prejudice. Many of those who returned to Asia went on to help create the film industries of their respective countries: China, Japan, the Philippines.

While much has changed since then, and progress has been made, the Asian film community in New York City still faces challenges, not unlike those faced by the creators of the Asian American International Film Festival, which began in New York in 1977. The festival, the nation's first film gathering dedicated wholly to screening works by filmmakers of Asian descent, was created at a time when the lack of opportunities for Asian American talent in the media was glaring, and finding distribution for Asian films in the United States was at best a challenge and at worst a shot in the dark.

Today, the problems of commercial distribution for foreign films continue. Still, the recent box-office successes of John Woo, M. Night Shyamalan (The Sixth Sense), and James Wong (Final Destination), as well as the continuing careers of Ang Lee and Wayne Wang, are clear evidence of the assimilation of Asian and Asian American talents into the American motion picture industry. This assimilation is part of the next stage of Asian and Asian American film in New York City.

PERFORMING ARTS

Traditional Asian performing arts have been alive in New York since at least as early as the 1930s, when Chinese, specifically Cantonese, opera could be found here. Up until the mid-Fifties, however, performers were brought to the metropolitan area only on a sporadic basis, and were often billed as exotic extravaganzas. The active role the Asia Society took in 1956 began to change this as the organization sought to de-exoticize performers and their art by presenting them in a cultural context. By the early '70s Asian performing arts were regularly scheduled in venues throughout New York City, with an emphasis placed on discovering performers that had never been exposed outside of their home regions—a sea change strongly influenced by the enthusiasm and vision of Beate Gordon, then-director of Asia Society's performing arts programs.

As part of an APA Heritage Month performance at the American Museum of Natural History, a Korean ensemble demonstrates playing a traditional hour-glass drum to a participant from India. (Photo © Corky Lee)

Activism in the Arts

The Asian American performing arts community has had a long, notable history of activism. Some artists, like the Asian American performance troupe **Peeling the Banana,** an ensemble whose members are always changing, even carry a mission statement "to use autobiography and community building as a departure point for performance pieces that concern Asian Americans as artists and as members of a larger, multiracial community." Composer **Fred Ho** and the band **Yellow Peril** frequently lend their talents to community causes such as rallies in support of anti-Asian violence and the Chinatown labor struggle. Ho even named his own production company Big Red Media, which presents such disparate entertainments as Black Panther music/video ballets, martial arts ballets, and "womyn" warrior operas. Arts collectives such as the **South Asian Women's Creative Collective** also use the arts as empowerment for individual and community advancement.

Today, the Asian presence in New York's glittering performing arts world is alive, well, and in evidence at the highest levels. The scene is wonderfully diverse, a mosaic that is as multifaceted as the arts themselves, with influences both multicultural and intergenerational. Traditional Asian forms—presented as faithful renderings of music, dance, and theatrical rituals—are regularly performed by a constantly rotating roster of visiting artists from Asia. But in the last quarter century or so, Asian American avant-garde artists have also become a force to be reckoned with. And for many of these artists, a recurring theme has been that of identity.

The term "Asian American" grew out of the 1960s American Civil Rights movement—and indeed, the theme of identity politics has manifested itself in the work of artists from different eras, class, and ethnic backgrounds in fascinatingly diverse ways. Today's Asian American arts scene offers a full range of identity politics that runs the entire gamut from experimentalists like rock/hip-hop/funk band **Yellow Peril** (whose raison d'être is to create work that is "in-your-face" vis-à-vis Asian American politics) to classical works by the **National Asian American Theatre**

Company (NAATCO), which features Asian casts performing European and American classics, and 1940s swing music from the bandleader **George Gee and His Make Believe Ballroom Orchestra**. Each of these artists, it could be said, makes a statement of sorts, bringing up the oft-asked question: Just what is Asian American art? Does it have to have an Asian face or "theme," or is it defined by the fact that its author or creator is an artist of Asian descent? No simple answer to this question exists; suffice it to say that this multifaceted genre is producing the kind of serendipitous inventions that bubble up wherever root cultures marinate in foreign soil.

Whatever their political bent, these talented artists have in New York City a wealth of showcase stages and venues to strut their stuff, from Broadway to the legendary **La MaMa** off-Broadway to the **World Music Institute, Asia Society,** and **Summerstage** to **P.S. (Performance Space) 122** and the **Brooklyn Academy of Music**. Performers are working in traditional art forms, reflecting their identity to their communities as well as to the greater New York population and pushing the envelope in less traditional venues as well, from hip-hop to comedy to performance art.

Homegrown Talent

New York draws artists, dancers, musicians, and actors from all points of the world to create and perform. But the multicultural gumbo that is Gotham is now seasoned with a rich homegrown group of artists, second- and third-generation Asian Americans who have fashioned thrilling new work from the melding of different cultures. Nowhere is this more apparent than in the Asian American performing arts community.

Right now, this scene is more robust and diverse than ever. But it is also spread out and somewhat disparate. Correspondingly, the Asian American arts scene in general is at a crossroads. It is no longer solely a grassroots community, but it has yet to become a commercially viable entity or a instantly recognizable brand—making the road a tricky but thrilling one for artists to navigate.

For some, the nebulous nature of the scene can pose problems. "Mainstream venues don't take us seriously, and the very few Asian American arts groups are very poor or too conservative," laments **Fred Ho,** a veteran musician/composer of musical theater works that have been staged at such venues as the Brooklyn Academy of Music's "Next Wave" festival, and the experimental emporium **The Kitchen,** among others.

Other artists, like the up-and-coming choreographer **Maura Nguyen Donohue,** founder of **In Mixed Company,** see the climate as inspiring in a different way. "I think it's a great time to be Asian in this city," she says. "It may be because front-running veteran artists like [Chen & Dancers founder] H. T. Chen and [Pan Asian Repertory Theatre founder] Tisa Chang have paved the way, or because all things Asian have suddenly become in."

If there is any center to the Asian arts world in New York, it is the **Asian American Arts Alliance,** an arts service and resource organization founded in 1983 to increase the support, recognition, and appreciation of Asian American arts. In addition to its busy schedule of workshops and public forums, the alliance also publishes a bimonthly calendar, an annual Directory of Asian American Arts Organizations and Touring Artists, and *Dialogue,* a fine, in-depth quarterly magazine about APA arts. Also check out its most informative website (www.aaartsalliance.org).

Theater: The play's the Thing

Of all the city's Asian American performing arts, the theater perhaps best mirrors the living experience of the Asian community in New York, with points of view almost as diverse as the city itself.

The longest-running Asian American theater company in New York, the **Pan Asian Repertory Theatre,** has specialized in first-class productions of Asian-themed plays for audiences of all ages since 1976. Specializing in Chinese-themed plays (in Chinese and English) for audiences of all ages is the **Yangtze Repertory Theatre,** who have worked out of many different spaces over the years. The **National Asian American Theatre**

Ping Chong and his performance group, Ping Chong & Company, have been pioneers in most aspects of avant-garde theater. (Photo © Josef Astor)

Company, an OBIE Award–winning theater group, features Asian casts performing European and American classics ranging from Molière's *School for Wives* to William Finn's *Falsettoland*. Since 1989, the **Ma-Yi Theatre Company** has been the premier Filipino American theater company in the country. They began their second decade by expanding the scope of their work to include that of any Asian American artist interested in tackling relevant issues.

On the more eclectic side is **Ping Chong & Company,** founded by performance artist Ping Chong in the early 1970s following his stint with the legendary New York City avant-garde performance artist and composer Meredith Monk. As David Henry Hwang, playwright of the Tony Award–winning M. *Butterfly,* reflects: "Ping Chong and Company has been a pioneer in so many categories that it's hard to comprehend them all. Dancer, performance artist, avant-garde innovator, Asian American interculturalist, director, choreographer, actor—Ping Chong has encompassed them all with his unique style, meticulous craftsmanship, and consummately theatrical voice. In the final analysis, this artistic giant cannot be categorized, because his work knows no limits."

And on the grittier side of the city's Asian American theatrical experience are such newer troupes as **SLANT,** composed of three men, Rick Ebihara, Perry Yung, and Wayland Quintero, who made an auspicious debut in 1995 with the not so subtly titled piece *Big Dicks, Asian Men.* "SLANT is the freshest performance art/small theater company in the U.S.," says Fred Ho. "Their work is irreverent, satiric, raucous, and thoroughly Asian American. It's no-holds-barred, 'go-for-the-jugular' stuff." Another new company to keep an eye on is **Second Generation Productions,** who specialize in Asian American–themed musical theater pieces.

The door was opened for many of the more avant-garde theaters—like Ping Chong, and SLANT—at the mother of all off-Broadway theaters in New York City, **La MaMa E.T.C.** (Experimental Theatre Club), where such groundbreaking works as *Hair* and *Godspell* first hit the boards. "[La MaMa Founder/Artistic Director] Ellen Stewart has opened the doors of La MaMa to a large net of Asian American artists and artists from all over the world for almost half a century, and nurtured an audience for a global vision of theater," says award-winning choreographer Muna Tseng, whose **Muna Tseng Dance Projects** has been produced at La MaMa since 1992. ". . . La MaMa E.T.C. has always been a home creatively and spiritually for me."

Dance:
Asian sensibilities/western forms

Both traditional Asian and modern forms of dance are on display in the wide-ranging dance scene in New York. One of NYC's foremost practitioners of traditional Asian dance is the **Chinese Folk Dance Company,** who perform a vast repertoire of Chinese classical, folk, and ethnic-nationality works. Through costume, movement, and music, these performances evoke the ancient, classical, and indigenous folk cultures of China. A highlight of their season is their Annual Lunar New Year Concert, held at the Tribeca Performing Arts Center, which includes Peking Opera with spirited acrobatics.

One of the first and still foremost movement image makers in the Asian American community is **Chen & Dancers,** founded by H. T. Chen in 1978, whom choreographer Maura Nguyen Donohue calls "the indomitable mentor for NYC's Asian American dance community." The company fuses the spirited energy of American modern dance with the poise of traditional and contemporary Asian aesthetics. While Chen & Dancers also started at La MaMa, they now primarily operate out of the Mulberry Street Theater in Chinatown, which has become a prime showcase for younger and emerging Asian dancers.

Since 1986, the aforementioned Hong Kong–born dancer/ choreographer Muna Tseng, a frequent Ping Chong collaborator, has built Muna Tseng Dance Projects into a company that has become world-renowned for their seamless fusion of Asian sensibilities and Western abstract forms.

Asian American dancer/choreographers have always been a vital part of New York's downtown modern dance scene—but not without the usual artists' struggles. "As a dancer/choreographer in NYC, life is hard—survival, paying rent, visa issues, etc.—and this is not the place for everyone," says choreographer Joyce Lim. "But because of the diversity of this city, New York has been a place where I can really explore issues about my culture, heritage, and race with other Asian people from around the world. I would not have contact with them in Malaysia or other parts of the U.S. It is amazing how many issues we as Asians have with each other; how much history and prejudice comes with our upbringing." As a Chinese Malaysian currently based in New York City, Lim finds the most successful way she communicates

Sam-Oeun Tes, a native Cambodian who teaches as well as performs, presents a traditional dance at the APA Heritage Festival in Union Square. (Photo © Corky Lee)

with an audience, regardless of culture, age, or background, is through the construction of images.

Veterans such as **Yoshiko Chuma and the School of Hard Knocks** and Donna Uchizono have, since the early 1980s, created and performed experimental and multidisciplinary dance and dance/theater works that were rooted in the postmodern minimalist aesthetic that predominated when they were first getting started. Newer artists like Joyce Lim collaborated with Nami Yamamoto in the 1999–2000 season on an irreverent identity piece entitled "Wan Dollah" at **Danspace Project**. In that same season, Maura Nguyen Donohue's In Mixed Company presented an evening of dances choreographed to the music of punk/folk "grrl" Ani diFranco entitled *Righteous Babes* (as a reference to her self-created record label of the same name) at P.S. 122.

music: An urban jam session

There may be no more diverse and electric arts scene for Asian American performers in New York than the music scene, ranging from such internationally renowned classical stars as Yo-Yo Ma, Sarah Chang, and Midori, to up-and-coming rappers like Double O and everyone else in between. "New York City is a jam session of all people and languages," says renowned composer and violinist **Jason Kao Hwang,** whose diverse resumé ranges from leading his own ensemble, the Far East Side Band, to composing an opera based on oral histories from New York's Chinatown, to contributing source music to the Martin Scorsese film *Kundun*. "Within this urban crucible, I am striving to create my own sound, an expression of the Asian American experience."

One group that Hwang has strong praise for is **Music from China,** which has performed a number of his contemporary compositions at both Lincoln Center's Merkin Hall and the Asia Society over the past two years. "They are an extraordinary ensemble that has performed both traditional and contemporary music for over twenty years," Hwang says. "I, along with all of Chinatown, love their annual productions. Last summer I attended one of their Cantonese Opera productions in Chinatown. During one of the last scenes, I found myself surrounded by Chinese American grandmothers crying softly during a tragic aria sung by a 'ghost.' It was a wonderful, extraordinary performance."

Japanese Americans celebrate together during the April ritual **Sakura Matsuri (Cherry Blossom Festival),** a weekend-long festival of Japanese American arts and crafts featuring the UJC Asian Jazz Ensemble at the Brooklyn Botanic Garden. The festival, which honors the blossoming of spring, includes the performance of taiko drums, whose name is derived from the pre-Buddhist phrase meaning "peaceful, harmonious drums." The taiko drum is said to represent the voice and spirit of the Japanese people. The first East Coast taiko performing troupe, **Soh Daiko,** who often perform throughout the city, have been combining exhilarating music and movement into a not-to-be-missed spectacle since 1979.

Among New York's East Indian population is a noted new presence on the avant-jazz/classical scene, pianist/composer Vijay Iyer, who is also a scholar of ethnomusicology and cognitive science. "I peer through a cloudy lens at my South Asian ethnic and American cultural heritages," says Iyer of his artistic process, "as well as at my own peculiar personal history. I also use my music as an occasion to conduct experiments: What would happen if . . . ?"

A burgeoning pop/soul, rock/hip-hop Asian American music scene features such new notables as rapper Double O, pop/soul diva **Toni Wang,** city folksinger/songwriter Angela Ai, and rock/funk bands such as 101 and Superchink. Asian hip-hop artists include Korean American Jamez and Filipina Kuttin' Kandi. These younger artists embrace the "sound-collage"–oriented approach to their music and frequently include audio samples that pay homage to their ethnic identities; **Jamez,** for example, fuses Korean instrumentation and vocalists into his modern hip-hop ensemble of DJ and studio. But, as Toni Wang says "It is difficult to identify a specific venue as Asian American artists are pretty dispersed in the places at which they choose or are chosen to perform." Wang suggests that anyone wanting to know more about these artists and where they are performing in the New York area should contact the Asian American Arts Alliance and **Coalition of Asian Pacific Americans (CAPA)**—the sponsors of the annual Asian Pacific American (APA) Heritage Festival. "Though these are not necessarily performing venues per se, they are homes where APA artists can go to for networking purposes and support."

And Javanese and Balinese gamelan, traditional forms of music that are based on melodic percussion, have found a home with the **New York Indonesian Consulate Gamelan.** This informal group normally holds practices every Tuesday evening at 6 p.m. at the Indonesian Consulate in NYC. Newcomers are always welcome to come and watch, or join in. Performances of both types of gamelan music are given a few times a year.

A very different weekly ritual is George Gee and His Make Believe Ballroom Orchestra, regulars at Lincoln Center's "Midsummer Night's Swing," who also let loose every Tuesday and Thursday at Swing 46.

Of course classical music has an equally strong voice–with collaborations by such artists as Yo Yo Ma and pipa virtuoso Wu Man, and Cho Liang Lin. Also, composers such as Zhou Long, Chou Wen Chung, and Tan Dun create contemporary new music with distinctly Asian and Western aesthetics.

A wide range of Asian and Asian-influenced artists are often programmed at the **WNYC-FM**–sponsored New Sounds Live concerts. And if you can't make it out for a live performance, an Asian mix may be heard periodically on both David Garland's Evening Music show (8–10 p.m., Monday through Thursday) and on the New Sounds show hosted by John Schaefer, every night from 11 p.m. to midnight at 93.9 FM. "Asian music has always been a part of our New Sounds programs, even though it is just that—a part. The show spans a wide range of contemporary music, from computer and electronic music to the traditions of Africa and Asia that provide the roots for so much of today's music. In that context, it's essential to recognize the importance and the beauty of the music, both old and new, being made in Turkey, Iran, India, China, Indonesia, Japan, Tuva, and throughout the whole Asian continent." He has recently featured avant-garde wizard of the toy piano Margaret Leng Tan; new music from Japan, with works from Ryuichi Sakamoto and others; classical Indian *dhrupad* music with Wasifuddin Dagar; and Pakistani *qawwali* music.

spoken word & performance Art

The stand-up-comedy scene in New York City has become much more than straight jokes delivered fast and furiously to the crash of a drum cymbal. These days, stand-up, spoken word, and performance art have become seamlessly meshed, creating a whole new genre, where long, in-depth monologues tell a story, and the literature—and in some cases even the author—leaps off the page and onto the stage.

This new genre is a prominent one in the Asian American performing arts community. This spoken word/performance scene ranges from limited engagements of full-blown autobiogaphical theatrical fare from the likes of **Margaret Cho** (who, even though she is a Californian was voted one of the 1999 New Yorkers of the Year in *New York* magazine) to actor **Aasif Mandvi,** who, with his acclaimed one-man show, *Sakina's Restaurant,* became the first South Asian performing artist to have an extended off-Broadway run, and noted up-and-coming "pure" stand-up comic and Bronx native **Alladin.** One of the city's foremost and quintessentially homegrown Asian American spoken word performance artists is **Regie Cabico,** who first earned his renown by winning poetry slams—poetry competitions in which performers are judged on an Olympics-style scoring system—at the now-legendary **Nuyorican Poets Cafe,** on Manhattan's Lower East Side.

"My memory of walking to a Wednesday night open mike at the Nuyorican Poets Cafe is the surreal experience of seeing barflies to my right and fledgling poets getting numbers for their reading to my left," says Cabico. "The pure Alphabet City pre-commercial theatricality was overwhelmingly magical. . . . The instant community I felt and the first time I won a Friday Night was electrifying. . . . A standing ovation from this audience is like being a matador." Cabico recommends that first-time visitors check out the Slam during Grand Slam or Semi-Final Slam time. In addition to his own performances, Cabico also curates "Writers on the Ledge," a monthly spoken word series at **Dixon Place** on East 26th Street. Other notable Asian American spoken word/performance artists include Aileen Cho and Beau Sia, who, like Cabico, also blend racial, sexual, and identity politics into bitingly irreverent and thoroughly entertaining works.

The ground-zero venue for Asian American spoken word/performance artists in New York is the **Asian American Writers' Workshop (AAWW),** which hosts readings and performance "caravans"—tours featuring authors conducting writing workshops and performing readings of their work. Mei Ng, author of the acclaimed novel Eating Chinese Food Naked, likens the Workshop to "a homecoming to a home that I never really had and never really knew to miss until I found it. Instead of plugging away in a vacuum, when you're doing readings at the space or participating in caravans, you can bond with other Asian American writers," Ng says, "and you don't have to explain what 'Chinese mom hair' is!" (For those who don't know, "Chinese mom hair" refers to the standard haircut of Chinese mothers of a certain generation.)

In addition to the AAWW, A/APA authors and spoken word/performance artists can also be heard and seen at the **Poetry Project at Saint Mark's Church,** as well as in more mainstream settings such as the **Asia Society, Joe's Pub** at the Joseph Papp Public Theater, and at the Maya Lin–designed room at the **Asian/Pacific/American Studies Institute** at New York University.

Beyond Manhattan:
More performing Arts

Adventurous souls should walk over to 14th Street and take the L train under the East River to Williamsburg, Brooklyn—New York's fastest-growing arts haven. Once there, check out the goings-on at **Galapagos,** a multidisciplinary performance art/music/dance space, and the **Williamsburg Art & Historical Center,** which frequently showcases Japanese art and performing artists.

In Queens, you'll find performances through organizations such as the Flushing Council on Culture & the Arts/Flushing Town Hall (718 463-7700; www.flushingtownhall.org), **Taipei Economic and Culture Office**, the Queens Museum of Art (718 592-9700; www.queensmuse.org), and at **Flushing Meadows-Corona Park,** as well as the **Queens Botanical Garden**.

For another "outer borough experience," take the Staten Island Ferry to see the excellent Asian American performing arts programs offered at the **Chinese Scholar's Garden** at the Snug Harbor cultural center, and at the **Jacques Marchais Museum of Tibetan Art.**

At the north end of New York City, the Bronx is home to Asian American programs as well. **The Bronx Museum of the Arts** often holds events in conjunction with similar-themed visual-arts exhibitions, and/or group shows that feature Asian American artists. Beautiful **Wave Hill,** along the Hudson River, is a frequent sponsor of outdoor dance performances that may feature Asian artists. And, the **New York Botanical Garden** often has performances related to their annual "Chinese Garden and Tree Peony Festival" in May.

film &
performing arts
THE LISTINGS

Cultural Offices

(see also Cultural Offices and Continuing Education in Services)

Asia Society. This is the major institution promoting cultural understanding between Asia and the United States. For almost fifty years, the Society has presented a world class performing arts and film program, featuring many artists in their U.S. debuts. Today, the organization is involved not only in presenting innovative works by Asian and Asian American artists but also in producing and commissioning new works (725 Park Ave., NY; 212 517-ASIA [2742]; www.asiasociety.org; 6 train to 68th St. *Note:* During renovations, the Asia Society is housed [until Fall 2001] at 502 Park Avenue; 4, 5, 6, N, R train to 59th St./ Lexington Ave.).

Asian American Arts Alliance. You can't do better than to consult its bimonthly newsletter—the Asian American Arts Calendar—an invaluable guide to all sorts of cultural events involving Asian and Asian American talent in New York City, for film screenings and the performing arts (75 Varick St., NY; 212 941-9208; www.aaartsalliance.org; 1, 9 train to Canal St.).

China Institute. The China Institute offers a number of different programs related to traditional and contemporary Chinese civilization, culture, and heritage. Besides art exhibitions, the Institute offers classes, lectures, book signings, films, and cultural performances to the public. Programs especially for corporations and educators are also available (125 E. 65th St., NY; 212 744-8181; www.chinainstitute.org; 6 train to 68th St.).

Chinese Information and Culture Center (Taipei Theater/Taipei Gallery). Run by the Taipei Economic and Cultural Office, the center's mission is to promote Taiwanese arts in New York City; it sometimes has film screenings as well as performances and exhibits(1221 Ave. of the Americas, NY; 212 373-1850; www.taipei.org; B, D, F, Q train to 47–50th sts./Rockefeller Ctr).

Coalition of Asian Pacific Americans (CAPA). Resource organization for Asian Pacific Americans and sponsor of the annual Asian Pacific American (APA) Heritage Festival (12 W. 18th St., NY; 212 989-3610; www.capaonline.org; 4, 5, 6, L, N, R train to 14th St./Union Sq.).

Japan Society. Home of one of the longest-running Japanese film programs, Japan Society always presents fascinating film series, including extensive retrospectives of major Japanese directors such as Ozu, Mizoguchi, and Kurosawa. The Society also presents the most interesting performers in traditional and contemporary music, dance, and theater from Japan. The auditorium is unusual because of the width, designed with the dimensions of Noh and Kabuki theater in mind. (333 E. 47 St., NY; 212 832-1155; www.japansociety.org; 6, E, F train to 51st St./Lexington Ave.).

Korean Cultural Service. The Korean Consulate sponsors Gallery Korea as well as monthly screenings of recent films from Korea at their consulate office (460 Park Ave., 6th floor, NY; 212 759-9550; www.koreanculture.org; 4, 5, 6, N, R train to 59th St./Lexington Ave.).

Philippine Center. Sponsors film screenings at other sites throughout the city, but maintains gallery space for exhibits; in 1998 and again in 2000, the Philippine Consulate co-sponsored a series of recent films from the Philippines at the Walter Reade Theater (556 Fifth Ave., NY; 212 575-4774; E, F train to Fifth Ave.).

Multidisciplinary Venues

The Bronx Museum of the Arts. Fine arts museum that regularly showcases Asian visual artists and related spoken-word, film, and performing arts events (1040 Grand Concourse, Bronx; 718 681-6000; D, 4 train to Yankee Stadium/161st St.).

Brooklyn Academy of Music. Presents the celebrated "Next Wave" festival of arts, which often features Asian and Asian American performers (30 Lafayette Ave., Brooklyn; 718 636-4100; www.bam.org; B, M, N, R train to Pacific St.; D, Q, 2, 3, 4, 5 train to Atlantic Ave.; G train to Fulton St.).

Brooklyn Botanic Garden. Many a tree grows in Brooklyn's sprawling landscape paradise that is ideal for idyll reflections and inspiring walks. Be sure to allot some quality time to be spent in the tranquil Japanese Garden, and if you're nearby in April do not miss the "Matsuri," or "Cherry Blossom Festival," a weekend-long festival of Japanese American arts and crafts featuring the UJC Asian Jazz Ensemble (1000 Washington Ave., Brooklyn; 718 623-7200; 2,3 train to Eastern Parkway).

Chinese Scholar's Garden at Snug Harbor. Chinese-themed garden and fine arts gallery located in Staten Island's world-class fine arts museum and cultural center, Snug Harbor. Asian cultural and performing arts events are regularly held in the Scholar's Garden and elsewhere on the grounds. On the weekends dim sum and other light food fare is available (1000 Richmond Terrace, Staten Island; 718 448-2500; Staten Island Ferry, then S40 bus to Snug Harbor).

Jacques Marchais Museum of Tibetan Art. Tibetan fine arts museum and cultural center that features an all inclusive and eclectic selection of lectures, spoken word, film, and performing arts events (338 Lighthouse Ave., Staten Island; 718 987-3500; Staten Island Ferry, then S74 bus to Lighthouse Ave.).

The Kitchen. A space for both emerging and established artists who wish to expand their fields through interaction and exchange of interdisciplinary ideas (512 W. 19th St., NY; 212 255-5793; A, C, E train to 14th St., www.thekitchen.org; L train to 8th Ave.).

P.S. (Performance Space) 122. An eclectic assortment of performances are presented here, usually involving dance or theater in one way or another (150 First Ave., NY; 212 477-5288. www.PS122.org; L train to First Ave., 6 train to Astor Pl.).

Summerstage. Wonderful outdoor performance venue in Central Park; showcases numerous music and theater pieces by Asian artists (72nd St. and Fifth Ave. at Rumsey Field in Central Park, NY; 212 360-2777; 6 train to 68th St., or B, C, train to 72nd St.).

Wave Hill. Set on a luxuriant twenty-eight acres of gardens and forest along the Hudson River, Wave Hill's mission is to facilitate the exploration of the complementary relationship between humans and nature. Dance groups that perform here are often selected from the many Asian and Asian American goups in the New York area (675 W. 252nd St., Bronx; 718 549-3200; www.wavehill.org; 1, 9 train to 231st St., transfer to the BX 7, BX 10 to 252nd St.; Metro-North from Grand Central to Riverdale Station)

film

Film and Video Organizations

Asian Cinevision. The premier Asian American media organization in New York City, which presents the annual Asian American International Film Festival each summer (133 W. 19 St., 3rd floor, NY; 212 989-7870, 989-1422; www.asiancinevision.org; 1, 9 train to 18th St.).

Downtown Community Television. One of the last of the community-based video organizations, founded by Jon Alpert and Keiko Tsuna; it has production workshops, screenings of documentaries, and many other activities (87 Lafayette St., NY; 212 966-4510; www.dctvny.org; A, C, E, N, R, J, M, Z, 6 trains to Canal St.).

Millennium Film Workshop. Holds media production workshops and weekly showcase for independent and experimental filmmakers (66 E. 4th St., NY; 212 673-0090; www.millenniumfilm.org; F train to Second Ave.).

Third World Newsreel. Documentary collective founded in the '60s, creating documentaries on social issues, often dealing with minority perspectives; distributor of films and videos by minority artists; holds media production workshops (545 Eighth Ave., NY; 212 947-9277; www.twn.org; A, C, E train to 34th St.).

Movie Theaters and Other Screening Rooms

(*see also Cultural Offices listings, above*)

American Museum of the Moving Image. Screens many historical and retrospective film programs, including international selections (35th Ave. at 36th St., Astoria, Queens; 718 784-0077; R, G train to Steinway St.).

Angelika Film Center. Six-screen independent movie house, specializing in the latest independent and foreign film releases (18 W. Houston St., NY; 212 777-FILM/531; www.angelikafilmcenter.com; B, D, F, Q train to Broadway/Lafayette).

Anthology Film Archives. Showcase devoted to independent and experimental film (32-34 Second Ave., NY; 212 505-5110; www.anthology filmarchives.org; F train to Second Ave.).

Brooklyn Academy of Music's Rose Cinemas (BAM Cinemathek). Eclectic and imaginative programming of international films (30 Lafayette Ave., Brooklyn; 718 623-2770; www.bam.org; B, M, N, R train to Pacific St.; D, Q, 2, 3, 4, 5 train to Atlantic Ave.; G train to Fulton St.).

Cinema Village. One of the earliest art houses in New York City, recently renovated to accommodate three screens. Shows independent and foreign films, as well as special rereleases of classic titles (22 E. 12th St., NY; 212 924-3363; N, R, 4, 5, 6, L train to Union Sq.).

Eagle Theater. One of the last of the ethnic theaters in New York, this one showing Indian films; this is an old-fashioned movie house, seating about 500, which has been outfitted with ethnic snacks and evocative posters. The usual fare is the latest from Bollywood, the Indian film industry commercial staples of melodramas and comedies with lavish musical interludes (73-07 37th Rd., Jackson Heights, Queens; 718 205-2800; E, F, G, R train to Roosevelt Ave./Jackson Hts.; 7 to 74th St.-Broadway in Queens).

Film Forum. A veritable institution, this three-screen movie house shows independent and foreign films, as well as a wide-ranging revival program. (209 W. Houston St., NY; 212 727-8110; www.filmforum.com; 1, 9 train to Houston St.).

Pioneer Theater/Two Boots. A brand-new movie theater, specializing in American independent and new foreign film releases; around the corner from the Two Boots Pizza Parlor (155 E. 3rd St., NY; 212 254-3300; F train to Second Ave., 6 train to Bleecker St.).

Quad Cinema. The first multi-screen movie house in New York City, dedicated to eclectic programming of American commercial, American independent, and foreign films (4 W. 13th St., NY; 212 255-8800; www.quadcinema.com.; F train to 14th St.; L train to Sixth Ave.).

The Screening Room. Eclectic programming of American independent and foreign films, with an attached restaurant (54 Varick St., NY; 212 334-2100; www.thescreeningroom.com; 1, 9, A, C, E train to Canal St.)

Walter Reade Theater. The best small movie theater in New York City, run by the Film Society of Lincoln Center, to showcase important foreign, American independent, and classic films (70 Lincoln Center Plaza, NY; 212 875-5600; www.filmlinc.com; 1, 9 train to 66th St.).

Video Sources

Anime Crash. Video store with a specialty in Japanese anime titles; for sale only. The store is a small, East Village storefront, with a distinct specialty air, filled with items that are for the aficionado of this particular form of animation (13 E. 4th St., NY; 212 254-4670; www.anime crash.com; 6 train to Astor Pl.).

HQ (High Quality) Video. Video store specializing in imported Japanese titles, specifically in anime and in softcore "pink" titles; for sale only (21 W. 45th St., 2nd floor; 212 221-0027; B, D, F, Q trains to 42nd St.; 7 train to Fifth Ave.).

Kim's Video. Paradigmatic Village video stores with students of film in mind; outstanding anime and Hong Kong action selections. Four locations (85 Ave. A, NY; 212 529-3410; 6 train to Astor Pl./6 St. Marks Pl., NY; 212 505-0311; 6 train to Astor Pl./144 Bleecker St., NY; 212 260-1010; A, C, E, B, D, F, Q train to W. 4th St./350 Bleecker St., NY; 212 675-8996; 1, 9 train to Christopher St.).

Kinokuniya Bookstore. Well-presented books, magazines, manga, and anime—in Japanese and English—plus an interesting selection of books of pan-Asian interest at the grande dame of Japanese bookstores (10 W. 49th St., NY; 212 765-7766; www.kinokuniya.com; B, D, F, Q train to Rockefeller Center).

Naghma House. Carries an extensive selection of videos and DVDs for both sale and rental from the Indian subcontinent, in languages such as Hindi, Tamil, and Telegu. A large collection of music is available as well, from classics to bhanghra for the younger audience. Indian musical instruments are also for sale (131 Lexington Ave., NY; 212 532-0770; 6 train to 28th St.).

Sunrise Mart. This ultra-hip East Village Japanese market carries a wide array of Japanese movies to rent (4 Stuyvesant St., 2nd floor, NY; 212 598-3040; 6 train to Astor Pl.).

TIC Akean. Video store on 9th Street toward Second Avenue that rents Japanese videos (not subtitled) and sells Japanese books and magazines (229 E. 9th St., NY; 212 982-6074; 6 train to Astor Pl.).

performing arts

Arts Education

Korean Traditional Music Institute of New York. This art and music school offers a range of classes, with an emphasis on traditional musical instruments and folk dance (137-45 Northern Blvd., Flushing, Queens; 718 961-9255; 7 train to Main St./Flushing).

Lotus Fine Arts Multicultural Music and Dance Studios. Offers a wide array of individual and group classes in many types of Asian music and dance (109 W. 27th St., 8th floor, NY; 212 627-1076; www.lotusarts.com; 1, 9 train to 28th St.).

Radio Hula. Specializes in all things culturally Hawaiian and features Hula dance classes (105½ Mercer St., NY; 212 966-3378; N, R train to Prince St.).

South Asian Women's Creative Collective. An activist collective that uses arts empowerment for individual and community advancement (located in the Asian American Writers Workshop—*see* Spoken Word and Performance Art, *below*).

Dance

Chen & Dancers/Mulberry Street Theater. Dance troupe founded by veteran artist H. T. Chen (70 Mulberry St., NY.; 212 349-0126; www.htchen dance.org; A, C, E, J, M, Z, R, N, 6 train to Canal St.).

Chinese Folk Dance Company/New York Chinese Cultural Center. Performing a vast repertoire of traditional Chinese classics (390 Broadway, 2nd floor, NY; 212 334-3764; www.chinesedance.org; A, C, E, J, M, Z, N, R, 6 train to Canal St.).

Dance Theatre Workshop. Chelsea dance workshop that often presents emerging artists (219 W. 19th St., NY; 212 924-0077; www.dtw.org; 1, 9 train to 18th St.).

Danspace Project. Performance space for dance (St. Mark's Church-in-the-Bowery, 131 E. 10th St., NY; 212 674-8194; 6 train to Astor Pl., N, R train to 8th St.).

The Joyce Theater. Chelsea performance space that often features contemporary and ethnic dance. (175 Eighth Ave., NY; 212 242-0880; www.joyce.org; A, C, E train to 14th St.).

Maura Nguyen Donohue Dance Projects/In Mixed Company. Cutting edge modern dance performance art troupe (917 207-5373; www.inmixedcompany.com).

Muna Tseng Dance Projects. World-renowned dance company that weaves Eastern and Western modern dance forms into a seamless quilt (e-mail: munatseng@aol.com).

Tribeca Performing Arts Center. Performance art space (199 Chambers St., NY; 212 346-8510; A, C train to Chambers St.).

Yoshiko Chuma and the School of Hard Knocks. Founded in 1984 as a collective of artists from diverse backgrounds and differing art forms under the direction of choreographer/director Yoshiko Chuma. Its purpose is to create, perform, encourage, and sponsor experimental and multidisciplinary dance and dance/theater works in a variety of venues (212 533 9473; e-mail: ychuma@aol.com).

Music

Chinese Cultural Arts Center (Taipei Economic and Cultural Office). Chinese musical instruments and masks on display. Also, the Haitien Hsiang-Yin Chorus rehearses here every Sunday. The bilingual choir, led by noted Taiwanese conductor Pi-Chu Hsiao, performs Chinese and American folk and religious songs (41-61 Kissena Blvd., Flushing, Queens; 718 886-7770; www.taipei.org; 7 train to Main St./Flushing).
George Gee and His Make Believe Ballroom Orchestra. Classic swing band plays at Swing 46 on Tuesday and Thursday nights (718 779-7865; www.georgegee.com; Swing 46; 349 W. 46th St., NY; 212 262-9554; www.swing46.com; C, E train to 50th St.).
Music from China. Musical ensemble performing both traditional and contemporary works all over the city (212 941-8733).
New York Indonesian Consulate Gamelan. A group promoting Javanese and Balinese gamelan music. Open practices held weekly, performances held several times a year (N.Y. Indonesian Consulate, 5 E. 68th St., NY; 212 879-0600; idt.net/~jvn/gamelan.htm)
Soh Daiko. East Coast taiko drum performing troupe (212 941-9208; www.sohdaiko.com).
WNYC-FM (93.9). New York's National Public Radio affiliate; often features cutting edge Asian music on their New Sounds program and, more occasionally, on the Evening Music show (93.9 FM; New Sounds is on every night at 11 p.m.; Evening Music airs Monday through Thursday from 8 to 10 p.m.).
World Music Institute. Specializing in Indian, Persian, and all South/East Asian music, WMI is a not-for-profit concert presenter—at different venues throughout the city—of traditional music from around the world. It also operates a CD and video retail outlet that features similar musical fare (49 W. 27th St., NY; 212 545-7536; www.hearthe world.com; N, R train to 28th St.).

Spoken Word and Performance Art

Asian American Writers' Workshop. Founded in the early 1990s, this book publisher and bookseller has fast become a cornerstone of NYC's Asian American cultural scene. Dedicated to the creation and dissemination of Asian American literature, the AAWW publishes award-winning anthologies and numerous literary journals and newsletters, while housing a busy schedule of readings, spoken word events, and the South Asian Women's Creative Collective and numerous other smaller organizations (16 W. 32nd St., NY; 212 228-6718; www.aaww.org; B, D, F, Q, N, R train to 34th St./Herald Sq.).

Asian/Pacific/American Studies Institute at New York University. Academic institution and regular presenter of lectures, spoken word, and visual arts events in a handsome gallery space designed by the award-winning architect, Maya Lin (269 Mercer St., NY; 212 998-3700; 6 train to Astor Pl., N, R train to 8th St.).

CBGB Gallery. Sunday night Poetry Slams at 8 p.m. (315 Bowery; 6 train to Bleecker St.).

Cornelia St. Cafe. Features music, play readings, and spoken word events (29 Cornelia St., NY; 212 989-9319; A, B, C, D, E, F, Q train to W. 4th St.).

Dixon Place. In addition to Regie Cabico's monthly "Writers on the Ledge," and other spoken word events, it also hosts a variety of theater, dance, music, and performance art events (309 E. 26th St., NY; 212 532-1546; 6 train to 28th St.).

Galapagos. A cutting edge, multidisciplinary performance art/music/dance space that is fast becoming the centerpiece of the burgeoning bohemian scene that is Williamsburg, Brooklyn (70 N. 6th St., Brooklyn; 718 384-4586; L train to Bedford Ave.).

Joe's Pub. The cabaret space at the legendary Joseph Papp Public Theater featuring spoken word and music events (425 Lafayette St., NY; 212 539-8770; www.publictheater.org; 6 train to Astor Pl., N, R train to 8th St.).

KAYA. A small literary publisher of innovative and challenging Asian and Asian American diasporic writing that also presents readings and other spoken word events (373 Broadway, NY; 212 343-9503; www.kaya.com; A, C, E, N, R, J, M, Z, 6 train to Canal St.).

Museum of Chinese in the Americas. Museum that features readings and much more (70 Mulberry St., NY; 212 619-4785; www.moca nyc.org; A, C, E, R, J, N, M, Z, 6 trains to Canal St.).

Nuyorican Poets Cafe. Friday Night Poetry Slams and more (236 E. 3rd St., NY; 212 505-8183; www.nuyorican.org; F train to Second Ave.).

The Poetry Project at St. Mark's Church. A leading forum for innovative poetry, the Poetry Project offers support for poets through weekly readings and writing workshops (131 E. 10th St., NY; 212 674-0910; www.poetryproject.com; 6 train to Astor Pl.).

Williamsburg Art & Historical Center. Cultural institution that frequently showcases Japanese art, spoken word, and performing artists in the heart of Williamsburg (135 Broadway, Brooklyn; 718 486-7372; www.wahcenter.org; L train to Bedford Ave.).

Theater

Fred Ho c/o Big Red Media. Composer and his production company present wide range of avant-garde and experimental works (212 760-4980; www.bigredmedia.com).

La MaMa E.T.C. (La MaMa Experimental Theatre). The mother of all performance spaces (74/A E. 4th St., NY; 212 475-7710; www.la mama.org; 6 train to Bleecker St.).

Ma-Yi Theatre Company. The nation's premier Filipino American theater company (212 581-8896; www.ma-yitheatre.org).

National Asian American Theatre Co. Asian performers act in traditional classics (718 623-1672; www.naatco.org).

Pan Asian Repertory Theatre. Performs at Playhouse 91 (316 East 91st St., NY; 212 505-5655; www.panasianrep.org; 6 train to 96th St.).

Peeling the Banana. Performance ensemble with changing repertoire and activist bent; also active as a writing and performing workshop (Contact: Asian American Writers' Workshop, 16 W. 32nd St., NY; 212 228-6718; www.geocities.com/tokyo/pagoda/2927).

Ping Chong & Company. Troupe founded by renowned performance artist Ping Chong. Performs most often at La MaMa. (212 529-1557; www.pingchong.org).

Rajkumari Cultural Center. This center works to preserve both the cultural traditions and contemporay creativity of the Indo-Caribbean community. Workshops are offered in various locations as is the annual Kitchrie Festival (no permanent location; for information call 718 805-8068).

Second Generation Productions. Theater company specializing in Asian American–themed musical theater (212 334-4777; www.2g.org).

SLANT. Small theater troupe specializing in satirical, irreverent works (212 714-7189; www.slantperformancegroup.com).

Yangtze Repertory Theatre of America. Specializing in Chinese-themed plays for audiences of all ages (2 Mott St., Suite 706, NY; 718 263-8829).

asia in brooklyn

It's a bright, brisk, beautiful spring day at Midwood High School in south-central Brooklyn. In a fourth-floor room, Ishaq Bukhari, 17, a junior from nearby New Utrecht High, is feeling just a tiny bit agitated. He shifts about in his seat, clutching a wad of neatly written notes. He glances out the window at the schoolyard below, where fellow students are both shooting hoops and shooting the breeze. Bukhari's light hazel eyes have the mildly concerned, slightly unfocused gaze of an Oscar nominee just before the results are announced. Then, his name is called and in an instant he seems to harness his emotions, nervous energy magically transformed into a quiet confidence. He walks up to the podium, turns to face the audience, and flashes a brief, brilliant smile. It's money time at the Urdu Bilingual Oratory Olympics, and Ishaq Bukhari is about to nail his speech.

Bukhari left Pakistan to join his immigrant parents in Brooklyn several years ago. He remembers the day he arrived. The first thing that struck him was "the smell of America. I could smell the difference. When I first arrived, I said, 'What is this place?' I thought I was dreaming." In the beginning, he says, "it was hard to adjust to American life. There was such a huge difference in society and culture." Now that he has been here long enough, Bukhari says he is used to the routine of everyday life in the United States—like attending a coeducational school. "In

The exquisitely restored Japanese Hill-and-Pond Garden in the Brooklyn Botanic Garden.

Pakistan, girls and boys don't mix in the same classroom. There, it's a separate society, and here it's a combined society."

With around 150 Pakistani students at New Utrecht, Bukhari has many friends he can relate to. They are devout Muslims for whom daily prayer and arranged marriages are cultural norms to be embraced and accepted, customs that most of their American counterparts can hardly begin to fathom. The sporting talk is of cricket instead of baseball. Bukhari and his buddies dream of cricketing glory and playing organized matches among high schools in Brooklyn. Medical school is still a few years away. "Life is not so bad," he says.

In Brooklyn, which could be the moon as far as most Pakistanis are concerned, Bukhari and his friends remain faithful to the strict mores dictated by their culture and religion. Here, where a grand cross section of people of all styles and backgrounds live in a borough of bridges and boardwalks and Brighton Beach summers, Asian children are raised under the watchful eyes of their tradition-minded parents. While life in America can provide the opportunity for a good education and lead to untold riches, many parents are loath to let their kids immerse themselves fully in the American experience. Education officials in New York are respectful of the various cultures represented in schools and work hard to find positive and innovative ways to integrate a foreign culture into the system.

Which brings us to the annual Urdu Bilingual Oratory Olympics. Several people in the room are not conversant in Urdu—the literary language of Pakistan—but it is still obvious to everyone that the students (representing seven Brooklyn schools) deliver their well-rehearsed speeches with deep pride, passion, and fiery conviction. Material ranges from treatises on traditional values ("The Dignity of Hard Work"; "Respect Your Teacher") to poems about love and religion. Bukhari explains that his recitation—"I Am Not the Merchant of Shining Rays"— is a contemporary poem about "the glories of the world and my nation's ancestors. It tells us to deal with our problems and not to blame fate." His friend Khalid Nawaz Shafi puts the day's pro-

Checker cab, Brooklyn-style. (Photo © Corky Lee)

ceedings into perspective: "It is not a matter of winning, it's a matter of making a statement about our culture."

Barbara Zaffran of the Brooklyn High School Superintendent's Office has been organizing the borough-wide foreign-language Olympics for many years. The Chinese equivalent, for example, is now in its tenth year. Says Zaffran: "This helps to showcase the multicultural population in Brooklyn. We want the students to value their traditions, and bring them to their future lives in America." Peter Kondrat, a bilingual instructor at the school, says it is important to emphasize the need for students to "hold on to their roots and strike a balance before 'finding' themselves in America. The cultural value that's placed on education shows a community in good stead. It's certainly an attraction for Asian immigrants to come to the U.S. and get their slice of the pie."

Nikes and *shalwar kameez*

The students at Midwood exhibit an ironic sense of the dilemma they face in their adopted country. It extends beyond simply wearing Nikes with their *shalwar kameez*—Pakistan's elegant

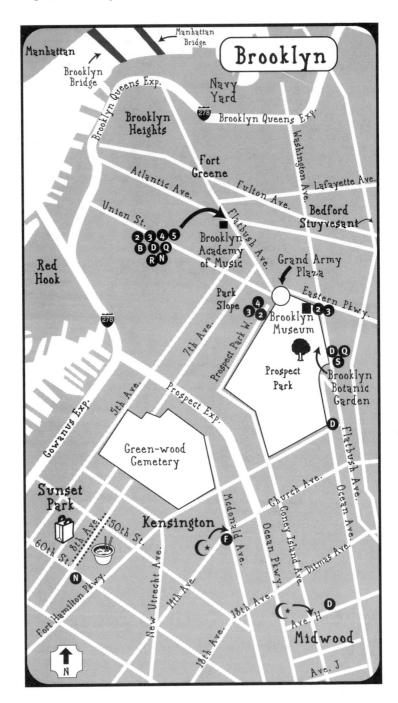

public transportation

KENSINGTON (Church and McDonald aves.) SUBWAY: F to Church Ave.; BUS: B67 to Church and McDonald aves.

MIDWOOD (Coney Island Ave. and Ave. H) SUBWAY: D to Ave. H; BUS: X29 to Coney Island and Foster aves., B68 to Coney Island Ave. and Ave. H

SUNSET PARK (8th Ave. between 50th and 60th sts.) SUBWAY: N to 8th Ave.; BUS: B70 to 50th St. and 8th Ave.

national dress of long shirt and baggy pants. It's difficult to douse the natural exuberance of teenagers, despite the fact that they are obliged to abide by strict social and religious rules. The conflict between stringent core values and a good old American sense of entertainment is brought into sharp focus after a performance by two female students who integrate traditional costumes, modern dance, and a Pakistani pop tune into an energetic welcome dance. They are admonished by Asghar Choudhri, a well-known community leader and invited judge at the Urdu Olympics. "Our culture doesn't start with dancing, it starts with the Koran," he says, eliciting heavy applause from the assembly, punctuated by whoops of approval from Ishaq Bukhari and his gum-chewing, earring-wearing pals. "It's more difficult for parents to adjust over here," says Choudhri. "The children don't feel it [the cultural differences] as much as the older generation."

According to Choudhri, 150,000 Pakistani immigrants live in the Midwood section of Brooklyn, with its epicenter at the junction of Coney Island Avenue and Avenue H. This claim might seem exaggerated in view of the City Planning Commission's 1998 estimate, which pegs the entire Asian population in Brooklyn at about 143,000, constituting 6.2 percent of the borough's total population of 2.3 million. An official at the Commission stresses that its figures are "only estimates" and that there is little doubt that the number of Asians is far greater. Choudhri, the unofficial "Mayor of Midwood," says that perhaps another 50,000 Pakistanis reside throughout the rest of the borough. "The problem with the earlier census is that people were afraid to give their names," says Choudhri, an accountant by training, who, because of his strong standing in the community, works tirelessly to solve problems for new immigrants, many of whom are undocumented arrivals. His modest second-floor office attracts a constant stream of visitors, not all of whom are here to seek his professional services. Some come to express concerns about the city's social services agency, for example. "They don't understand our culture, our way of life. It would help if we could get case workers to have sensitivity training with us."

Choudhri first arrived in Brooklyn in the mid-1960s, but he traces Midwood's birth as a Pakistani enclave to 1982, when the **Makki Mosque** was built on Coney Island Avenue, followed by the opening of the Punjab Grocery in 1984. "The early arrivals were single construction workers and taxi and limousine drivers," says Choudhri. "When they earned enough money, they started their own businesses. Now, lots of people own real estate, and there are many stores and services catering to the community, with more opening all the time. Businesses are thriving."

The Asian subcontinent is also represented by a small but significant Bangladeshi community centered near the F train stop at Church and McDonald avenues in the Kensington section of the borough. Just as in Midwood, the area is anchored by a mosque and a vibrant strip of shops and grocery stores. New York Times reporter Somini Sengupta says there are some very good reasons why this has become a South Asian hub. "The very early Bangladeshi immigrants were sailors who jumped ship and ended up in the construction trade—a low-wage entry into the economy," she says. "They worked in the brownstone renovation industry, and Brooklyn is the perfect place for that. The community sprung up around the subway station, and housing in the area was also relatively inexpensive." Today, the entire borough, Sengupta notes, is a very integrated place. "The Pakistanis in Midwood live side-by-side with Orthodox Jews—two deeply religious communities in apparent harmony." There is another

Bangladeshi enclave in the Bedford Stuyvesant area, but compared with that in some other parts of the city, "Brooklyn doesn't have the same concentration of Asians. They happen to be newer immigrants." Still, says Sengupta, "all you have to do is walk up and down the streets of these neighborhoods and you can feel the Asian presence."

The city's second chinatown

Asian Americans are the fastest-growing group in New York, and the Chinese community undoubtedly accounts for the dragon's share of Asians in Brooklyn. According to official 1998 statistics, about 140,000 ethnic Chinese are spread primarily among the adjoining neighborhoods of Sunset Park, Bensonhurst, Bay Ridge, Borough Park, and Sheepshead Bay. Another 70,000 or so live in the rest of Brooklyn. As with the Pakistani community, though, undocumented arrivals make it more than likely that the actual numbers are much higher. Paul Mak, President of the **Brooklyn Chinese-American Association,** says that the move to

Barber shop along Eighth Avenue in the heart of Sunset Park's growing Chinatown.

Brooklyn began in the early 1980s, as part of an overflow situation from Chinatown in Manhattan. "In the mid-'80s, more new immigrants chose to concentrate around Sunset Park because the N train provided a direct link to Chinatown." Mak says moving to Brooklyn provided plenty of opportunities at that time, because of low rents and empty storefronts. The migration continued through the early 1990s, and today, the neighborhood is more than 90 percent Chinese. "Even if you have money, you can't buy a house here," Mak says.

A stroll along Eighth Avenue between 50th and 60th streets in Sunset Park will verify Mak's assertions. The street is bustling with activity and lined with Chinese food stores, restaurants, travel agencies, and video outlets. "Dollar vans"—ubiquitous vehicles that charge about $1.50 per passenger—ply the neighborhood streets, providing door-to-door shuttle service for workers, many of whom still make the commute to Manhattan. Mak estimates that there are 200 garment factories and 700 Chinese-owned businesses in Brooklyn, making the community an economic force in the borough.

The importance of Sunset Park lies in the fact that, unlike Flushing or Queens, the Chinese community there is a direct extension of Chinatown in lower Manhattan, according to Peter Kwong, director of Asian American Studies at Hunter College in Manhattan and author of several books on the immigrant experience. "We're talking about a community where non-English-speaking Chinese can find a job and work and operate without knowing English," he says. Kwong admits that such rapid development is not without its pitfalls. "The growth of the Asian population has provided a great deal of cheap labor for the city, but the proliferation of garment factories in Brooklyn is cause for concern, partly because they don't have unions and partly because many of the workers are illegals."

Social issues aside, visitors to Sunset Park will find much to savor, not least of which is the excellent quality of its restaurants. At **Ocean Palace,** a dim sum and seafood restaurant that the *Zagat Restaurant Survey* says is "just like Hong Kong," owners Danny Tsoi and Jimmy Ching epitomize the immigrant success story. "When we came here in 1989, a lot of people said we were crazy, but we wanted to take a shot at a new neighborhood," says Tsoi, who started his career as a busboy in Chinatown. "A year later, everyone was saying we had very sharp business sense." Now, Tsoi employs over 100 full-time staff. According to Ching, who runs the duo's second restaurant, on Avenue U, the reason for their success is that they cater to the different needs of different clientele. "Brooklyn," he says, smiling, "has been wonderful to us."

Back at Midwood High, Ishaq Bukhari collects his gold medal, and Asghar Choudhri stands up to address the students one last time. It is as much a summation as a lesson in survival. "Always remember," he says, "in this country, your unity is strength."

diversions by day & night

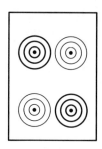

7

It's been said that New York is a place where people play as hard as they work. The Asian immigrant community is no exception. Throughout the five boroughs, the city's Asian population immerses itself in both traditional forms of recreation and thoroughly Americanized fun. Asian youths fill the city's pool halls; Japanese men and women alike play shogi chess and flock to area golf courses. The emerald cricket fields of the city's universities and parks are populated largely by South Asians, who now dominate a sport first introduced to their native countries during the time of British colonial rule. Pakistani men gather in Queens' **Flushing Meadows–Corona Park** each weekend to compete at the ages-old game of kite fighting, their fingers wrapped in duct tape to protect against the glass-coated strings they hold, the kite-fighter's best weapon. Meanwhile, East Indian music comes to the metropolitan area by way of popular all-night music festivals, a centuries-old tradition in India.

In Manhattan's Chinatown, while the fortune-tellers set up rickety tables in Columbus Park, Chinese youths pound the pavement on the park's basketball courts. Just around the corner, a Chinese chess club discusses the intricacies of xiangqui. Even the

A father shows his son how to play "Kuling-Tang" gongs, as dancers from a performance celebrating Filipino Moro culture at the Public Library in Woodside, Queens, look on. (Photo © Corky Lee)

A sampling of Vietnamese food at one of the annual Asian Pacific American Heritage Festivals, this time at Lincoln Center. (Photo © Corky Lee)

traditional Chinese funeral is a form of entertainment, with a brass band wailing as it accompanies the funeral procession up Mulberry Street. The bustling business at local OTB parlors testifies to the community's recreational interest in gambling. Behind steel doors, basement rooms hold privately-run gaming parlors, where the diversion of the hour might be pai-gow, fan-tan, mah jongg, or straight poker.

In the evening, when the city's nightcrawlers head out to play, Koreatown opens its private karaoke rooms for business. The blissful warbling goes on until the wee, wee hours of the morning. Late-opening sake bars, selling lesser known—and often pricey—varieties of the traditional Japanese drink, stay busy throughout the night in the East Village and Nolita.

At different seasons, traditional Asian festivals and holidays are celebrated with vigor and pageantry throughout the city. In fall, the Korean Harvest Moon Festival and the Hindu Festival of Lights, or Diwali, take place; in late winter, there's Chinese New Year of course, and Tet, the Vietnamese New Year; then, in May, myriad events celebrating the birth of Buddha, take place, to name a few.

Even a perhaps unexpected destination like the **Bronx Zoo** gets into the act, with special festivals of its own. The Zoo regularly presents weekend-long events like the "Festival of Mongolia" and the "Journey to China," which feature dance, storytellers, folk arts, and interactive arts and crafts in conjunction with its permanent animal viewing areas: Asia Wild, the Himalayan Highlands, and Jungle World.

Throughout the city, New York's populace goes about its business—working, learning, building homes and careers. And when they are finally able to take a break, they find ways to relax and enjoy themselves. For Asians, such leisure-time activities may involve adapting historical customs and traditions to local soil.

sports & games

Asians in New York love their recreational sports as much as any group, and have smoothly tackled traditional all-American games like hoops and baseball. Some sports and hobbies like cricket and ping-pong, and games of strategy, such as go, chess, and mah jongg, hold particular appeal.

Simply Cricket

Starting in late April or early May, the sports fields of the metropolitan area welcome the cricketers, with their cork balls and their willow bats. In New York, cricket is largely a sport played by South Asians, who, judging by their continued success in the World Cup, have emerged as some of the best cricketers in the world. How did people from India, Pakistan, Sri Lanka, and Bangladesh come to be so cricket-crazy?

"Cricket was introduced in South Asia during the British

colonial days, at a time when there wasn't a lot of entertainment and no real national sport in the respective countries," says Hassan Safdar, president of the Columbia University Cricket Club. "It didn't require a lot of equipment, and as it caught on, everyone started playing in the streets. Plus we've excelled at it—India, Pakistan, and Sri Lanka have all won World Cup titles."

The Columbia University Cricket Club has an impressive pedigree—it is the oldest sports club at the university. And, it plays in one of the oldest tournaments in the country, the Ivy League Tournament. While its 50 members hail from 13 cricketing nations, most are South Asians. They play throughout New York on Saturdays and Sundays from April through October, first in the Ivy League Tournament, and then in the Commonwealth League games.

Chess, Asian Style

Chess in all its forms is thought to have one ancestor, *Chaturanga*, which was invented in India around the 6th or 7th century. One offshoot evolved into *xiangqi*, or Chinese Chess, today one of the world's most popular games. Its name is derived from the Chinese for "elephant chess" because the pieces are wide and the game is played with pounding vigor. New York has a couple of Chinese Chess clubs, the **New York Chinese Chess Association** and the **United East Athletic Association**. *Shogi*, or Japanese chess, differs from other chess games in that the pieces taken from the opponent can be used as reinforcements. *Shogi* is represented in New York by the **New York Shogi Club,** which recently hosted the largest *shogi* tournament in the world outside Japan.

Anime Jones

In a dark room on the third floor of the School of Visual Arts at 5 p.m. on a Sunday, the window blinds are drawn shut. Some 30 people are sitting, rapt, staring at a small TV monitor. They have been here since noon, watching Japanese cartoons, and talking about Japanese cartoons. It's the monthly meeting of the **Metro Anime** club, formed to share in and celebrate a passion for the singular genre of animation unique to Japan called anime.

The Metro Anime club was formed to give New York anime aficionados a forum to discuss anime and share videotapes, laser discs, and CDs. Because the anime hobby can get pretty pricey (imported Japanese CDs cost from $30 to $40), the club has formed a lending library, which allows members to check out subtitled anime tapes free of charge.

What is it that draws New Yorkers to spend so much time watching and trading anime (pronounced "ah-nee-may")—Japanese animated stories—and reading *manga* (Japanese comic books and magazines)? What is so compelling to young girls about the adventures in the TV series *Sailor Moon* and *Card Captors*? Why are young men drawn to *Trigun* and sci-fi epics like *Gasaraki*? What has made Pokémon such a commercial phenomenon?

"Well, all I can say is that there are a lot more Americans influenced by Japanese animation than the other way around," says Joe Mazzel, who works at **Forbidden Planet**, a comics store near Union Square. Unlike most of American animation, Japanese anime covers a wide variety of issues and subjects. "It's not just about good guys and bad guys," says Angela Washington, the president of Metro Anime's lending library. "Anime is much more complex and more filled with symbolism than American animation."

Seth Robertson, another Metro Anime member, conceded that while Japanese graphics, with its limited movement and slow frames, had little of the dazzling innovation of Disney, in the art of anime, plot and characterization were considered more important than the graphics. "The story is given more depth," he says. "The plot builds, revealing little bits of information, and in the end you find the characters and pieces of plot are all connected."

Joe Mazzel says that one reason for the wide-ranging and sophisticated nature of anime is that American animators have had to kowtow to broadcast standards and restrictions, while their Japanese counterparts have been more free to experiment. Adults have as much to choose from as kids. "In Japan, everyone reads comics, not just kids," he says. "It's every bit as accepted a medium as television, and it has something for everyone, both adults and children."

Indeed, there were no children present at the meeting of the Metro Anime club, which appeared to be composed of an equal mix of Asians and non-Asians, ranging from college age to people in their late thirties. Many of the anime videos shown during the meeting dealt with adult themes and problems—but they were also full of fun and wit and imaginatively conceived.

Night falls in the city

New York brings out the nightcrawler in everyone, and the Asian population is no exception. From the young South Asian club kids out to bhangra the night away to the sedate traveler from Tokyo sipping a fine junmai-shu at a sophisticated sake bar, there are options in this city for virtually any kind of Asian nightlife experience.

Karaoke Madness

Karaoke, of course, is a Japanese invention, having originated in Kobe, Japan, some 20-odd years ago. But the entertaining practice of standing on stage and singing into a microphone to the background accompaniment of a popular song has been thoroughly co-opted throughout the world. In New York, karaoke clubs have become as ubiquitous as Gap stores—well, almost. There are karaoke bars, karaoke rooms, karaoke jockeys, karaoke rentals. You can sing your heart out in places like **Winnie's,** a divey Chinatown bar that packs 'em in with an eclectic songlist; **Lucky Cheng's,** in the East Village, which has a nightly drag Kabuki Karaoke lounge; or **Onigashima,** a cool, sedate Japanese restaurant and bar that offers private party rooms with karaoke machines. Many of the Japanese karaoke clubs in New York are private rooms rented out by the hour or are connected to a

καmpαι! To share sake is to perform *oshaku*—to pour for one another. And there are more and more sake bars in which to do so in New York as the variety of sake available here widens to include an impressive number of types and grades. "You don't have to take a trip to Japan," says Bon Yagi, proprietor of **Sakagura**.

Sake is often served warm in bottles called *tokkuri* or *ochoshi*. The small cups from which sake is drunk are called *sakazuki* or *ochoko*. Traditionally, one doesn't pour one's own sake. And when someone is pouring for you, the cup should be picked up and lifted toward the pourer. Sake is also served cold, in *masu*—small wooden boxes—with a little bit of salt sprinkled on the sipping corner. Cold sake is considered by many to be the more sophisticated presentation of the beverage, particularly for the higher quality sakes.

Izakaya sake shops such as **Yajirobei, Decibel,** and Sakagura also serve *sakana* or sake food—small dishes of sashimi, yakitori, broiled mackerel, grilled bonito, eggplant with miso, simmered tofu, pickled daikon radish, tempura, croquettes, *tataki*—a menu selected to complement the taste of the sake.

Japanese restaurant. Openings and closings occur with enough frequency that you should call ahead to make sure the karaoke club is in operation before you go.

One of the hippest spots for karaoke is in Koreatown. Picture this weekend night scene: **B.l.u.e.,** an understated place, with handsome wood floors, minimalist metal chairs and blue couches; the tables are backlit by cool blue neon, and a laser beam scrawls a sassy red zigzag on the ceiling. Pounding music fills the room, easily muffling the chatter from the young, attractive, and laid-back crowd sitting at scattered tables around the club. The waitresses are long and lanky, with iron-straight hair and fashionably high heels. Many of the waiters wear short, spiked haircuts, moussed and gelled to beat the band, some dyed platinum blond. All are buffed, toned, and downtown urbane. No question, it's a good-looking, stylish crowd, even by Manhattan standards.

By 10 p.m., the tables start filling up. B.l.u.e. could be any trendy nightclub in New York, except that here patrons are digging into big, steaming bowls of noodle soup, and the two video monitors are playing Korean hip-hop to choreographed videos—videos that are easily as polished as those on VH1, but restricted to Korean songs—both Korean translations of American songs and original hits by Korean bands. Everyone in the room, it seems, is young and Korean, with a few Japanese mixed in here and there.

At 11:30, the background music stops and the karaoke singing starts at this karaoke nightclub and restaurant on 32nd Street in the heart of Manhattan's Koreatown. Depending on the mood of the KJ (karaoke jockey), the themes range from hip-hop to reggae to teen-throb ballads. B.l.u.e. may be the only karaoke club in Manhattan that plays Korean songs—and only Korean songs. Even the Japanese who come here sing in Korean. Non-Asians are rare patrons, generally arriving with Asian friends. Max Yi, a Korean American who grew up in Texas, said that most of his Korean friends only patronize Korean spots. "They're more comfortable doing so," Yi says, as he works the tables in B.l.u.e. "It's like people in Texas who'll only go to steakhouses."

As a karaoke "club," B.l.u.e. is the rare exception in Koreatown. But wander up and down 32nd Street, between Broadway and Madison Avenue, and you'll see plenty of lighted signs that say KARAOKE, with arrows pointing upward. The signs lead to the neighborhood's wildly popular karaoke rooms, often a floor or two above one of the many Korean barbecue restaurants at street level. These businesses rent out private karaoke rooms by the hour. Many of the rooms, which hold two to twenty people, have flashing strobes in psychedelic colors and serve beer, wine, and food, or let you bring your own. Some places will even record your singing for posterity on a cassette tape.

The karaoke rooms are open all night long, generally closing around 6 in the morning. The businesses stay busy into the wee hours, and the peak time for patronage runs from 11 p.m. to 3 a.m. Each room has a windowed door, which the managers check periodically to make sure everything is aboveboard. All of the karaoke rooms in Koreatown are run by Koreans, but the people who come in are a range of ethnicities. At **MBC Music**

Studio, on West 32nd Street, a choice of three songbooks are offered, one in Korean, one in Japanese, and one in English. The English songbook has a staggering array of offerings, from Elvis's "All Shook Up" to "Begin the Beguine." Koreans use the English songbook to sing along to dance songs by pop singers like Brittney Spears, and ballads by bands such as the Backstreet Boys.

Why are these karaoke rooms so popular? For Brian Kim, who works at MBC Studio, the answer is simple: show biz. "They want to sing! They want to sing! They want to sing!" he says, laughing. Indeed, a glance into any room reveals a throbbing jungle beat, flashes of strobe, and giddy patrons making love to a microphone. For one hour, a stone's throw from the touristed thoroughfares of Manhattan and in the shadow of the Empire State Building, anyone can find stardom in the city.

Bhangra Nights

It just may be the hottest party in New York—and it was born across the seas in the Punjab region of India more than four centuries ago. Bhangra is an electrifying musical hybrid that combines festive traditional Indian folk music with the latest in hip-hop, house, techno, jungle—you name it. It is the focus of the phenomenally popular bhangra party/dance events overseen by Asian American DJs at clubs all over Manhattan since the late '90s. **Basement Bhangra** has been a huge success at S.O.B.'s, where patrons dance against a running backdrop of Bollywood movies, the first Thursday of every month. The **Mutiny Club Night** bhangra parties, held regularly at the Frying Pan at Chelsea Piers' Pier 63, have been equally popular. The DJs work the crowds into dancing frenzies by combining live drum (the haunting Indian dhol) and bass with electronic sounds. "It's very energetic party dance music," says Vijay Balakrishnan, a New York writer. He's one of thousands of hip South Asian Americans attending the parties—although the events are becoming increasingly assimilated, with more and more Anglos joining the throngs. Still, even the parties tend to break down according to group and class. Some events target the South

Asian professional class, with strict dress codes, steeper cover prices, and more pop-style sounds. Other events take a cue from inner-city parties; they're more hardcore, both musically and otherwise. The bhangra DJs—many of them women—have won national renown, as much for their synergistic skills as their innovative use of sounds. DJ Rekha (aka Rekha Molhotra) comes to Basement Bhangra lugging a heap of records and discs with an intriguing collection of sound effects, from classic song samples to car horns blaring to recorded speeches by Malcolm X. As she has pointed out, bhangra is more than just dancing till you drop. Many events are used to raise money for social causes, such as a recent bhangra night for acid-burn victims in Bangladesh.

festivals & celebrations

Traditional celebrations are meaningful and integral to Asian American life—full of ritual and pomp and the comforting reaffirmation of family and friendship. From the lunar New Year to other observations both religious and secular, somber and joyous, the calendar is overflowing throughout the rest of the year.

The Chinatown New Year, in late winter, is a riot of color, music, and street celebration, accompanied by the pounding of drums. The Cherry Blossom Festival (Sakura Matsuri) is held at the Brooklyn Botanic Garden at the end of April or early May. Events celebrating the birth of Buddha follow later, in May. Obon, the Buddhist festival of the dead, usually takes place in July. In August, the Hong Kong Dragon Boat Festival brings a thousands-year-old Chinese sport to Queens, accompanied by a day-long celebration of cultural performances. The Korean Harvest Moon Festival, held annually at the end of September in Flushing Meadows-Corona Park in Queens, offers performances and games. The Japan Society's "Matsuri on 47th Street" festivities follow, and then, later in the fall the Hindu festival of lights—Diwali—a joyous event celebrating the Hindu New Year, is held at South Street Seaport.

Happy New Year!

For most Asian cultures New Year is the celebration of the new lunar year. It usually occurs in late January or early February and starts with the new moon and ends on the full moon 15 days later. Koreans welcome it in with the distinctive sounds of their hourglass-shaped drums; Tibetans gather for a colorful procession that meanders through Greenwich Village; and the Vietnamese observe it as Tet. However it's marked, this is a holiday that even non-Asian cultures are aware of, and it is always a welcome harbinger of spring. For many people living or working in New York's Chinatown, the first day of the new year is the only day of the year they will have off from work. It is a day for friends and families to gather together. Guests may come bearing gifts of oranges, which represent abundant happiness. New Year traditions reflect the region in China a family is originally from, and the level of observation may vary between households. But for many Cantonese, the largest ethnic population in Chinatown, the old customs are still honored and celebrated.

"First you have to clean house," says Rita Leong, a daughter-in-law of Eileen and Larry Leong, the owners and operators of **Canton,** one of Chinatown's most venerable and acclaimed restaurants. "But don't wait for New Year's Day to clean; that's bad luck. Do it before." Some people believe that dust and dirt should be swept out the back door, not the front, which would sweep all the good fortune out of the house. Not only should your house be thoroughly clean, Lee says, but everyone in the family should be wearing new clothes, preferably red, considered a lucky color, on New Year's Day. "Even the underwear should be new," she laughs. In a tradition called hong bao, children and older singles are deluged with money presented in lucky red envelopes by married couples.

Traditions have a special meaning to the Leong family, four generations of which have owned and operated Canton over the course of 40 years. The family is particularly proud of the restaurant's special Chinese New Year's menu, which lets New Yorkers sample traditional Chinese foods eaten during the holiday. The

In Flushing, Queens, a small boy tries out a mini-version of the traditional lion head—usually a three-person operation—here, in celebration of the Chinese New Year, though a lion may be used at many other events throughout the year. (Photo © Corky Lee)

Chinese believe that certain foods help usher in the New Year with good fortune and bonhomie. It is customary, for example, to eat vegetarian food on the first day of the new year as a way to honor the Buddha. Oysters represent wealth, and noodles symbolize long life. Chicken is considered good luck and a sign of prosperity—but it should be served along with the head, neck, and feet. Mandarin oranges and fish are also recommended to guarantee prosperity.

During the 15-day celebration, Chinatown patrons are treated to colorful lion dances that are performed in the doorways of

Chinese businesses. These distinctive drum-and-lion rituals are rich with symbolism. The lion—a large puppet, generally manipulated by three people—is there to scare away evil spirits; the drums are there to make the lion dance. The lion listens to the drums, and dances accordingly. Many different Chinese clubs and associations prepare all year for these rituals, and each club's lion strives to be more flamboyantly colored and designed than the last. Indeed, the lion is a powerful symbol in Chinese culture, representing vigor, strength, courage, and inspiration; it is also a common emblem in Chinese architecture.

For centuries, the sound of popping firecrackers has been an essential part of Chinese New Year celebrations. Since the late '90s, a citywide ban on such goods has put a damper on holiday spirits. Once the streets of Chinatown at New Year's were a cheerful cacophony of admittedly nerve-wracking explosions. Since the ban, however, the numbers participating in the local celebration have dwindled radically. Apparently, many Chinese revelers have sought out other, firecracker-friendly venues outside New York City in which to set off the new year.

A Chinese dragon is a much more elaborate affair than the lion—up to 40-feet long, it takes as many as 20 people to handle it. The most important animal in Chinese mythology, the dragon bestows blessings at the New Year. Here, a Taoist priest "wakes the dragon" by dotting its eyes. (Photo © Corky Lee)

Not all Chinese celebrations involve firecrackers and 40-foot-long dragons. Here are some examples of what to expect if you happen to be invited to a more intimate Asian celebration:

Birthdays and Babies

Long life, to the Chinese, warrants a big party, and milestone birthdays are celebrated with a bang. The honoree is traditionally showered with gifts of Chinese gold and treated to a multi-course banquet. Foods include abalone, lobster, and shark's fin soup. Brandy—thought to boost healthy circulation—is the drink of choice.

Bringing new life into the world is another reason to celebrate, which many Chinese do one month after the baby is born. The celebration is actually called a "One-Month Party." According to custom, this is the appropriate period to wait to ensure the health and well being of both mother and child. At it, friends and family join together to meet the new baby; hard-boiled eggs dyed lucky red are served, symbolizing good fortune and fertility.

Weddings

Nuptial traditions in America are followed to varying degrees by people of Chinese descent. Dowries for marriages are still honored in many families. The marriage of Kevin and Rita Leong (of Canton restaurant fame) is a good example. The groom's gifts to his in-laws included a pair of live chickens, a green coconut, and pastries as well as a whole roasted pig. Kevin's in-laws in turn gave him a new suit, a wallet, a belt, and a pair of shoes. The wedding banquet had many elaborate courses; before the banquet, Rita changed from her wedding dress into a long red *cheongsam*, adorned with dragon and phoenix images. The bride and groom were presented with gifts of Chinese gold jewelry, made of soft, 24-karat gold.

Life Is Like a Bowl of Cherry Blossoms

Sakura Matsuri, the annual Cherry Blossom Festival at the Brooklyn Botanic Garden, offers a virtual smorgasbord of Japanese arts and music. Set amid clouds of pink and white blossoms, the spring (late April, early May) festival celebrates the blooming of the Sekiyama (Kwanzan) cherry trees along the garden's Cherry Esplanade. Past events have featured bamboo flute concerts, bonsai exhibits, Japanese storytelling for kids, and workshops in block-printing, calligraphy, and *kyudo* (archery). Visitors can watch artisans create Mataro dolls, startlingly realistic-looking dolls fashioned literally from sawdust and glue, and sing along with the Japanese folk song "*Sakura, Sakura*," ("Cherry Blossom Song") to the accompaniment of the koto, a large wooden instrument with 13 strings that has been around for thousands of years. (*Note: Other aspects of Sakura Matsuri are explored in* Little Tokyo *and* Film & Performing Arts.) Celebrations in honor of the beauty of spring continue into May and June at the New York Botanical Garden. Here, the spectacular display of peonies in full bloom at the **Chinese Garden and Tree Peony Festival** captures everyone's admiring attention.

Buddhism: Birth & Death

The traditional Buddhist festivals in observance of the Buddha's birthday, and that of Obon—commemorating the deceased—are both, in their way, about celebrating and appreciating life itself. Whether honoring those who have moved on, or welcoming the good fortunes we encounter each day, these festivals are wonderful experiences for Buddhists and curious New Yorkers alike.

On the Eighth day of the fourth month in the lunar calendar (generally sometime in May), Buddhists world-wide celebrate the birthday of Sakyamuni Buddha. Events of the day are cen-

The APA Heritage Festival

Held the first weekend in May at either Union Square Park (17th Street and Broadway) or Damrosch Park (behind Lincoln Center), the **Asian Pacific American (APA) Heritage Festival** is a great place to start your journey into different Asian cultures and their local communities. This all-day outdoor festival, which kicks off APA Heritage Month, features continuous music, dance, spoken word, and folk arts performances, and a rotunda with arts and crafts, food, and information booths. The APA Heritage Festival is the centerpiece of the **Coalition of Asian Pacific Americans (CAPA),** a nonprofit organization created in 1979 when President Jimmy Carter proclaimed the very first Asian Pacific American Heritage Week (now, officially, a month).

Kimono-clad dancers perform during the Japanese festival of Obon—observed to commemorate the deceased—in New York's Bryant Park. (Photo © Corky Lee)

tered around local temples in the area (*see* Religion & Spirituality) and include musical performances, food (vegetarian, please), meditation and prayer sessions and a traditional lantern parade honoring both the memory of Buddha and the hope for an enlightened soul. Some of the larger of these parades and ceremonies take place in Flushing, Queens.

On a more solemn note than the Buddha's birthday, Obon is a week-long celebration centered around the Buddhist day of the dead, a time to remember and reconnect with loved ones who have passed on. Rather than mourn the losses, however, the Obon festival finds joy in the remembrance of those close to us. Along with offerings of food for the spirits who are believed to have returned for the event, the festival includes traditional Japanese dancing, music, and games. Most events take place at local Buddhist temples, but Bryant Park has been a site for it, usually with fabulous traditional attire and music. The annual event sponsored by the New York **Buddhist Church** at Riverside Park is another large public observation.

Row, Row, Row Your Dragon

In Hong Kong, in the 3rd century B.C., a poet and reformer named
Qu Yuan drowned himself in the Mi Lo River to protest the cor-
ruption of the government. According to Chinese lore, the towns-
people tried to rescue him by beating their paddles against the
water and pounding on drums to scare the fish away from him.
When it seemed that this wasn't working, they threw dumplings
(*zongzi*) into the water as an offering to Qu Yuan's spirit. The legend
of his death evolved into the **Hong Kong Dragon Boat Festival**,
one of the most important and popular festivals in China—and,
for the past decade, in New York too. Every year in early August
scores of New Yorkers take to the waters of Meadow Lake in

The Hong Kong Dragon Boat Festival, an important and extremely popular
event in China, is gaining popularity here too, drawing thousands of people to
the annual late summer competition in Flushing Meadows-Corona Park. (Photo
© Corky Lee)

MOON FESTIVALS

Probably the second most important festival in Asian culture (after the lunar New Year, of course) is the Autumn Moon Festival, held to honor the full moon. Determined by the Lunar calendar, it generally falls in late August or September. Koreans celebrate it with the **Korean Harvest Moon and Folklore Festival,** a two-day event in Flushing Meadows-Corona Park. This festival actually takes place at a number of locations throughout the city. The celebration at the Staten Island Botanical Garden is of particular interest, as it is located in the unique Chinese Scholar's Garden there. Their **Autumn Moon Festival** features a tea ceremony with Moon Cakes (*see below*), lion dancing, lantern-making, and live music and dance presentations, such as the Chinese Folk Dance Ensemble. The festival also features ceremonies to honor ancestors as well as a lively assortment of traditional games, music, and dancing.

The Moon Cake Story:

In Chinatown, at least, the observation would not be complete without Moon Cakes—very rich, potently sweet cakes made with lotus seed, egg yolks, and sugar—which are eaten after dinner along with fresh fruit, and can range from homemade to expensive imports from Hong Kong, cooked in century-old bakeries using vintage recipes. (*See* Food & Drink *for bakery locations.*) Moon Cakes symbolize togetherness—and indeed the Moon Festival is a family day. After dinner and a sampling of moon cakes, everyone in the family goes up on the roof—a distinctly New York pleasure—to enjoy the evening moon.

Flushing Meadows-Corona Park in long, flat boats to compete for prizes—the biggest being the $10,000 team prize. Each boat seats 20 to 22 rowers, sitting two by two on narrow, thinly padded wooden slats. There is also a drummer, beating out the rhythm for the rowers, at the bow, and a steersperson, keeping them on course with a long wooden oar, at the stern. Each boat has been transformed into a seaworthy dragon, with scales painted down the sides and elaborately carved and painted dragon heads coming off the bow.

Due to its enormous popularity in Asia—and its growing popularity around the world—dragon boat racing is said to be the second most popular sport on earth. The competition in the races in Hong Kong is stiff. Here in New York, aside from the few teams trying to qualify for the Hong Kong racing finals, the mood is much more relaxed. But no matter where you are, the races are much more than just races. They are, as the New York Dragon Boat Racing organization states, "multicultural celebrations and sporting events." There are arts and crafts on display and for sale, dance performances, musical performances, and a parade to start the whole thing off. And there's food—of which *zongzi* are, of course, the focal point. *Zongzi* are made of glutinous rice and filling—traditionally dates, meat, and egg yolks—wrapped in bamboo leaves in a triangular or pyramidal shape.

Matsuri on 47th st.

Each year in September or October the Japan Society of New York invites anyone and everyone to a street festival on 47th street. The highlight of the festivities is a traditional mikoshi shrine procession. The mikoshi shrine (or portable shrine) is used to not only celebrate and give thanks to the spirits, but to rejuvenate ones own spirit through dancing, drumming, and ecstatic shouts from participants and enthusiastic onlookers. The Japan Society festival also includes martial arts demonstrations, art exhibits, and a wonderful assortment of Japanese dishes for tasting.

Diwali

Diwali (or Deepavali), the Hindu festival of lights and new year celebration, usually falls in late October or early November. Diwali both commemorates Ram's journey home from exile and celebrates Lakshmi, the goddess of wealth. The holiday is traditionally celebrated by the lighting of small oil lamps said to guide Ram back to his ancestral home and to welcome Lakshmi into homes for the upcoming year. In New York City, Diwali is celebrated with a massive street festival at South Street Seaport organized by the Association of Indian Associations. The festival includes stalls selling traditional food, two stages for cultural performances, and events such as a re-enactment of scenes from the epic Ramayana and a fireworks display.

diversions

THE LISTINGS

Sports and Recreation

Championship Ping Pong. Where the serious players—and those that want to be—go to compete (78-14 Roosevelt Ave., 2nd Floor, Jackson Heights, Queens; 718 478-7000; E, F, G, R train to Roosevelt Ave./Jackson Hts., 7 train to 74th St./Broadway).

Columbia University Cricket Club. For information on games or joining the club, check out the club's website at www.columbia. edu/cu/cricket or contact Hassan at shs43@columbia.edu or the club secretary Diptabhas Sarkar at ds579@columbia.edu.

Flushing Meadows-Corona Park. Tai chi, Pakistani kite-fighting, and cricket are some of the many activities that can be enjoyed at this historic World's Fair site, which also boasts the Queens Museum of Art, Queens Theater in the Park, the New York Hall of Science, Shea Stadium, and the USTA Headquarters, along with public tennis courts, an ice rink, and fields for recreational use (Flushing, Queens; nyc parks.completeinet.net; 7 train to Willets Pt./Shea Stadium).

New York Chinese Chess Association. (21 Division St., NY; 212 219-8858; F train to East Broadway).

New York Shogi Club. Established 50 years ago; recently sponsored one of the largest shogi tournaments outside Japan (330 W. 45th St., Rm. 11B, NY; nyshogi@pop.interport.net; or contact Shigeki Masui, executive director of public relations and communications at smasui @banet.net; A, C, E train to 42nd St.).

Singh's Sporting Goods. Advertised as "the cricket store for the new millenium," Singh's may indeed have the widest selection of cricket equipment in North America and is conveniently located in the heart of New York's cricketing population (100-06 101st Ave., Ozone Park, Queens; 718 925-9058; www.singhsport.com; A train to Rockaway Blvd.).

United East Athletic Association, Xiangqi Club. (70 Mulberry St., Room 201, NY; 212 227-9452; www.txa.ipoline/club.htm; A, C, E, N, R, J, M, Z, 6 train to Canal St.).

Anime and Manga

Anime Crash. Considered the tip-top shop in NYC for anime tapes and merchandise (13 E. 4th St., NY; 212 254-4670, 212 254-4730; www.animecrash.com; N, R train to 8th St.).

Asahiya Bookstore. Big Japanese bookstore with loads of manga (52 Vanderbilt Ave., NY; 212 883-0011; www.asahiyausa.com; S, 4, 5, 6, 7 train to 42nd St./Grand Central).

Bulletproof Comics & Games. The top comic shops in Brooklyn, with three locations (2178 Nostrand Ave., Brooklyn; 718 434-1800; 2, 5 train to Flatbush Ave., Brooklyn College; 4507 Fort Hamilton Pkwy., Brooklyn; 718 854-3367; L train to Rockaway Pkwy., Canarsie; and 8109 Flatlands Ave., Brooklyn; 718 531-6415; L train to Rockaway Pkwy.).

Forbidden Planet. Though the focus here is admittedly on science fiction, there is a healthy manga selection (840 Broadway, NY; 212 473-1576; 4, 5, 6, N, R, L train to 14th St./Union Sq.)

Hyper Hobby/Image Anime Co. Good for toys, posters, and other merchandise (103 W. 30th St.; 212 631-0966; www.imageanime.com; B, D, F, N, Q, R, to 34th St./Herald Sq.).

Kinokuniya Bookstore. Large Japanese bookstore with equally large manga selection (10 W. 49th St., NY; 212 765-7766; www.kinokuniya.com; B, D, F, Q train to 47–50 sts./Rockefeller Ctr.).

Metro Anime. Anime club meets monthly for discussion/viewing of anime tapes. Members have free use of lending library of anime tapes (metroanime.org; meetings are held at the School of Visual Arts, 209 W. 23rd St., Room 311; N, R, 6 train to 23rd St.).

Octopus Kingdom. Anime tape and CD outlet (150 Lafayette St., Suite 28, NY; 212 941-8380; A, C, E, J, M, Z, N, R, 6 train to Canal St.).

Karaoke

B.l.u.e. Karaoke & Restaurant. Koreatown karaoke starts nightly around 11:30 (9 W. 32nd St., NY; 212 947-3028; B, D, F, N, Q, R train to 34th St./Herald Sq.).

East Japanese Restaurant. Private karaoke rooms; two hours includes unlimited beer, sake, wine, soft drinks, and sushi (253 W. 55th St., NY; 212 581-2240; B, D, E train to 7th Ave.).

Elbow Room. Popular Wednesday night karaoke rocks from 11 till 4 in the morning; celebrity sightings likely (144 Bleecker St.; 212 979-8434; www.elbowroomnyc.com; A, B, C, D, E, F, Q train to W. 4th St.).

Hagi. Private rooms rented by the hour. Japanese songbooks; only a few in English (152 W. 49th St., NY; 212 764-8549; N, R train to 49th St.).

Lucky Cheng's. Drag Kabuki Karaoke lounge nightly till 4 a.m. (24 First Ave., NY; 212 473-0516; F train to Second Ave.).

MBC Music Studio. Karoake rooms for rent till 6 a.m. (25 W. 32nd St., 3rd Floor, NY; 212 967-2244 or 212 967-3030; B, D, F, N Q, R train to 34th St./Herald Sq.).

Onigashima. Japanese restaurant and bar with private karaoke party rooms; both English and Japanese songbooks (43-45 W. 55th St., NY; 212 541-7145; B, Q train to 57th St.).

Village Karaoke. Private rooms offer songbooks in Japanese, Korean, Chinese, and English (27 Cooper Sq., NY; 212 254-0066; 6 train to Astor Pl.).

Winnie's. Small joint with killer songlist (104 Bayard St., NY; 212 732-2384; A, C, E, J, M, Z, N, R, 6 train to Canal St.).

Sake Bars

Chibi's Sake Bar. (238 Mott St., NY; 212-274-0054; N, R train to Prince St.)

Decibel. (240 E. 9th St., NY; 212 979-2733; 6 train to Astor Pl.)

Hapon. (211 E. 43 St., NY; 212 986-1213; 4, 5, 6, 7 train to 42nd St./Grand Central)

Sakagura. (60 E. 42 St., NY; 212 953-7253; 4, 5, 6, 7 train to 42nd St./Grand Central)

Typhoon Lounge. (79 St. Marks Pl., NY; 212 979-2680; 6 train to Astor Pl.)

Yajirobei. (8 Stuyvesant St., NY, 2nd floor; 212 598-3041; 6 train to Astor Pl.)

Bhangra Events

Basement Bhangra. Held on the first Thursday of each month, with resident DJs Rekha and Joy in the house. Changing venues, generally S.O.B.'s (204 Varick St., NY) or Irving Plaza (15 Irving Pl., NY). For information, go to www.sangamsounds.com/basement.

Mutiny Club Night. Regular bhangra parties held at Chelsea Piers' Frying Pan (Pier 63, NY; 212 252-2397; www.sangament.com).

Festivals and Celebrations

(see also descriptions in Asia in Queens, Chinatown,
Film & Performing Arts, and Little Tokyo)

Asian Pacific American (APA) Heritage Festival. Generally held in Union Square on the first Sunday in May to celebrate Asian Pacific American Heritage Month (Coalition of Asian Pacific Americans; 212 989-3610; www.capaonline.org).

The Autumn Moon Festival (see also Korean Harvest and Folklore Festival below). This fall festival, held each year at the Staten Island Botanical Garden in the unique Chinese Scholar's Garden, features traditional lion dancing, lantern making, and a tea ceremony with delicious Moon Cakes (Staten Island Botanical Garden, 1000 Richmond Rd., Staten Island; 718 273-8200; www.sibg.org; Staten Island Ferry).

Bronx Zoo (International Wildlife Conservation Park) NYC's most famous and legendary zoo regularly presents weekend-long events like "Festival of Mongolia" or "Journey to China" which feature dance, storytellers, folk arts, and interactive arts and crafts booths in tandem with their permanent Asian-themed viewing areas, Asia Wild, the Himalayan Highlands, and Jungle World (2300 Southern Blvd., Bronx; 718 367-1010; www.wcs.org; 2 train to Pelham Parkway).

Burmese New Year Water Festival. This traditional celebration of the people and culture of Burma is based on the idea that water cleanses and renews the spirit. Family and friends splash each other with water while enjoying the food, fashion, and culture of the Burmese people. The event is held each year in July at the Queens Botanical Garden (Queens Botanical Garden, 43-50 Main St., Flushing, Queens; 718 886-3800; 7 train to Main St./Flushing).

Cherry Blossom Festival/Sakura Matsuri. The Brooklyn Botanic Garden celebrates the arrival of spring and the blooming of the garden's cherry trees with this festival at the end of April. Features traditional Japanese taiko drumming (900 Washington Ave., Brooklyn, NY; 718 623-7200; www.bbg.org; 2, 3 train to Eastern Parkway/Brooklyn Museum).

Chinese Garden and Tree Peony Festival. Here, the preening is done by Chinese peonies; generally, early May through early June (New York Botanical Garden, 200th St. and Southern Blvd., the Bronx; 718 817-8700; www.nybg.org/events/peonyfest.html; B, D train to Bedford Park Blvd.).

Chinese New Year. Chinese celebration of the new lunar year starts with the new moon on the first day of the new year and ends on the full moon 15 days later. The 15th day of the new year is called the Lantern Festival, which is celebrated at night with lantern displays and children carrying lanterns in a parade.

Hong Kong Dragon Boat Festival New York. The 2,000-year-old Chinese rowing tradition comes to Queens, each year in early August. A lively cultural celebration accompanies the races, with food, drink, music, dance performances, and a parade. (Races held at Meadow Lake in Flushing Meadows-Corona Park, Queens; 718 539-8974; www. hkdbf-ny; 7 train to Main St./Flushing).

Korean Harvest and Folklore Festival. Held annually at the end of September; stage performances and games (Sponsored by the Korean Produce Association, 718 842-2424, or contact the *Korea Central Daily* newspaper in Flushing for details; 718 358-8900).

Matsuri on 47th Street. Besides regular programs that features performers in traditional and contemporary music, dance, and theater from Japan, the Japan Society sponsors a street-long community festival (47th Street between 1st and 2nd aves.) that features a traditional *mikoshi* shrine procession, as well as music, dance, crafts, and food. (Japanese Society, 333 E. 47th St., NY; 212 832-1155; www.japanso ciety.org; 6, E, F train to 51st St./Lexington Ave.).

New York Buddhist Church and American Buddhist Academy. On the second Sunday in July, this Church runs the annual Obon festival to commemorate the deceased with traditional music and dance, right across the street in Riverside Park (331-332 Riverside Drive, NY; 212 678-0305; 1, 9 train to 103rd St.).

Asian festivals in NYC

JANUARY/FEBRUARY: Chinese Lunar New Year, Tet (Vietnamese New Year)

APRIL: *Sakura Matsuri* (Cherry Blossom Festival)

MAY/JUNE: Asian Pacific American (APA) Heritage Festival, Buddha's Birthday, Chinese Garden & Tree Peony Festival

JULY/AUGUST: Obon, Burmese New Year Water Festival, Hong Kong Dragon Boat Festival

SEPTEMBER/OCTOBER: Autumn Moon Festival, Korean Harvest Moon and Folklore Festival, Matsuri on 47th Street, Diwali (Hindu Festival of Lights/Hindu New Year)

little
manila

S pread around the intersection of 14th Street and First Avenue, on the edges of the East Village and Stuyvesant Town, is the tiny neighborhood burg of Little Manila—and unless you know what you are looking for, you just might miss it altogether. It's only a handful of restaurants and a couple of markets, dotted around a small area. All are a short distance from Beth Israel and Bellevue hospitals, Mount Sinai Hospital for Joint Diseases, and hospital-owned housing. In fact, Manhattan's Little Manila owes its very existence, in large part, to these centers of healing.

The Filipinos who live in New York—and any Filipino, for that matter, who lives outside the Philippines, the islands of the Malay Archipelago—call themselves "pinoys." The estimated number of pinoys in New York City is 30,000. But because they have settled all over the metropolitan area, their presence is sometimes hard to detect. One sure place to find many Filipino immigrants in New York, however, is working in the area hospitals. The influx of Filipino emigrant doctors and nurses and other professionals into the city began after the 1965 Immigration Act. In the ensuing years, Filipina nurses were actively recruited to fill a nursing shortage, and by the early '90s comprised 10 percent of the city's nursing staff. By the start of the 21st century, it was estimated that 72 percent of all women from the Philippines in the city were employed as trained nurses. The Filipina nurse has

The Immaculate Conception Church in Manhattan welcomes New York's Filipinos, many of whom are Catholic, to mass that is held in Tagalog, their native language.

become an archetypal New York immigrant, like the West Indian nanny, the Indian or Pakistani cab driver, and the Korean grocer.

Of course, pinoys are employed in plenty of other professions around the city: They are writers, artists, laborers, priests, chefs—just to name a few. While West Coast Filipino emigres started arriving in the 1920s as agricultural workers and formed identifiable ethnic enclaves, the East Coast's newer, smaller Filipino community is widely scattered throughout Manhattan, Queens, and the suburbs of New York and New Jersey. But Filipinos from far and wide come together to worship at **Immaculate Conception Church** (414 East 14th St.), which holds mass in Tagalog, the language of the Philippines. Built in 1894 to accommodate a less fortunate congregation than that of nearby Grace Church (it was called Grace Chapel and Hospital), it has been serving a Catholic parish of diverse ethnicities since 1943. It also houses a Catholic school.

The United States–Philippines history is long and complex. When Spain lost the Spanish-American War in 1898, the Philippines, then a Spanish colony, was purchased by the United States government for $20 million. In 1934, the U.S. granted the Philippines a ten-year period of transition leading up to full independence, a process that was stalled in 1942 when Japan

public transportation

LITTLE MANILA (14th St. between Ave. A and 2nd Ave.) SUBWAY: L to 1st Ave; 4, 5, 6, L to 14th St./Union Sq. BUS: M14 on 14th St., M15 on 1st and 2nd Ave.

invaded the country. In 1945, the Philippines finally became a fully independent nation.

The result of this multinational tug-of-war is a culture influenced by both Spanish and American societies. The use of English as the other official, bureaucratic language, plus a colonial educational system, may explain why the pinoys in the U.S. have been able to succeed in such a relatively short time. Today, Filipinos are the third-largest group emigrating to the U.S., behind Mexicans and Chinese. (Interestingly, the high rate of immigration, especially by Filipino professionals, has raised concerns about a "brain drain" out of the Philippines, a concern shared by other developing countries in Asia and Central Europe.)

As in many other ethnic neighborhoods, food plays a central role in Little Manila. The cuisine reflects the country's varied Chi-

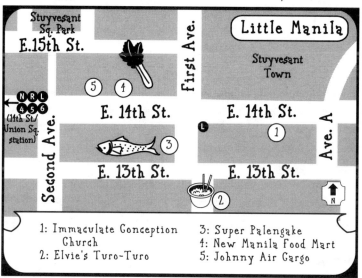

1: Immaculate Conception Church
2: Elvie's Turo-Turo
3: Super Palengake
4: New Manila Food Mart
5: Johnny Air Cargo

The New Manila Food Mart, located on East 14th Street in Little Manila, is a source for Filipino specialties.

nese, Malay, and Spanish influences. A meat or fish, a stew or soup, and a vegetable accompanied by rice make up a typical meal. The dominant flavors are soy sauce, vinegar, garlic, black bean sauce, shrimp paste, coconut milk, and citrus fruits, which are used to flavor pork and other meats. In the clean and small dining room at **Elvie's Turo-Turo** (214 First Ave.), which is mostly a takeout joint, you are guided to *turo-turo* ("point, point") at the steam table filled with a dozen or so Filipino specialties, including the national dish, *adobo*, flavorful grilled pork marinated in soy sauce and vinegar. You can also try whole fried fish or sweet and delicious barbecued pork on a stick. The majority of Elvie's diners are Filipino, so you know it's the real deal. The many traditional specialties are made accessible to non-Filipinos by a descriptive menu and a helpful staff.

Filipino foodstuffs are available at the nearby markets. A small grocery offering Asian and Filipino foods, **Super Palengake** (231 First Ave.), also has Filipino videos, music tapes, newspapers, and phone cards for calling the Philippines. **New Manila Food Mart** (351 East 14th St.) is an even smaller grocery store that's also a small diner, eat in or take out. The magenta-colored eggs are a national favorite—they're hard-boiled and soaked in salt and vinegar for a couple of weeks.

While you're in the neighborhood, you can mail a package to the Philippines via **Johnny Air Cargo** (331 East 14th St.), a company that only sends parcels to the Philippines, by air or by sea.

Little Manila in Manhattan may be small today, but a Filipino presence is well established in the New York area (for example, see *Asia in Queens* for a tour of the culinary enclave in Woodside). Little Manilas are likely to expand and develop wherever Filipino families are setting up shop, moving into apartments, and sharing their native identity via the four weekly Filipino newspapers and a cable station in New Jersey. At night, the savory scent of *adobo* sends out welcoming smoke signals to the new arrivals, fellow pinoys making their homes throughout the city.

[services]

New York City has a wealth of Asian-specific community, educational, human-service, and media resources. You may already have discovered a number of them in earlier chapters. Here, we focus on some special areas in greater detail. Perhaps you've seen an art exhibition that whetted your appetite for further study. You may require health or legal advice, or seek sources for adoption. You may be seeking a particular media organization. You may simply be looking for information on specific Asian cultural and educational opportunities, business and media resources, and community organizations. Here, then, are some invaluable informational sources on all things Asian in New York.

cultural offices & continuing education

Cultural organizations fulfill several functions. First, they serve the immigrant community already residing in New York by celebrating their heritage through lectures, art groups, films, and social activities. They also safeguard the history of the community through libraries that archive documents, newspapers, photographs, and books. For both new immigrants and visitors, they provide a familiar language and new network of information about the city, and their own ethnic community. Another objective of these organizations is to demystify Asian cultures through language classes, art exhibitions, and other cultural activities, beginning the process of understanding and appreciation. For prospective students, many institutions have curricula that cover Asian literature, history, and language; some offer programs that take place in Asian countries.

Asian American Arts Alliance. A key resource for Asian and Asian American arts in New York City. Their newsletter is an invaluable guide to cultural events involving Asian and Asian American talent throughout New York City (75 Varick St., NY; 212 941-9208; www.aaartsalliance.org; 1, 9 train to Canal St.).
Asian American Arts Centre. Creates and develops a wide range of cul-

tural, artistic, and education programs for the Asian American community to preserve its cultural heritage. Also publishes *Artspiral*, a biannual periodical (26 Bowery, NY; 212 233-2154; B, D, Q train to Grand St., A, C, E, J, M, Z, N, R, 6 train to Canal St.).

Asian/Pacific/American Studies Program and Institute at New York University. An undergraduate program that focuses on Asian Pacific Americans through an interdisciplinary study of literature, history, arts, and gender studies. The institute sponsors conferences and events on these and other subjects (269 Mercer St., NY; 212 988-3700; www.nyu.edu/apa; B, D, F, Q train to Broadway-Lafayette, 6 train to Bleecker St.).

Asia Society. A pan-Asian cultural organization dedicated to fostering an understanding of Asia and the communication between Americans and the peoples of Asia. The Society provides a forum for building awareness of the more than thirty countries broadly defined as the Asia-Pacific region—from Japan to Iran, and from Central Asia to New Zealand. (725 Park Ave., NY; 212 517-ASIA [2742]; www.asiasociety.org; 6 train to 68th St. *Note:* During renovations, the Asia Society is housed [until Fall 2001] at 502 Park Ave.; 4, 5, 6, N, R train to 59th St./Lexington Ave.).

China Institute. Dedicated to the appreciation and enjoyment of traditional and contemporary Chinese civilization, culture, and heritage, the China Institute offers a number of different programs to the city of New York. Art exhibitions showcase Chinese paintings, calligraphy, textiles, and architecture; Mandarin language classes specifically for children, adults, and travelers are offered for all levels of proficiency; and lectures, book signings, films, and cultural performances of the Institute are open to the public. Programs especially for corporations and educators are also available (125 E. 65th St., NY; 212 744-8181; www.chinainsti tute.org; 6 train to 68th St.).

Chinese Information and Culture Center. As the cultural wing of the Taipei Economic and Cultural Office, the Chinese Information and Culture Center promotes appreciation and celebration of the culture and traditions of China and Taiwan. The Information Center has a library with 40,000 volumes in English and Chinese and an extensive audiovisual section. The Cultural Center consists of the Taipei Theater, Taipei Gallery, and the Chinese Culture Program, which offers classes in Mandarin, calligraphy, and tai chi (*Info:* 1230 Ave. of the Americas, 2nd Floor, NY; 212 373-1800; *Culture:* 1222 Ave. of the Americas, NY; 212 373-1850; www.taipei.org; B, D, F, Q train to 47-50th sts./Rockefeller Ctr.).

performing Arts classes Just as multifaceted as the Asian American performing arts community are the educational activities related to these art forms. One of the leading lights in this area is **Lotus Fine Arts Multicultural Music and Dance Studios,** where a wide array of individual and group classes are available in many types of Asian music and dance. **Chen & Dancers** and the **Chinese Folk Dance Co.** offer dance classes ranging from traditional Asian dance to modern dance and ballet. Acting and directing classes are available at the **Pan Asian Repertory Theatre,** while the **Asian American Writers' Workshop** has classes in playwriting, screenwriting, and all other genres with some of the most distinguished Asian American wordsmiths in the greater NYC area. There's also **Radio Hula,** which specializes in Hawaiian hula classes. These establishments usually have a variety of classes that can accommodate students of all levels and ages, along with the occasional master class.

Coalition for Asian Pacific Americans (CAPA). Promotes cooperation and understanding among New York Asian American social arts and historical organizations, and seeks to provide a conducive environment for Asian Americans to use their history, culture, and art to foster self-esteem and respect for their heritage. (12 W. 18th St., NY; 212 989-3610; www.capaonline.org; 4, 5, 6, L, N, R train to 14th St./Union Sq.).
Columbia University's East Asian Languages and Culture Program. In-depth studies at all levels in religion, history, literature, and the languages and cultures of South and East Asia. Program features include the renowned Southern Asian Institute and the Department of Middle East and Asian Language and Culture (MEALAC) (W.116th St. and Broadway 212 854-1754; www.columbia.edu; 1, 9 train to 116th St.).
Japanese American Association of New York, Inc. (JAA). Promotes friendly relations among Japanese and Japanese Americans in New York (15 W. 44th St., 11th floor, NY; 212 840-6942; 7 train to Fifth Ave., 4, 5, 6, 7 train to 42nd St./Grand Central).
Japan Society. Promotes intellectual and cultural interchange to maintain a vibrant relationship between U.S. and Japan. The center houses a gallery, the C. V. Starr Library, a research archive, and the Toyota Language Center (333 E. 47th St.; 212 832-1155; www.japansociety.org; 4, 5, 6, 7 train to 42nd St./Grand Central).
Korean Cultural Service. Housed in the same building as the Korean

Consulate, it has a library containing information about Korea and Koreans in the U.S. (460 Park Ave., 6th floor, NY; 212 759-9550; 4, 5, 6, N, R train to 59th St./Lexington Ave.).

Korea Society. Sponsors lectures, Korean language programs, a Korean Club, touring Korean art groups, and other programs to promote understanding of Koreans and Korean culture in the U.S. (950 Third Ave., 8th floor, NY; 212 759-7525; www.koreasociety.org; 4, 5, 6, N, R train to 59th St./Lexington Ave.).

Museum of Chinese in the Americas. A nonprofit educational organization documenting the history of Chinese immigration to the U.S. Walking tours of Chinatown and an archive library can be accessed by appointment (70 Mulberry St., 2nd floor, NY; 212 619-4785; www.moca-nyc.org; A, C, E, J, M, Z, N, R, 6 train to Canal St.).

New School University (The New School for Social Research). Chinese and Japanese language programs. English as a Second Language program. Culinary Institute courses in Japanese, Chinese, and Indian cooking, and shopping and walking tours of Chinatown and other Asian districts (66 W. 12th St., NY; 212 229-5600; www.nsu.newschool.edu; call for bulletin; 1, 2, 3, 9, F train to 14th St.).

New York University's East Asian Studies Program. Undergraduate program with emphasis on language and literature of East Asia (715 Broadway, 3rd floor, NY; 212 998-7620; www.nyu.edu/pages/east.asian.studies; B, D, F, Q train to Broadway-Lafayette; N, R train to 8th St.; 6 train to Bleecker St.).

The Philippine Center. In the same building as the Philippines Consulate, it sponsors concerts, symposiums on Filipino culture, art exhibits, and conferences with Filipino government officials (556 Fifth Ave.; 212 575-4774; 7 train to Fifth Ave., 4, 5, 6 train to Grand Central).

Queens Public Library. The branch in Flushing has an extensive collection that includes a large Asian section, and the Lefferts branch occasionally features Indian storytelling and dance, and is the site of the Namaste-Adaab collection (41-17 Main St., Flushing, Queens; 718 661-1200; 7 train to Main St./103-34 Lefferts Blvd., Richmond Hill, Queens; 718 843-5950; A train to Lefferts Blvd.).

Tibet House. A cultural center with a gallery and a library to preserve and restore Tibet's cultural and spiritual heritage. Various events and exhibitions on-site (22 W. 15th St., NY; 212 807-0565; www.tibethouse.org; N, R, L, 4, 5, 6 train to 14th St./Union Sq.).

community & Human services

Contrary to the stereotype of a high-achieving, upwardly mobile group, the Asian American community, especially the newer generations, does experience social problems typical of urban populations. Family violence, alcohol and drug abuse, unemployment, poverty, and problems with youth do occur—here in New York City, for example, one source says one out of three Asian American high school students fails to graduate. In response to these problems, community and service groups have been founded in the Asian community to educate, protect, and support its members.

Human services organizations help Asian Americans overcome problems common to immigrants and help them combat racial prejudice by educating them on their political and civil rights. They act as watchdog organizations against labor infringements, police brutality, and anti-Asian violence. They also act as research centers that collect data for federal and state policy-making and funding. There are also resources for getting in touch with an international network of gay and lesbian Asians, as homosexuality is still taboo in many Asian countries and in much of the Asian American community. Health-oriented centers are crucial to the lives of those living with HIV/AIDS, as they give referrals to clinics and social services. The following organizations work at the community level to better the standard of life for many Asian Americans.

Asian American Legal Defense & Education Fund (AALDEF). Since 1974, it has served the Asian American community on the East Coast by promoting voting rights and equal opportunity, and combating anti-Asian violence and police brutality. It also seeks to stamp out sweatshops and promote a fair immigration policy (99 Hudson St., 12th floor, NY; 212 966-5932; www.aaldef.org; 1, 9 train to Franklin St.).

Asian Professional Extension (APEX). Similar to the Big Brother/Big Sister and other mentoring programs, this organization seeks to promote the personal development of Asian American youths by pairing them with an Asian American adult as a mentor and a tutor (120 Wall St., 3rd floor, NY; no phone; www.apex-ny.org; 2, 3, 4, 5 train to Wall St.).

Asian Americans for Equality. Founded in 1974 to insure equal opportunity for Asian Americans. Offers courses on taxes, tenant rights, and buying a house, and counsels low-income housing residents (111 Division St., NY; 212 964-6023/2288; F train to East Broadway).

Asian Health Center of Flushing. Nonprofit, community-based health care center offers free vaccinations. Its staff speaks Cantonese, Mandarin, and English (136-26 37th Ave., 2nd floor, Flushing, Queens; 718 886-1200; 7 train to Flushing/Main St.).

Asian Pacific Islander Coalition on HIV/AIDS (APICHA). To support Asian and Pacific Islander community members with HIV/AIDS, it offers health-related services, education, and research. It has two offices (275 Seventh Ave., Suite 1204, NY; 212 620-7287; 1, 9 train to 23rd St.; 74-09 37th Ave., Suite 400, Jackson Heights, Queens; 718 457-9662; E, F, G,R train to Roosevelt Ave.; 7 train to 74th St.-Broadway).

Brooklyn Chinese-American Association. A multifaceted social service agency serving Sunset Park, Borough Park, and Bay Ridge (5002 Eighth Ave., Brooklyn; 718 438-9312; B, M train to 50th St.).

Chinese-American Planning Council. One of the largest and most comprehensive social service organizations serving the Chinese American population in the U.S. Wide scope with many services offered (150 Elizabeth St., NY; 212 941-0920; B, D, Q train to Grand St.).

Committee Against Anti-Asian Violence (CAAAV). A political organization of the immigrant and working-class Asian American community, formed in response to anti-Asian violence and police brutality. Programs include immigrant rights advocacy, referrals, and organizing skills training (191 E. 3rd St.; 212 473-6485; www.home.dti.net/caaav; F train to Second Ave.).

Gay Asian and Pacific Islands Men of NY (GAPIMNY). A membership organization that is a forum for gay, bisexual, and transgendered people of Asian heritage. It also hosts a variety of workshops and social events (P.O. Box 1608 Old Chelsea Station, New York, NY 10013; 212 802-7423; www.gapimny.org).

Indochina Sino-American Senior Center. Provides social services helping low-income and older (55 and up) Chinese and Southeast Asians integrate into the mainstream culture. Buddhist temple on-site (81 Bowery, 2nd floor, NY; 212 226-0317; B, D, Q train to Grand St.).

Japanese American Social Services Inc. Provides social services and assistance to the Japanese American community in New York City (275 Seventh Ave., 12th floor, NY; 212 255-1881; 1, 9 train to 23rd St.).

Korean Family Counseling & Research Center. Offers referrals to social services in Korean and English for women and children (41-25 Kissena Blvd., 2-F, Flushing, Queens; 718 321-2400; 7 train to Flushing/Main St.).

Korean Social Services Center of New York. Provides referrals and social services to the Korean American community in New York City (16 W. 32nd St., Room 301; 212 564-2772; B, D, F, Q, N, R train to 34th St./Herald Sq.).

Long Yang Club, NYC Chapter. An international social club for gay Asians and non-Asian friends with chapters in many cities. It organizes group outings and social events (212 835-8788; www.longyangclub.org).

National Korean American Service & Education Consortium. Advocates Korean American civil rights and offers free legal clinics, income tax help, naturalization services, and referrals to Medicaid and WIC (50-60 Parsons Blvd., Flushing, Queens; 718 445-3939; www.nakasec.org; 7 train to Flushing/Main St.).

Nav Nirmaan Foundation. Provides counseling and social services to the South Asian community, and educates to prevent child abuse, alcoholism, and domestic abuse (87-08 Justice Avenue, Room LA, Elmhurst, Queens; 718 478-4588; G, R train to Grand Ave.).

New York Asian Women's Center. Provides shelter, counseling, and other social services to Asian women dealing with domestic violence and sexual assault. Founded in 1982, it promotes self-sufficiency, independence, and an end to violence against women (39 Bowery, Box 375, New York, NY 10002; 212 732-5230; hotline: 888 888-7702).

Sakhi for South Asian Women. Founded in 1989, Sakhi, which means "woman friend," is committed to ending domestic violence and helping women of South Asian origin by offering a variety of services. It also publishes *Voices of Sakhi*, first-person accounts by survivors of domestic violence (P.O. Box 20208, Greeley Square Station, New York, NY 10001; 212 868-6741; hotline: 800 621-4673; www.sakhi.com).

South Asian Lesbian and Gay Association of New York (SALGA-NY). A social and political group for the South Asian gay and lesbian community (P.O. Box 1491, Old Chelsea Station, New York, NY 10113; 212 358-5132; www.salganyc.org).

Vietnamese-American Cultural Organization. Provides a wide array of social services to the growing Vietnamese community in New York City, including youth services, unemployment and job assistance, and assistance on mental health issues (113 Baxter St., NY; 212 343-0762; A, C, E, J, M, Z, N, R, 6 train to Canal St.).

International Adoption

In 1999, American families adopted more than 4,000 Chinese infants and children, almost all of them girls. In the same year, nearly 2,000 Korean children became Americans. About 500 children were brought in from Vietnam, the same number from India. International adoption from Asia began after the Korean War, as a way of dealing with war orphans and Amerasian children fathered by American GI's. Today, there are an estimated 100,000 Korean adoptees in the U.S. and another 20,000 in Western Europe. The Korean adoption numbers peaked from the mid-'70s through the '80s, when Korea struggled economically. In the '90s the number of Korean adoptions decreased, though it has remained steady. China's strict one-child policy and a society that favors boys have left many baby girls orphaned. Since 1994, China has allowed the number of international adoptions to increase significantly.

also-known-as, inc. A nonprofit membership group for adult inter-country adoptees. Organizes educational and community events, including a "Motherland visit" to Korea. A great web resource (P.O. Box 6037, FDR Station, NY 10150; 212 386-9201; www.akaworld.org).

Families with Children from China (FCC). For those interested in adopting from China or who have a child from China, FCC provides a valuable resource on the web. Excellent place to start researching for a private agency. FCC also has a local chapter in the New York City metropolitan area with over 1,000 families. Membership is $29 and includes a quarterly newsletter and invitations to events (P.O. Box 237065, Ansonia Station, NY 10023; 212 579-0115; www.fwcc.org).

Families with Children from Vietnam. A web resource for those who have already adopted from Vietnam or are considering doing so (www.fcvn.org.).

Family Service of Westchester. Another private agency in the area that specializes in adoptions from China (1 Summit Ave., White Plains, NY; 914 948-8004; www.fsw.org).

Spence-Chapin Services to Families and Children. A New York City–based agency that not only specializes in international adoptions from Korea, China, and Russia, but also has an African American Infant Program (6 E. 94th St., NY; 212 369-0300; www.spence-chapin.org).

Media

Locally published newspapers help to bind together immigrants in a new land. Often the newspapers are satellite papers owned by companies in the home country in Asia. Each day or week, the majority of the content is transferred electronically from Asia, and in New York (or in other large metropolitan cities with sizable Asian communities), it goes into print with additional local coverage. Such papers also play a vital role in the local economy since they are important venues for advertising and commerce. The same applies for radio and television, though the West Coast's Asian American broadcast media is far more developed, because of its longer history. In addition, wire services and professional associations for Asian American journalists and professionals try to ensure a fair and visible coverage of Asia and Asian Americans in the American media.

Media Organizations and Services

Asian American Journalists Association. A national organization that promotes Asian American presence in journalism; the chapter in New York is the group's largest, with 250 members (National Office, 1182 Market St., Ste. 320, San Francisco, CA 94102; 415 346-2051; New York chapter, contact Pradnya Joshi, President, at pjoshi@newsday.com; www.aaja.org/chapters/newyork).

Korean Press Agency, Inc. (KPA). Korean and Korean American newswire service to American and Korean media (29 W. 30th St., Room 1003, NY; 212 594-0493).

Press Trust of India. Newswire service to North America and India (405 E. 42nd St., NY; 212 751-0850).

South Asian Journalists Association (SAJA). A professional networking group for South Asian journalists that seeks to improve the standards of journalistic coverage of South Asia and South Asian America. Keeps a SAJA stylebook for covering South Asian news (c/o Sreenath Sreenivasan, Columbia Graduate School of Journalism, 2950 Broadway, NY; 212 854-5979; www.saja.org).

Television and Radio

You will need to check your local cable listings for where to find the stations or programs produced by the following:

Fujisankei Communications International. Weekend cable TV programming of Japanese entertainment and news (150 E. 52nd St., NY; 212 753-8100).

Japan Media Productions. Late-night Japanese magazine cable TV show. (576 Fifth Ave., Suite 1103, NY; 212 661-1211).

Korean Broadcasting Corporation. Broadcasts Korean-language news and entertainment on cable TV (42-22 27th St., Long Island City, Queens; 718 426-5665).

KTV. Korean programming, on cable TV, 24/7 (136 39th Ave., Flushing, Queens; 718 358-3301).

The Korean Channel (TKC). Broadcasts many TV programs from Korea, as well as local news (35-11 Farrington St., Flushing, Queens; 718 353-8970).

Sinovision. Wide range of Chinese-language programming—drama, variety shows, news—on Crosswalk Cable, Sunday through Thursday evenings (15 E. 40th St., NY; 212 213-6688).

U.S. Broadcasting System (TV Korea). Boadcasts nine hours of Korean-language programming a week (820 River Rd., Edgewater, NJ; 201 592-7445).

U.S. Nippon Communications Network (WYNE). Weekend news and entertainment in Japanese, with subtitles, two hours per week (220 East 42nd St., 27th Floor, NY; 212 983-7070).

WKCR/Chinese Radio Network FM 89.9. Broadcasts news, information, and entertainment in Mandarin, Saturday mornings on Columbia University's radio station (64 Fulton St., #603, NY; 212 513-0233).

WCAV/Chinese American Voice FM 104.3. Radio programming in Mandarin, with one hour per day in Taiwanese (42-25 Kissena Blvd., Suite 131, Flushing, Queens; 718 961-6490).

WGBB/AM 1240. Mandarin Chinese programming weekdays (45 John St., NY; 212 513-0233).

WMBC. Multilingual 24-hour cable station featuring Chinese, Japanese, and Korean programming in the evenings throughout the week (460 Bergen Blvd., Suite 355, Palisades Park, NJ; 201 944-9622, 973 697-0063).

World TV. News and entertainment programs in Cantonese and Mandarin daily (141-07 20th Ave., Whitestone, Queens; 718 746-8889).

WZRC/Radio Seoul AM 1480. A variety of programming, broadcast entirely in Korean, 24/7 (136-56 39th Ave., Flushing, Queens; 718 358-9300).

Stack of Chinese-language newspapers.

Newspapers and Magazines

aMagazine. A bimonthly national Asian American lifestyle magazine published in New York City. Beginning in 2001, it will be published monthly. Its website is an excellent resource (697 Fifth Ave., 3rd floor, NY; 212 593-8089; www.aonline.com).

Asahi Shimbun. Established in 1986 and popular among expat Japanese businessmen and their families. It also publishes a monthly supplement, *Plaza Asahi*, which is about the Japanese American community, and an English version of the paper, twice a month (845 Third Ave., NY; 212 317-3000).

China Press (Qiao Bao). A Chinese-language daily that prints news from China and abroad (15 E. 40th St., NY; 212 683-8282).

China Times magazine. A free weekly magazine in Chinese to be found on Saturdays where Chinese newspapers are sold (203 Lafayette St., NY; 212 219-9025).

The Filipino Express. A weekly newspaper based in Jersey City. In English (2711 John F. Kennedy Blvd., Jersey City, NJ; 201 434-1114).

Filipino Reporter. Established in 1972, it reports, in English, Filipino news from other parts of the U.S. on a weekly basis (Empire State Bldg., 350 Fifth Ave., Ste. 601, NY; 212 967-5784/7980).

India Abroad. Published since 1970, this is the oldest Indian newspaper in North America and the largest outside India. Published in English in six cities. In New York, it hits the newsstands on Fridays (43 W. 24th St., NY; 212 929-1727; www.indiaabroadonline.com).

India Tribune. Weekly paper in English with editions in New York, Atlanta, and Chicago (100 W. 32nd St., 6th floor, NY; 212 564-7336; www.indiatribune.com).

Korea Central Daily News (Joon Ang Ilbo). Korean-language daily, published every day except Sundays, that covers Korean American happenings on the East Coast (32 W. 32nd St., 4th floor, NY; 212 239-1774).

Korea Times (Hanguk Ilbo). First published in L.A. in 1967, this Korean-language newspaper is published every day except Sundays (42-22 27th St., Long Island City, Queens; 718 482-1111).

Little India. Published monthly, the magazine and its online version look at life for Indians living in the U.S. from many points of view (1800 Oak Lane, Reading, PA; 610 396-0366; www.littleindia.com).

Ming Pao Daily News. A daily newspaper in Chinese that covers national news and news from Hong Kong, Taiwan, Mainland China, and the Chinese American community (43-31 33rd St., 2F, Long Island City, Queens; 718 786-2888).

News India Times. A national weekly published in New York City, in English. Comes out on Fridays (244 Fifth Ave., 4th floor, NY; 212 481-3110; www.newsindia-times.com).

Pakistan Calling. A free English-language weekly for the Pakistani community that covers news from Pakistan, the subcontinent, and the tri-state area. (303 Fifth Ave., Suite 1310, NY; 212 779-0942; www.pakistancalling.com).

World Journal. Independently run Chinese-language daily. Most widely read Chinese-language paper in North America. Parent company in Taiwan (141-07 20th Ave., Whitestone, Queens; 718 746-8889).

About the Authors

The **Asia Society** is America's leading institution dedicated to fostering understanding of Asia and communication between Americans and the peoples of Asia and the Pacific. A nonprofit, nonpartisan, educational organization, the society presents a wide range of programs that include major art exhibitions, performances, media programs, and international conferences and lectures at its headquarters office in New York and regional centers throughout the world. The Asia Society brings prominent Asian and American leaders in government, business, the arts, and academia together with the growing audience of people with an abiding interest in Asia. Asia Society, 725 Park Avenue, New York, NY 10021; 212 288-6400; www.asiasociety.org

Sandee Brawarsky's articles and essays have appeared in various publications including the *New York Times*. Her latest book, *Two Jews, Three Opinions: A Collection of Twentieth Century American Jewish Quotations*, will be reissued in paperback this fall. . . . **Daryl Chin** co-founded the Asian American International Film Festival, and is Associate Editor of *PAJ: A Journal of Performance and Art*. He is finishing his monograph on the video artist Shigeko Kubota, to be published by Johns Hopkins University Press. . . . **Alvin Eng** is the editor and compiler of *Tokens? The NYC Asian American Experience On Stage* (Asian American Writers' Workshop/Temple University Press, 2000). His plays, poetry, and lyrics have also been published in *Action: The Nuyorican Poets Cafe Theater Festival* (Touchstone/Simon & Schuster, 1997) among others. . . . **Geoffrey Eu** edits the Insight Guides series of travel books. . . . **Letha Hadady, D. Ac.,** is the author of *Personal Renewal* and *Asian Health Secrets* (Random House). She stars in *Asian Health Secrets*, a popular Winstar video shot in New York's Chinatown. . . . **Bruce Edward Hall**'s *Tea That Burns: A Family Memoir of Chinatown* (Free Press) was the Booklist Editors Choice for 1998. He has also written about China and Chinatown for the *New York Times*, and won the Best Magazine Article award from the Society of American Travel Writers. . . . **Betty Hallock** attributes her interest in Asian food to a Japanese mother whose appetite for sushi is unmatched. Betty was born in Japan and grew up in southern California. She is currently a reporter at the *Wall Street Journal*. . . . **Reena Jana** is the New York Contributing Editor to Hong Kong's *Asian Art News* and *World Sculpture News* magazines, a U.S. Correspondent to *Flash Art International*, and a contributor to *Artforum, Art Asia Pacific, Art & Auction, Wired*, the *New York Times Magazine* and *Time Out New York*. . . . **Theresa Kimm** is a freelance writer and fiction writer living in Brooklyn. Born in Seoul, South Korea, she immigrated to Minnesota at the age of 10. After graduating from University of Minnesota at Minneapolis with a B.A. in American Studies, she moved to New York City to become a writer. . . . **Alexis Lipsitz** is an award-winning writer and editor living in New York City, and is currently an editor at Frommer's Travel. . . . **Arthur J. Pais** has taught journalism at New York University, Marymount Manhattan College and Montclair State University. His articles have appeared in the *New York Times*. He has also written for *Variety*, the *Chicago Tribune*, *Newsday* and *India Today*. . . . **Kenneth Wapner** is an author, editor, journalist, and book packager. The books he has worked on include the L.A. *Times* bestseller *Bones of the Master*, (Bantam, 2000). *Photography:* **Carrie Boretz** is a photojournalist who has been published widely in newspapers and magazines including the *New York Times*, the *New York Times Magazine*, *Fortune*, *U.S. News and World Report*, *People*, and *Newsweek*. She lives in New York City with her husband, photographer Edward Keating and their two daughters, Caitlin and Emmy. . . . **Corky Lee** was born and raised in Queens, N.Y.; Lee is a second-generation Chinese American. When studying American history at Queens College, he began his career in photography. Since then, his mission as a photojournalist has been to document the incredibly diverse Asian American communities ignored by mainstream media. Corky Lee lives in New York City.

Acknowledgments

All guidebooks are collaborative efforts, and this one is no exception. Indeed, *Asia in New York City* is the result of almost fifty years of institutional interaction with the metropolitan area, now encapsulated in this volume. What began as an in-house publication with limited distribution in 1980 is now a book with an online companion that has the potential to reach and be used by a wide and enthusiastic audience with a passion for all things Asian. Special appreciation goes to Marshall Bouton, Executive Vice President, Asia Society, for knowing that the time was right to reinvent the concept of a resource guide on discovering Asia in New York. Over the four-year development period, many members of the Asia Society contributed their ideas, knowledge, contacts, and time.

The editors, publishers, and writers have faced rather unusual and extenuating circumstances in the process of bringing this project to completion. The commitment of Will Balliett and F-stop Fitzgerald has been unerring. It would have been much easier to throw in the towel. Nancy Su and Alexis Lipsitz steered the book through an unclear future. Sue Canavan provided a wonderful design, and Mike Walters took the book through production with grace and speed. Lynne Arany made it all work in the end, and we are very thankful for her skillful approach. The generosity of The Freeman Foundation has made the website component possible. The Asia Society also would like to thank Peter Anderson for his guidance in all matters of a legal nature. Finally, enormous gratitude goes to Karen Karp and Susie Park for having the vision, doggone stubbornness and blind enthusiasm to survive every obstacle that could have prevented the publication of *Asia in New York City*. For all involved, it has truly been a labor of love.